Augsburg College
George Sverdrup Library
Minneapolis, Minnesota 55404

Freedom and the Administrative State

FREEDOM
and the
ADMINISTRATIVE STATE

by JOSEPH ROSENFARB

Author of THE NATIONAL LABOR POLICY AND HOW IT WORKS

HARPER & BROTHERS PUBLISHERS
New York and London

To the Memory of My Mother

FREEDOM AND THE ADMINISTRATIVE STATE

Copyright, 1948, by Harper & Brothers. Printed in the United States of America. All rights in this book are reserved. No part of the book may be reproduced in any manner whatsoever without written permission except in the case of brief quotations embodied in critical articles and reviews. For information address
Harper & Brothers
B-X

CONTENTS

		PAGE
	Introduction: The Chosen Generation	ix

BOOK ONE: The Genesis and Evolution of the Administrative State

I	*Man and Power*	3
	1. Man and Society	
	2. Man's Quest for Power	
II	*Socialization of Power*	9
	1. Mechanisms for Increasing Means of Satisfaction	
	2. Mechanisms for Controlling Man's Wants	
III	*Organization and Power*	21
	1. Political Power	
	2. The Nature and Principles of Organization	
IV	*Man and the State*	29
	1. The Nature of the State	
	2. The Origin of the State—The Family State	
V	*The State in Precapitalist Economies*	37
	1. Familial, Feudal, Town and Mercantilist Economies	
	2. The Dawn of the Modern World	
VI	*The State in the Capitalist Economic Order*	44
	1. The Mechanism of a Self-regulated Economy	
	2. The Pathologies of an Unco-ordinated Economy	
	3. Government Regulation of the Economy	
VII	*Proposed Approaches to Planning*	55
	1. The Employment Act of 1946	
	2. The Return to Absolute Capitalism	
	3. Government Ownership	
	4. Government Spending	
	5. Distribution Schemes	
VIII	*A Planned Economy for Private Enterprise*	63
	1. A Program for Direct Planning	
	2. Planning of Needs	
	3. Resources Planning	
	4. Production Planning	
	5. Planning Techniques and Agencies	
	6. The Meaning of the Administrative State	

CONTENTS

BOOK TWO: Freedom and Democracy in the Administrative State

		PAGE
IX	*Economic Freedom under Planning*	79
	1. The Choice Before Us	
	2. The Meaning of Freedom	
	3. Freedom and Security	
	4. Consumer Freedom	
	5. Free Enterprise	
X	*Cultural and Political Liberties under Planning*	87
	1. Cultural Freedom	
	2. Civil Liberties	
	3. A Program for Freedom of Information	
	4. Liberty and Antidemocratic Forces	
XI	*Power Distribution and Political Systems*	99
	1. Inquiry Into the Distribution of Power	
	2. Leadership and Social Structure	
	3. Sources of Leadership	
	4. Recruitment and Control of Leadership	
XII	*Democracy in a Planned Economy*	120
	1. Conditions of Democratic Viability	
	2. The Problem of Transition	
XIII	*Property and the Social Order*	128
	1. Property and Social Status	
	2. Stages of Economic Development	
	3. Property and Political Systems	

BOOK THREE: Labor Relations in the Administrative State

XIV	*Compulsives in Labor Relations*	139
	1. Government Intervention in Postwar Strikes	
	2. The Growing Strength of Labor	
	3. The Impact of Strikes on a Modern Economy	
	4. The Wage-Price Relationship	
	5. The Integrating Role of Government	
XV	*Industrial Democracy and Freedom*	159
	1. Industrial Democracy and Civil Liberties	
	2. Plant Democracy and Security	
	3. Intra-union Democracy	
	4. Freedom of Organized Labor under Planning	
	5. Freedom of Employment under Planning	
	6. Union Restrictive Practices	

		PAGE
XVI	*Labor's Role in Politics*	175
	1. Retrospect and Prospect	
	2. Techniques and Forms of Political Action	

BOOK FOUR: Law and Government in the Administrative State

		PAGE
XVII	*The Role of Law and Government* 1. Concepts and Meanings 2. The Mechanism of Control: Power and Responsibility	191
XVIII	*Political Integration of the State* 1. The Stages and Process of Integration 2. The American Pattern 3. Functional Federalism under Planning	195
XIX	*Differentiation of Government and Law* 1. Differentiation of Functions and Forms 2. The Role of the Fatherhood Symbolism	202
XX	*Integration of Representative Government* 1. The Historical Pattern of Government Integration 2. The British Cabinet System 3. The American Presidential System 4. A Program of Government Reorganization	212
XXI	*Administrative Integration* 1. Democratic Controls of the Administrative Process 2. Structure and Function 3. A Proposal for Administrative Reorganization 4. A Microcosm of Democratic Administration	224
XXII	*Freedom through Government* 1. Freedom and Organization 2. Sanctions, Remedies, and Incentives 3. Liberty and Authority	231
	Footnotes to Chapters	241
	Index	260

Acknowledgments

It is with deep gratitude that I wish to acknowledge my indebtedness to many from whose help I greatly benefited in the preparation of this study. Miss Leah Lappin's advice, editorial and research assistance were invaluable. Dr. Ordway Tead's incisive editorial revisions and critical suggestions were particularly useful. Thanks are due the following for reading and commenting on the manuscript: Senator Robert F. Wagner; Senator Wayne Morse; Chairman Arthur S. Meyer of the New York State Board of Mediation; Mr. Merlyn S. Pitzele, Member, New York State Board of Mediation and Labor Editor of Business Week; Dr. George W. Taylor, Professor of Economics, University of Pennsylvania; Mr. A. A. Berle, Jr.; Dr. Ruth Foster; Dr. James C. Charlesworth, Professor of Political Science, University of Pennsylvania; Dr. Lyman Bryson, Counsellor on Public Affairs, Columbia Broadcasting System; Dr. Bernard C. Meyer; Judge Thurman W. Arnold; Mr. Robert R. Nathan; President Walter P. Reuther of the U.A.W.-CIO; Mr. Boris Shishkin, Economist of the American Federation of Labor; Mr. Abe Fortas; Mr. Donald Montgomery, Economist of the U.A.W.-CIO; and Joseph McMurray, Administrative Assistant to Senator Wagner. The responsibility for the views expressed in this study is solely that of the author.

To Miss Elbertha Ackley I am grateful for typing the manuscript; and to Columbia University and its library staff for making its library facilities available to me.

I wish to thank the editors of the following publications for permission to use in revised form matter from the author's articles which first appeared in their pages: "Labor's Role in the Elections," *Public Opinion Quarterly*, Fall 1944; "The Administrative State: Compulsives in Labor Relations," *North Carolina Law Review*, February 1945; "Trend of Labor Laws," *Barron's Weekly*, July 15, 1946; "Protection of Basic Rights," in symposium, "The Wagner Act After Ten Years," Louis G. Silverberg (Ed.), Bureau of National Affairs.

THE AUTHOR

January 15, 1948

INTRODUCTION

The Chosen Generation

"The hell this ain't the most important hole in the world. I'm in it," says Mauldin's Willie. Every generation has the illusion that it is living through one of the most important periods in history. Yet it cannot be denied that our generation has indeed, as President Roosevelt declared, "a rendezvous with destiny," not for ourselves alone, not for the generation to come, but for mankind as a whole. We are preoccupied with social and political problems of surpassing magnitude, including the atomic bomb. We are confronted with no less than the problem of assuring the survival of our civilization and even of mankind itself.

The stream of human events has become a torrent. Providence, it would seem, impatient of the ever-widening gap between man's power over nature and his moral helplessness to restrain his own aggressions, confronts this generation with the ultimate decision. Either we pull ourselves up by our moral bootstraps in order to banish war and insecurity or we shall be hurled without trace into the bottomless pit. We are the chosen generation.

We have been living through not only war but economic and sociopolitical world revolution. The world over, we are witnessing the twilight of planless capitalism. Outside the United States the struggle is not between the capitalist and the communist economic systems, but between various forms of democratic socialism, on the one hand, and communism, on the other. All operate within the framework of a planned economy.

In America, we still have to face the crisis. We face it because, despite the passage of the Employment Act of 1946, we are yet to make and implement irrevocably the national decision that it is the function and duty of our democratic society, acting through its national government in co-operation with industry and labor, to plan our economy to provide by whatever means necessary for full employment.

Under the aegis and impetus of government controls we have

achieved the highest peacetime records in employment, production, and national income. We have experienced shortages because our great industrial machine has been unable during reconversion to keep up with our expanding demands and pent-up purchasing power. We have been told that our salvation lies in a return to the good old days of the economic system that produced the one shortage to cure all shortages—the shortage of jobs.

The wartime controls over production and the wage-price relationship have now been removed. There has been abroad in the land the lure to return to the unregulated private enterprise of the pre-Roosevelt era, though the siren call has been silent on how we were going to avoid the reefs of destruction on which once before our economy was brought to collapse. Significantly, within a year after the removal of wartime controls the Truman Administration asked Congress in November 1947 for enabling legislation to regulate our economy, including price, wage and materials allocation controls. The economic conditions which called forth this program may be accentuated, but have not been created by the projected Marshall Plan of aid for European economic rehabilitation. The need for government regulation of our economy is a permanent feature of our society.

The trend toward the interpenetration of the economic and political processes is one of the chief characteristics of at least the past half century, and has manifested itself in every economy in the world. It has varied in its pace of development and form of manifestation, but it has become the common denominator of modern socioeconomic evolution. There must be some vital need in our economy which this phenomenon fulfills for it to survive in the process of historical selection.

Obviously, such universality must be in response to a condition. We are dealing here with a fundamental condition of present-day society.

It is the thesis of this study that an economy in which continuous planning is essential is inherent in our economic system, and that a managed economy founded on private enterprise, and democratically controlled and oriented, should be America's contribution to modern statecraft and social systems.

We, the world over, are now entering what may be called the "administrative state." In order to appreciate its character, the nature, origin, and evolution of the state as an institution will be traced, not alone in structural form but as embracing the social, economic, legal, psychological, geographic, military, cultural, and political forces that have influenced the development of society and of the state. A definite pattern of the evolution of the state becomes evident from the analysis and the governing principles are crystallized. Only by knowing whence we have come can we know whither we are going. Only by distinguishing the possible from the futile can we embrace the vital and discard the fatal.

In this study we observe how the pattern and principles of political evolution found expression in the precapitalist economies. We watch the interplay of the same pattern and principles in the context of the historical evolution of the capitalist system, and note the same inexorable trend to the interpenetration of the political and economic processes and to the evolution of a managed economy. Some of the chief approaches to planning, including the Employment Act of 1946, are tested in the light of historical, social development and of our own cultural experience. It is these decisive criteria which point the way to the dynamically managed economy for private enterprise which is calculated by actual experience to achieve and maintain an expanding economy of full employment within the framework of our democratic tradition.

As the contours of our economy and social structure are changing under the impact of forces not altogether understood, and as we are required to make difficult and at times drastic adjustments to the changing pattern of our society, we are compelled to undergo individual and collective soul searching. Whither democracy? Whither liberty? As the world is agonizingly pressing forward in its search for economic security, age-old problems have risen to the fore again in the matrix of present-day circumstances. Are liberty and security incompatible? Are authority and democracy irreconcilable? Is an economy in which planning is integral inimical to our democratic values?

The meaning and incidence of democracy and of all types of freedom are set forth as well as the character of their expression in a managed economy. Though we cannot avoid the triumph of the administrative state, we can not only preserve freedom and democracy but can bring them to unprecedented fruition in the administrative state. This goes for economic and political freedom and for our civil liberties. A specific program is outlined to make freedom of expression by press and radio more widespread.

In conformance with the task of making the administrative state free and democratic, the crucial role of labor relations in our economy is explored: in their effect on the evolution of the administrative state, in the realities of industrial democracy and freedom, and in the implications of organized labor's political activities. All this is analyzed in the light of the Taft-Hartley Labor-Management Relations Act of 1947, which drastically amends the Wagner Act. A specific program is advanced for modifying our national labor policy in the sectors of the wage-price relationship, management-union rights and obligations, and intra-union democracy; and definite proposals are made in regard to the role of unions in politics.

The universal trend to multiplication of governmental functions has brought into focus the issue whether government administrators are to be the servants or the masters of the people. The evolution of the realm of law and of governmental forms, organs, and functions and of sanctions and incentives is explored to determine what tools and techniques are at our disposal to endow the administrative state with the power to perform effectively its great tasks and at the same time to exact responsibility to the people by the government. The traditional issues of federalism and the interrelationships of the legislative, executive, judicial, and administrative processes are re-examined in the context of a dynamically managed economy. From this emerges a program for an all-embracing government reorganization to bring our government machinery in line with the needs and imperatives of the democratic administrative state.

The great task of securing freedom in the democratic administrative state is all-pervasive and involves every aspect of the modern state including its relationship to the world order. The latter problem, however, is the subject of a companion volume which is soon to follow.

We are now at the crossroads of decision. The era of the Great Debate has opened in America. This is an opportune time to sound a warning against a return to the boom-bust cycle implicit in an unregulated economy. We can be certain of the emergence of the events analyzed, but not of the timetable. There may, of course, be an interlude in which laissez faire might prevail because of the pent-up domestic and foreign demand, but it will be only an interlude, and a costly one at that. The consequence will be another economic collapse of even greater magnitude than that of 1929. The great lesson learned by our generation—that a democratic people can be the master of their economy and provide for themselves both security and freedom through government—is in danger of being discarded. It will not be forgotten. It is in the hearts of Americans, and will rise to their lips as do-nothing government ends, as it must, in depression.

A politicist can afford to be ahead of his time. A statesman is one who keeps abreast of the times. A politician tries to catch up with the times. A reactionary is one who would bid the sun turn from west to east. It may be that those who will have the power will recognize that the government's function in our economy, analyzed in this study, is dictated by a condition and not a theory. If so, then those who will hold the power of decision, and who act upon convictions similar to those expressed in this study, will be considered not academicians but statesmen, and America and the world will be spared a dangerous crisis.

If we are to preserve democracy, it is up to our generation, in the economic realm, to commit ourselves to implementing Lincoln's philosophy of government: "The legitimate object of government is to do for a community of people whatever they need to have done, but cannot do at all, or cannot do so well, in their separate and individual capacities."

BOOK ONE

The Genesis and Evolution of the Administrative State

CHAPTER I

Man and Power

1. MAN AND SOCIETY

God created man in his own image, and ever since man has striven to become one with his creator.

Man's desires are limitless. To Cicero, "the thirst of desire is never filled, nor fully satisfied."[1] To Hobbes, mankind is in the throes of "a perpetual and restless desire of power after power that ceaseth only in Death."[2] For Buddha, "To conquer sorrow a man must annihilate the thirst of desire and the attachment of life."[3] To Hsun Tzu, the Confucian, "The nature of man is evil. His virtue is only an acquired goodness. Everyone is bent on profit. From following his lust for gain arise strifes and contentions, and the harmony of life is lost." And to Lao Tzu, "The holy man hoards not . . . [his] reason is to accomplish but not to strive."[4]

Being man, he is forever driven to discover the workings of the universe, to glimpse into the outermost reaches of space, to conquer distance and time, and to harness the forces of nature to his will. He tries to scale the impenetrable barrier of the grave by dreaming of immortality. Like his creator, man wants to be omniscient, omnipotent, and eternal. Man conceives of God in the image of his own boundless drives and vaulting ambitions.

In fulfilling himself, however, man comes into contact with other men who like himself feel themselves to be centers of the universe. Man is an individual and yet a member of society. This dualism is fundamental in the history and destiny of man.[5]

The society of man is dynamic. Man has certain drives of a physiological and perhaps psychic nature: hunger, thirst, sex, reproduction, companionship—these are drives, needs, wants, which must be satisfied. But the manner of their satisfaction is not governed or determined instinctually.

Man is neither wholly rational nor wholly irrational. Man's drives or wants are irrationally determined but reason is mobilized for their fulfillment. Man's reason is not the mistress but the handmaiden of his strivings. There may yet come a time when man will reach that state of cultural maturity with which we associate the primacy of reason and its control over man's strivings. Until the dawn of that bright day it is both a consolation and a promise that reason is not merely a metaphor and a symbol but a biologically verifiable part of human nature.

Since reasoning is not automatic, the connection between man's instinctual drives and their satisfaction is not as certain, invariable, and inexorable as is true of insects, whose instincts are all determining. The mode of fulfillment varies greatly. Man's nature within limits is highly malleable. Individual and cultural mores show a variegated pattern. Another element producing variation in human society is that man is able to exist in more varied physical environments than any other animal. More important, man is able and does continually change his environment, creating new environments and new needs and modes of adjustment. Man's knowledge and intelligence serve to alter not only man's mode of satisfaction but also man's physical and cultural environment. Man's society is in constant flux due to the interaction of his organism, environment, social milieu, and the conflict among individuals in the same society, as well as the struggle among different societies. Therefore, no permanently static human society is likely to arise, as is true of the society of insects.[6]

The totality of man's modes of adjustment and fulfilling of his needs constitutes his culture and social environment. To individual man, his social environment is of much more consequence than his physical environment. In it he finds the accumulated wisdom and mores of the race which it evolved in the process of adjusting to the world. Individual man is not only the creature of his social environment but also to a varying degree the creator, for in living his life he adds to and modifies the common treasure of the race. Even if his nature has not changed during the historical era, man is not putty, formless, shapeless, and without imperatives of his own inherent equipment.

Man is truly plastic and has shown greater flexibility in scope of adjustment than any other representative of life, but man's malleability has its limits. Since it has been assumed that human nature does not change, there has been a tendency among interpreters of culture and history to consider the human factor as a constant and therefore to ignore it in favor of one or another factor in man's variable environment. It may be suggested that even the factor of constancy in human nature needs amplification if confusion is to be avoided, for, contrary to democratic dogma, man is not born equal but with varying potentialities in instinctual drives and reasoning capacities. But to assume the factor of constancy does not justify excluding human nature from the influences molding society and culture. Geography[7] and economics[8] have emerged to claim priority as determinants of human destiny but have proved insufficient as exclusive or even principal agents of change. Yet there is no doubt that each of these and other factors[9] are powerful influences in varying degree and in different aspects.

What is objectionable in cultural interpretation is the search after a deterministic key, which suggests a wholly quantitative mechanistic approach. It is impossible to weigh and evaluate factors which differ qualitatively. It is profitless, for instance, to compare and weigh the influence of climate, ownership of means of production, and contents of cultural ideas. The old controversy of heredity versus environment has no meaning, just as it would be meaningless to claim that in a chemical compound one element is twice as important as another because their ratio is two to one. The proper scientific question to propound in social causation is not what priority to assign to each factor but how each component exercises its peculiar influence on the result. Our fate is neither wholly in the stars nor wholly in ourselves, but in both.

Turning our back on the deterministic view of history does not, however, enthrone the equally erroneous polarized attitude that history and social evolution are a caprice and no generalizations are feasible.[10] No two human beings are exactly alike, have precisely the same social environment, or respond in the very same manner to the same stimuli, yet human beings do exhibit the same physiological and psychic drives conditioned by their culture, and their differences in intellectual abilities are only of degree and not of too wide a character at that. It is impossible to predict with certainty what a particular individual is going to do in a certain situation, for there is as yet no adequate technique for fully exploring the totality of an individual personality and its background. Nevertheless, we may formulate statistical generalizations concerning mass behavior in a given social configuration. We may also examine the interaction of man's natural potentialities with the various phases of his physical and social environment.

2. MAN'S QUEST FOR POWER

The satisfaction of man's needs is not the consequence of automatic instinctual process, which is self-regulating and limited by fulfillment. It is the result of general drives which propel the thinking faculty to explore and manipulate the environment for the purpose of obtaining the means of satisfaction. Emphasis is on quest. The search for satisfaction is accompanied by psychic states, on the conscious and subconscious levels. Ambition, envy, love, hate are manifestations of man's search for fulfillment. If the process were automatic there would be no psychic overtones. Our reflexes, for instance, are specific automatic responses devoid of psychic accompaniment.[11]

Our drives with their psychic concomitants do not, however, cease upon achieving satisfaction. The release of tension that accompanies satisfaction is not only temporary but does not suspend activity or striving.[12] Man is the only animal that is aware of the phenomenon of time and therefore of death. He is the only one with a consciousness of past, present, and future. He is therefore driven to plan the satisfaction of his future needs and wants. Since the environment differs for each individual and the mode of satisfaction is not automatic, man's gratifications differ in degree according to the interaction of the means available and the individual involved. One man's frustration may be another man's fulfillment.

Our social institutions and activities reflect and reinforce man's implacable search for ever greater satisfactions. Our economic institutions provide a constant channel for the expression of our drives for the satisfaction of hunger, thirst, and the need for shelter. The family is man's universal institution to satisfy his drive for sex and reproduction. Our romantic literature, the movies, and our other escapist entertainment are evidence of man's unsatisfied cravings in the realm of sex.

Man's constant drive to satisfy his needs, when multiplied by the totality of his wants, may be viewed as the drive to conquer his environment, social and physical. But in seeking to master his environment man also changes it, creating a new one while escaping the shackles of the old. Man builds a technology with which he increases his economic satisfaction, but in so doing he also builds cities with compulsions of their own which he seeks to master. Man's quest for power and mastery over his environment is endless.

One wonders, indeed, whether it is not quest for power over the environment rather than simple survival that is the driving spirit of evolution. That man is a social animal has been proclaimed by Aristotle, and anthropology and psychology have sustained the assertion. To fulfill his physiologic needs and wants of sex and reproduction and even of hunger, thirst, and protection man must live in society. Even for the fulfillment of his psychic needs society is indispensable. Whatever its ideological uses, historically and biologically the idea of the "social contract," that man lived in a state of nature outside of regulated society, is without foundation.[13] It is no fun to live alone.

Although man is inseparable from society and an integral part of it, he is nevertheless an individual, the fulfillment of whose needs comes in conflict with the needs of others, while depending on them for satisfaction. It is not true that man's interests are necessarily opposed to those of society, for society affords man positive goods he cannot afford to be without. Not being an automaton, man must manage somehow to adjust himself to an ever-changing social flux. In this process he comes in conflict with other men similarly intent and engaged. Man must both compete and co-operate. It is this dualism in man's relatedness to society that underlies human conflict. No science of man can be meaningful and fructifying unless this duality is centrally recognized. It is this dualism that underlies man's psychic, social and political maladjustment. It is this dualism that underlies psychoanalytic inquiry, particularly in its explicit Freudian formulation.[14] To synthesize this duality is to usher in the dawn of the good society.

Of particular significance is the dualism of man's relationship to society when we realize that society is the sphere of man's urge to power.

Man's quest for power can be viewed in conjunction with activities directed to satisfy his particular wants. To the extent that man's quest for power is directed to the gratification of his elementary physiologic needs, it is not of social importance for it is dissipated in its limited task. Grubbing for a living leaves no energy for anything else except mating, which has ever been the lot and preoccupation of the mass of mankind.

It is that residue of the quest for power which remains after the elementary needs have been satisfied that makes the world go round. It is this aspect of power that is socially important, for it is in the social field that it finds its expression. It is this type of power that serves as an end in itself. This is ego power, for through it the ego expresses itself and thrives or shrivels.

Since man's quest for mastery of his environment is endless, the psychic manifestations of that activity have been detached from any tangible goals and have become themselves a distinct and recognizable psychic want, the lust for power. Individual men of course differ in the intensity of their power drives but there is no question that in one form or another in greater or less degree it is common to all men.[15]

The difference here between the abnormal and the normal is one of degree and not of kind. Grandeur delusions are a manifestation of certain types of insanity. The asylums are populated with Napoleons, Caesars, and even gods. But megalomania is not the exclusive possession of the asylums. Not in ancient times, but in the twentieth century, not in some isolated habitat, but in the midst of a pragmatic mechanical civilization, Father Divine is "God Himself" to his thousands of followers. Who said the age of faith and god-making is over?

Man's impulse to power need not take pathological or antisocial expression. Ambition to excel in one's work or profession, which often entails real sacrifice, may be shared by many long after economic need has been left behind. The scientist or the inventor is driven not solely by need to gain the applause of his fellow men but by curiosity to discover the secrets of nature and to manipulate them for his purpose. But this activity itself is obviously power motivated and manifested. That knowledge is power is generally acknowledged. To solve a riddle, to put together a puzzle picture affords pleasurable sensations because the ego is enhanced by overcoming obstacles. The excitement experienced by those pursuing creative intellectual labors may sometimes approach ecstasy. Philosophers need not be pitied. They are incontinent in their lust for power of a kind. The great and the good among us as well as the evil have drives for power. The difference is in the form in which the drive for power expresses itself, whether it is or is not socially beneficial or approved.

CHAPTER II

Socialization of Power

1. MECHANISMS FOR INCREASING MEANS OF SATISFACTION

How, then, does society socialize man's lust for power? For socialize it it must. Otherwise society would explode and dissolve from the internal conflict of man against man. Socializing power means curbing, conditioning, or taming it to socially approved and useful expression. We are not concerned in this connection with any value judgment of cultural concinnity and as to whether the communal goals or criteria are generally valid.

What are the mechanisms of socialization of power? For an answer we must probe into man's religion, ethics, psychology, sociology, and history. There are generally two ways to satisfy our drive for power. The first, and the direct, approach is to increase the means productive of satisfaction. The second, and indirect, approach is to curb our desires.

In dreams, in which one's power is infinitely magnified, man, the individual man, escapes reality.[1] Daydreaming may be considered as another normal expression of the same tendency. Certain philosophic systems, solipsism, for instance, serve the same purpose.[2] The most important institutionalized form of unlimited satisfaction is institutionalized religion. One of the most socially significant inventions of mankind is the concept of a life beyond the grave. In return for abiding by the social conventions of the community, the utmost desires and the deepest cravings of the individual are to be satisfied in the hereafter. Pie in the sky.[3] Each cultural community, including Mohammedan,[4] Hebrew[5] and Christian,[6] creates heaven in the image of its own wants, deprivations, and social aspirations.

But life in the hereafter is a place not only of rewards but also of punishments. Those who flaunt the will of the community are consigned to hell. In the hereafter, not only one's expressions of love and friendliness receive fulfillment but also one's hates, hostilities, and aggressions. Hell can be made rugged for those we do not fancy. Moreover, the salutary separation of the incidence of hate and love in hell and heaven, respectively, removes any ambivalent and conflicting reaction and consequent guilt feeling. A complete catharsis and power satisfaction is achieved.[7]

Marxist conception of religion as the "opium of the masses" and Freud's calling it an illusion do not of course stigmatize this phenomenon out of existence.[8] Since mankind as a whole has had to subsist throughout history on an economy of scarcity, a well-stocked heaven has served an indispensable need. Religion has persisted too long and too universally to be dismissed as a planned device to keep the masses in subjection and a racket for the benefit of the priesthood, though there is no denying the recurrence of such uses of religion. Religion, like every human institution, has its pathology. Certain church excrescences no more explain religion than prostitution explains sex, or graft is the whole of politics.

It is significant that communism's original hostility to religion gave way in Russia to a revival and absorption of the national Russian Orthodox Church by the Soviet dictatorship. Both communism and nazism lacked the supernatural or at least superhuman element to make them all-sufficient in the long run as mass faiths. Since dictatorships emphasize the transference of the father image to their leader by apotheosizing him, dictatorships more than democracies have need of a state religion.[9] Thus communism and fascism had the alternative of either going to the bother of creating their own supernatural symbolic system or coming to terms with and using one already in existence. The latter of course is preferable, since the masses of the people are already conditioned to the old symbolism and there is no need to resort to the difficult task of breaking old patterns and creating new ones.

This is actually what happened in Russia, Germany, and Italy. The difficulties that the Catholic Church and the Soviet government have experienced in trying to work out a modus vivendi are not due to inherent imcompatibilities between the two ideologies but to the reluctance of a totalitarian dictatorship to share power over the masses with another imperium. The Russian church is nationally controlled. Not so the papacy.

Freud's condemnation of religion has not, however, prevented him from paying it the strongest compliment—emulation. The psychoanalytic interview and the confessional must ultimately be based on the same validation. Religious conversion and psychoanalytic reorientation are not unlike. Understandably there are variations in modes, rationale, and sanctions but that may amount to differences in terminology. Advances in the knowledge of human behavior and relationships may frequently be no more than restatements suitable to the spirit of the times.

Religion, though historically perhaps the principal, is not the only means of socializing power by deflecting its expression to desirable channels. The ideologies of modern dictatorships are instructive in this respect. By the supplementary device of identification with the leader, the cause, and the race, the masses are goaded into expanding their egos vicariously to world-wide scope through the triumph of the leader and the country. Full scope is afforded in the war dance for the expression of mass aggressions, hostilities, and hate by directing them against a scapegoat, at first internal and then external.

In Nazi Germany, the Jews were the first victims and then came the English, French, and Russians—all in league to encircle the peaceful Germans. In Russia the Trotskyist and other purgees absorbed all the accumulated resentments and aggressions resulting from the privations and sacrifices the masses had to undergo, and then came the hated foreign reactionaries. Now it is the "monopoly capitalists," principally of the United States, who allegedly seek to encircle Russia. The social value of this technique is obvious. All love and attachment is directed toward the community and its leadership while all blame, hostility, and resentment for dissatisfaction are deflected against the conspiring foreigners. Not only is internal peace and national cohesiveness thereby served, but national expansion is advanced. The myth of encirclement, if persistently propagated, must lead to war because the accumulated emotional tensions must seek release.[10]

Another technique for encouraging the full expression of power in socially approved channels is to transfer its application from man to things, from domination of man to control over nature and art, from fighting to work. Work as a compulsive expression is familiar in psychiatry. On the social level this phenomenon is dominant in pioneer countries and at the beginning of an industrial era when capital goods must be built up, often at the expense of the standard of living of the masses.[11] Lassez-faire capitalism was its economic expression in England and the United States; Stakhanovism and other characteristics in the Russian system.[12] The phenomenally rapid development of North America is inseparable from the complete free play that was given to the American to indulge his drive for power in terms of acquisitiveness. So preoccupied became the American empire builders with internal development that, except for a few haphazard imperialistic ventures, there was no surplus energy and interest for a consistent expansion outward of a territorially imperialistic character once the continental limits were reached.[13]

To the extent that an individual sublimates his power drives in what Veblen called the "instinct of workmanship,"[14] he has less need for dominating drives toward his fellow man. Striving for excellence and perfection in one's labors in the arts and sciences is one way, a salutary one not always on the conscious level, of establishing implied dominion over man. Sublimation involves the gratification of a need not by the direct method, which may be blocked, but by substitute expression, socially approved.[15]

Canalizing man's quest for power into work drives, when combined with the proper economic system, contributes to the creation of economic abundance, which is an important mechanism for the socialization of power. This is especially important in its effect on the mass of the people. Economic privation sharpens competition for the means to satisfy man's elementary needs. Man's insecurity and aggressions are increased. The mass of the people are then more susceptible to hate propaganda and less amenable to humanitarian impulses. Particularly in democratic countries, where the mass exercises some influence on the framing of policy, no political system can be considered stable unless it provides economic security for the mass of the people.

Similar to work drives as agencies for the socialization of the quest for power among the masses are sports. Man's combativeness, aggression, and sadism, which find their greatest freedom in war, are sublimated in sports, both for participants and for spectators. As sublimated expression mass sports are superior to work, for they involve directly the conflict of man against man. Just as an inoculation induces a disease but in a minor, harmless form, so do sports re-enact the war drama in full emotional tone but without the terrific actual cost. There is the same fascination of the horror of direct physical conflict, blood, striving, devils, enemies, heroes, defeat, victory, anger, brotherhood, and mass solidarity—all the psychological equivalents of war. Men being what they are, it is indicative of a far higher cultural level for Americans to shout for the sleep-inducing blow than for the Germans to Sieg Heil the extermination of millions.

2. MECHANISMS FOR CONTROLLING MAN'S WANTS

Up to this point the mechanisms of socializing power that increase the means of gratification have been analyzed. The second, the indirect, method of satisfaction is by reducing and controlling the drive for power. Some of the mechanisms already discussed contribute to both—controlling drives and furnishing means for their gratification. Religion is pre-eminent in this. While affording free play to the expansion of the ego in its afterlife phase, organized religion has almost universally preached curbing man's desires. "Vanity of vanities, all is vanity," broods Ecclesiastes. Asceticism has been an almost universal phenomenon in all religions. It has probably received its extreme expression in Buddhism. Nirvana, the Hindu heaven, is the state of complete absence of any desires. It is the essence of the stoic discipline reduced to the ultimate.[16] Self-control, moderation, humanity, reasonableness are recurrent themes in religion and ethics through the ages.[17] They have become the attributes of maturity, the norm of modern psychiatry.[18]

The one great exception to the emphasis on curbing our inordinate wants has been German Kultur. The German atrocities in both world wars were not acts of passion but measures of policy adopted to achieve the German purpose of demographic superiority over Germany's neighbors. The highest purpose of our Judeo-Christian ethic is to tame our animal instincts and our lust for power. The German has looked within himself[19] and found the Nazi beast to be good and worthy of survival and domination. He bade him to cast off all human inhibitions and act openly as the beast.

Control of the drive for power has been achieved by the mechanism known as identification. The individual's quest for power is curbed so far as his own personality is concerned through his identification with some other individual or cause whose power quest he adopts as his own. In our society it is usually the wife who identifies herself with her husband and expresses her urge to power through his strivings. The extent of this identification is a good measure of the cohesiveness of the marital relationship. A disadvantaged minority indulges to the utmost its tendency to identification with some prominent member of the group who has achieved success. The rise of Al Smith symbolized the triumph of their aspirations to the urban immigrant population. Union members find personal gratification when their leaders walk with the mighty of the land.[20]

Identification is important in the realm of politics. It is the essence of the relationship between leaders and followers. The latter, depending upon the intensity of the movement, find a greater or lesser degree of ego satisfaction through identification with the personality and cause of the leader. Submission is the role of the followers and domination that of the leader. Although sadistic and masochistic tendencies are present in the same individual, in the leader the sadistic tendencies are predominant while the masochistic characteristize the followers, particularly in their attitude toward the leader. In dictatorships, where the core of political morality is found in abject obedience to infallible authority, the leaders must be deified, so that the ego drives of the mass may find superlative gratification in the godlike leader.[21] Observe the apotheosis of Hitler and Stalin.

In democracies, on the other hand, where the leaders have to obtain the consent of the governed, they are not revered during their lifetime.[22] Although there is still identification between leaders and followers, democratic ideology gives primacy to the people, not to the leaders. The voice of the people, not that of the leader, is the voice of God. Not the leaders but the people are infallible. Through democratic identification, the individual participates in all aspects of the government, although actually this may be wide of the mark. The ultimate expression of follower-leader identification is in religion, where humility and resignation is a great virtue and ecstasy is experienced by the believer in surrendering his will completely to that of the Almighty. Man becomes one with God by fusing with him.[23]

Identification can be with the community or an organization. In this way the latter receives the benefits of the power exertions of the members working themselves out in the aggrandizements of the common association. An interesting illustration is the Roman Catholic Church. The institution of celibacy deprives the priesthood of the varied normal expressions of power drives which might deflect them from the church. There is no family to absorb the hopes and aspirations of the priests. The church is the only avenue open through which their power drives can be satisfied. The egos of the priests can find expression only through the power and glory of the church.

Identification with ideas has played an exceptionally dynamic role in history. Man projects his personality and ego to the things about him and appropriates them by making them part of his ego. Ownership is an extension of the ego and its elimination is painful to man. Throughout history, men have invested their personalities in ideas and have therefore zealously defended them, to preserve the integrity and security of their egos. One of the greatest hindrances to a scientific approach to social problems is that men convert suitable ideas into faiths or ideologies, which satisfy deep-seated human yearnings. No amount of rational argumentation is likely to succeed in breaking the tie between the believer and his ideology, for this would cause a breach in the ego and would undermine its security. Only where some event creates a conflict between the ego and those who personify the idea will a divorce take place. The process of divorcement or disillusionment is so painful, because of the void created by the removal of certainty, that unquestioning devoutness is transformed to unreasoning opposition.

Marxist ideology has exercised a tremendous influence on the minds of recent generations. The liberals and radicals of the Western world, expressing their quest for power by seeking to reform or make over the economic system, shared and were conditioned by the same terminology as the Russian revolutionists. Their ego satisfactions were therefore closely identified with Soviet destiny. Businessmen, because fascism presumed to defend private property, easily forgave Mussolini and Hitler the excesses of fascism and nazism as long as they made the trains run on time and eliminated free labor unions. Having been seduced by fascist terminology into identifying their fate with fascism, they could not see that fascism does not lead to the triumph of the businessman's civilization but to the emergence of a new ruling class that would lead capitalism to catastrophe. Similarly with Western liberalism. Having clothed their aspirations with Marxist nomenclature, many among the liberals have been prone to identify Russia with their dreams of a proletarian revolution leading to a free, peaceful, and classless society. That Russian reality did not conform with their wishes made many of them impervious to reason and ready to lapse into a schizophrenic double-standard political morality. Civil liberties, democracy, disarmament, nonintervention—all these are quite proper for the United States and Britain, but not for Russia. The more the class-ridden imperialist absolutism of Russia becomes exposed, the more infallible the Russians become. Stalin can do no wrong and never changes his mind. Any apparent changes in the party line is deceptive to the uninitiates. It is really history that changes.

It is only when some sensitive devotees come in contact with Russian realty or have their emotional gears stripped by the frequent shifts in the party line that disillusionment sets in and the believer is cast adrift. But man abhors insecurity, for it undermines his ego. And so, many a former fellow traveler finds anchor in the harbor of extreme antisovietism.

Idea identification is not the monopoly of the masses. In its extreme intensity it is the characteristic of the select who dedicate their lives to a cause. We call them fanatics but for good or evil it is these intense natures who build religions, formulate ideologies, propagate scientific truth, and prophesy and organize revolutions. Inflamed by the vision, they are ready to embrace martyrdom for themselves as well as for others. When a concatenation of these molders of destiny with the right combination of social circumstances takes place, history echoes their fury and the face of society is transmuted.

When the troubled earth begins to subside and the revolutionary lava starts to cool off, it is not the orators, the theoreticians, who survive but the organizers and the manipulators of political machines. The idea men are among the first of its children to be devoured by revolution.[24] Danton gives way to Robespierre and Trotsky and Bukharin to Stalin. Intellectualism is a hindrance to enduring day-to-day political leadership. Intellectuals have too close an identification with their governing ideas to be able to shed them easily as a sacrifice to the expediency of remaining in power. The party machine has only one loyalty: to gain and hold power. Loyalty to ideas is a hindrance to a machine politician, although ideas must be used as symbols in the political arena for the benefit of the customers. It is statesmen like Lincoln and Roosevelt who possess the politician's flexibility within the framework of long-term tenacity of purpose.

The displacement phenomenon is another device of power socialization of importance in the political and economic fields. It may be considered another aspect of the identification mechanism and operates through the process of cultural conditioning. Through it the attitudes, emotions, loyalties, and configurations of the family are displaced toward the state and other organizations.[25] The king has been referred to as the father of his children and the employer conceives of himself as the paterfamilias of one great happy family. When the employees of this type of employer join a union, he takes it as a personal affront to a devoted father by ungrateful children.[26] In displacement, filial devotion becomes school spirit or even patriotism.

One of the most effective devices for socialization of power to induce socially approved behavior on the part of the mass of the people is the proclivity of mankind to conform. Some consider the need for approval by his fellows as man's strongest motivation.[27] The gang spirit, climbing on the band wagon, the warming sense of belonging, all these are reflections of man's fear of being alone and out of society. Even the rebel is no exception, for he chooses a select loyalty which gives him the strength to defy the prevailing social climate. To gain the approval of his fellows and thereby express his impulse to power, man will to a limit sacrifice on occasion the satisfaction of his biologic needs, even life itself. It is the stuff of which heroism, sacrifice, and patriotism are made. When cultivated with the proper indoctrination it is the cement of society, enabling a community to survive at the expense of its individuals.

The desire for conformity is the driving force for the transformation as well as the endurance of mores. From the desire for conformity and adjustment may be deduced the principle that theories of human behavior and motivation carry within them the germ of their own validation. The masked savage goes through the motions of the beast whose likeness he wears.[28]

Man's need for conformity is chiefly responsible for society's exercising its authority over man through the irrational aspects of conscience, or what Freud has called the superego.[29]

Reason is the solvent of irrational social authority but not of social ties. On the contrary, reason seeks to strengthen the social bonds by exposing the irrationality of the conflict between man and society. Its purpose is to provide socially acceptable modes of expression for the human drives, which do not depend on irrational sanctions as do the other modes of socializing power. Because of that, reason's role in reorienting and canalizing irrational drives has not been notably successful in history. Only the select few may claim that they have synthesized man's duality on the plane of reason. That, however, does not mean that social intelligence has been completely powerless.

Reason must be distinguished from rationalization, which is the process of defending antisocial expressions of ego power by assigning to them socially approved motives.[30] The objective of rationalization is to counteract and defeat the socialization of power. While the purpose of society is to convince the individual that what is good for society is good for him, by rationalization the individual seeks to convince society and himself that what is good for him is good for society. This underlies most of the propaganda of the pressure groups. Rationalization is at the bottom of every philosophy, particularly political theory. When faith begins to crumble philosophy comes to the rescue.[31] Thomas Aquinas lends a helping hand to Paul of Tarsus. In the Declaration of Independence the Founding Fathers, like all revolutionists, evidenced a need to justify their cause before the world. The need for justifying our desires in terms of the common good is abundant proof of the hold that the community has over the individual. It is also the measure of the triumph of democratic ideology as a moral mechanism. Even Hitler found it necessary to justify his leadership by proclaiming that he knew best what was good for the people. Rationalization is the shield of the elite against the encroachments of the masses.[32] It is one of the chief ingredients of ideologies.

One more mechanism for socialization of power needs to be considered: tangible checks to its exercise. These checks may be in the form of competition from other individuals in the community or from the coercive powers of the community as a whole. They are present in all societies, and at all times. When the individual's quest for power comes in conflict with these checks or where such conflict impends, in most cases it is to some extent curbed in its direct expression, and socially approved avenues are resorted to for its exercise. The manner of the adjustment of the individual to these social checks on his quest for power is of the essence of social and political struggle.[33]

To implement the various mechanisms for the socialization of power society resorts to a number of instruments and sanctions. It uses the symbolism and ceremonials of religion, of class, group associations, and of nationalism. It utilizes the propaganda of the deed as well as of the word. It resorts to all forms of power: military, economic, political, ideological, and rational. It has had at its disposal throughout history all sorts of myths and sanctions of authority: deity, race, will of the people, reason, science.[34] Most of these appear in combination in any given social situation. The nature of the combination of mechanisms of socialization of power and their instruments and sanctions varies with the type or form of government.[35]

Where the social situation is such that the mechanisms of socialization of power work with reasonable success, the society is said to reach an equilibrium in which the conflicts among men's quests for power are reduced to governable proportions. However, where circumstances alter to such an extent that the mechanisms for socialization of power no longer operate successfully, social upheavals and revolutions are the result and man's quest for power sheds the restraining influence of traditions and mores and seeks direct expression.[36] Everything is fair in love and war—and in revolutions. In revolutions the mailed fist is stripped of the velvet glove. Naked power, violence, combined with deceit, fraud, and cruelty, becomes the ultimate sanction of authority, and the crown of success adorns the brow of the most determined and ruthless. Those who seek the places of the mighty will not cast aside needful weapons, nor will those who are dethroned. The struggle for power then exhibits its Machiavellian character, for both the ins and the outs lack individual security, the necessary condition for a peaceful society.[37] The operation of the mechanisms for socialization of power produces an emphasis on security which pleases, shelters, and tames the ego. In times of upheaval the ego's security is undermined and the quest for power must begin all over again to find gratifications. Insecurity activates the quest for power, and when that insecurity operates in the economic field the struggle is embittered and sharpened to extremes. The quest for power then takes the elementary form of a struggle for survival to satisfy the elementary wants of food and shelter.

It has become commonplace to observe the cruelty, ruthlessness, deceit, violence, bloodiness, and unreason of our times.[38] The revolution of our day in the domestic and international realms has weakened and destroyed the mechanisms for the socialization of man's quest for power, thereby creating chaos, insecurity, and a relentless struggle for power. Not until the social, economic, and political forces internally and externally reach a degree of balance in the power struggle will peace prevail and man's inhumanity to man become manageable.

This does not end the analysis of man's drive for power. A further examination can most advantageously be undertaken by analyzing its ramifications in the various aspects of the state.

In conclusion, two questions should be dealt with. First, does man's quest for power have also an opposite tendency? The doctrine of opposite tendencies in human drives is widely accepted. We have seen that man's impulse to power may express itself through identification with a leader's lust for power through abject submission to that leader. Whether such submissiveness exists as a direct and not a derivative impulse of the drive for power is not certain. In other words, whether Aristotle's dictum that men are "masters" or "slaves" by nature has some psychological basis or is merely an attempt to justify a social system by its results is shrouded in doubt.[39] What is probable is that men differ in the strength and character of their impulse to power as in all other physical and mental traits. Ambivalent as each man may be in his tendencies to domination or submission, one or the other tendency is usually dominant and is conditioned in the interplay of man's innate equipment with his total environment. What may also be posited is that man's drive for power may be subject to degeneration as is his sex drive or his other capacities.

The second objection that might be raised to the foregoing analysis is that the concept of man's drive for power does not sufficiently allow for man's so-called altruistic inclinations. Yet the power theory is amoral, for the drive for power may have so-called self-regarding as well as altruistic expressions. Hitler's drive for world domination and a scientist's striving for achievement may both be different expressions of the same impulse to power, but what a difference in expression or result. Both Hitler and the scientist may be considered selfish, since both do what pleases them. But if Hitler's cruelties, aggressions, hostility, and hatred are expressions of innate potentialities for evil present in man, it is also true that in varying degree man has great potentialities in his nature for good as well.[40] Perhaps man's altruistic impulses of love, tenderness, and sacrifice for others are, as it has been suggested, derivatives of man's sexual and reproduction drives. But in any case the probability is that these potentialities are equally innate. Man carries within him the seeds of God and of the devil. It is the altruistic impulses that facilitate the socialization of man's lust for power.

CHAPTER III

Organization and Power

1. POLITICAL POWER

Political power arises from man's striving to master his social environment.[1] Since the social environment is based on the wills of the individuals who compose a community, mastery of the social environment involves control of the wills of the members of society or community. Exercise of control over the wills of others is the function of political power. Politics is the struggle of wills for mutual control within a sphere of power.[2] Political control is not coextensive with domination. It may include domination, but is not limited to it. Cooperation also is a mode of control.

The most obvious sphere of power for the exercise of political control has traditionally been the state, but political power is not limited in its application to the state. It is present in any association of individuals. Common speech gives recognition to this social phenomenon. That there is too much politics in a lodge, fraternity, business, church, or some charitable organization has been a frequent observation. Nor is the family free from politics. However subtly and imperceptibly it works itself out, the marital relationship involves a struggle of wills for supremacy. Since the control of wills in the marital relationship expresses itself on the psychic level, a definite decision in the contest of wills is as satisfying to the subordinate as to the dominant partner, if both positions correspond to their psychic needs.

In economic activities, political power is utilized wherever it is necessary to organize the wills of the participants for a common purpose. Here is the distinction between economic and political power. Tilling the soil, operating a machine, or performing directly any work is economic in character, but the act of organizing, directing, and supervising men in the performance of economic tasks is political in character. Industrial management is political power applied to the economic realm.

Similarly, in church, fraternal, and other associations political power consists of controlling the will of the members to advance the common purposes. Military organizations more than any other type of association are characterized by the prevalent use of political power. Unquestioning obedience to the commands of a superior and the rigid hierarchical structure of military forces bespeak absolutist dominance—the most primitive form of controlling the will of man.

While political power is universally present in all types of organized activities, it also makes use of all types of power. Men are made to obey commands by military or physical force or by the fear of its application, by the fear of economic retaliation or by expectation of economic rewards, or because they are convinced that their obedience is sanctioned by authority or is to their benefit. The latter result is obtained by the use of myths, symbols and ceremonials, which are found in all religious and secular ideologies and are transmitted through law, custom, propaganda, and education. The means employed to obtain and exercise political power may be as broad in scope as the mechanisms and sanctions used to socialize power.[3] In fact, socialization of power may be viewed as a political act when it has as its purpose the control of the individual wills composing a community.

What is the purpose of political power as distinguished from its function? Since man in the satisfaction of his needs finds himself in competition with his fellows, he seeks to control the wills of his fellows in order to protect and increase his share of the total means available for gratification of his wants. As one student put it, politics is "who gets what, when, how."[4] Political power, however, is not limited to competition to obtain means of satisfying our physiological wants. It is useful in the competition to satisfy man's drive for power over and above what is necessary to satisfy his elementary needs, in other words, that which we have called his ego power. In fact, political power has been the chief means for the most extravagant expression of man's quest for power. Alexander and Napoleon, Genghis Khan and Hitler—the world's conquerors throughout history have not been those with shrinking egos given to self-abnegation.

The reason why politics has throughout history been the main field for the expression of power is that up to modern times man lacked the technology to make much of a dent in his quest for mastery over his natural environment. His drive for power even to satisfy his material wants was canalized into a drive for power over his fellows. To escape from the dreariness of monotonous backbreaking toil man sought control over others. The only way to get sufficient of the world's goods for oneself has been to deprive others of their share. The reason that the Greeks never called slavery into question is that their economy was not sufficiently productive to enable everyone to enjoy the goods, and particularly the leisure, required to cultivate the virtues of the good life. The good society had therefore to be limited to the few.[5]

What is perhaps a more significant factor in fashioning political power as a most powerful weapon is the psychic need that man has for his fellow creatures. His dependence on them for such ego satisfactions as love, glory, prestige, and achievement makes control over them highly gratifying and failure of control frustrating. Man's evaluation of himself is not absolute, but is relative to the position of others in the social hierarchy. The process of controlling one's fellows has involved the expression of man's most primitive and emotionally most productive drives and impulses, sex, murder, sadism, masochism. More men want to be Napoleon than Newton.

2. THE NATURE AND PRINCIPLES OF ORGANIZATION

Out of the competition of wills to establish control within a power system or relationship organization is born. As soon as control is established between two or more individuals, organization is present, for organization is the control of the wills of individuals directed to a definite purpose. Since the function of political power is to exercise control over the wills of others, political power is the basis of organization irrespective of the purpose of a particular organization. Nor is the purpose ever lacking when two or more wills enter into a control system, whether that control is achieved by domination or cooperation, for man seeks to control the wills of his fellows to ensure the means of satisfying his needs. The great organizations of society may be classified according to the elementary needs they purpose to satisfy.[6] Economic organization supplies us with the means of satisfying our hunger, thirst, and need of shelter. The family organization furnishes us with outlets for the satisfaction of our sex hunger and reproduction drives. Through the state organization we obtain protection against internal disorder and the external enemy. Nor are our psychic needs neglected as the multiplicity of churches, schools, libraries, theaters, and fraternal societies indicates.

A prerequisite to the birth of organization is the existence of a system of power, that is, a sphere or area of experience where two or more individual units come in contact or in relation to each other. The most obvious type of a sphere of power is spatial. For people to form an organization they must be in contact or in communication with one another. Geographical propinquity is therefore indispensable in the formation and development of primitive communities and loses its importance as means of communication develop. The concept of a sphere of power in geographical terms is essential to an understanding of international relations.

Spheres of power may be determined also by the type of activity involved. Those engaged in the same business or profession in the same community may be said to be contained in the same economic power sphere, where their competition to establish a power control results in the organization of men along common economic interests: employer associations or labor unions.[7]

The organization that comes into being when control of wills is established within a power system may be temporary or permanent, depending upon the purpose that animates the participants and their capacities as organizers. The transitory, organizationally rudimentary character of a lynching mob may be contrasted with the highly crystallized millennial Roman Catholic Church.

The tendency, however, of social organizations is to project themselves in terms of time as much as possible within their system of power. This and other characteristics of organizations are due to the fact that organizations are the vehicles for the operation of man's drives or quest for power. Since man's impulse to power is limitless, organizations too exhibit the same power drives. Organizations and institutions have a tendency to continue their existence long after the reason for their being has evaporated.

Another tendency of organization due to man's limitless quest for power is to expand in size. In this connection man's lust for power expresses itself in a drive for monopoly in behalf of a particular organization within its system of power. The psychological weakness of the classical capitalist theory is that its basic assumption of self-regulated competition does not sufficiently recognize man's use of political and economic power to avoid competition.[8] Man abhors competition. He seeks to avoid it in love, in business, and in international relations, for it undermines his security and is a check to his quest for power. We are less than fond of the competitor for the affections of those we love. Monopoly is man's goal, not competition, even in games and sports where the results are not fraught with as much import as in conflicts where the stakes are men's lives and fortunes. It is not competition that we seek, but competition which leads to victory. Unless competition is enforced by some supervising authority it tends to disappear from its system of power and be replaced by monopoly.[9]

Another reflection of man's quest for power is the tendency of organization to increase the scope of its activities and functions, thereby enhancing the intensity of organization. Power can be multiplied extensively or intensively. Organization may grow by an increase in membership or in the controls over members. Both methods are cultivated.

Christianity began with the injunction to give unto Caesar the things that are Caesar's but, as the church became secure it sought to establish its dominion over Caesar. The struggle between church and state is one of the great issues throughout history and is evident even in democracies, where church and state are separated.[10]

What contributes to the trend toward expansion of organizational functions is the complex character of our society and the consequent difficulty of drawing lines of demarcation between various spheres of activity. The increasing conflict and overlapping of activities of government agencies is one example.[11] The complexity of society contributes to increasing the power systems or spheres within which organizations operate. This obviously expands the scope of monopoly drives of organizations in terms of functions as well as size.

Another principle of organization is the tendency to evolve from the simple to the complex. Increase in the size of an organization and in the scope of its functions contributes to making it more complex. How this complexity is proliferated and the nature of the process constitute one of the most significant elements in social and political evolution.

The initial governing principle to be considered is the differentiation of the status of the individual wills in relation to the control system established by organization. When two individuals enter into a control system of wills, an indispensable differentiation occurs in the status of the component wills. The differentiation in their status may be identified as that of superordination and subordination. However covert and subtle this may be, the psychic relationship at least is one of superior to inferior status, one of command to obedience, one of leadership to following, irrespective of the type of power used to establish a control of wills or organization.

This hierarchical relationship of wills crystallizes itself into a differentiation of function, between the one who does the controlling and the one who is controlled, between the manager and the worker, between the ruler and the ruled. The hierarchy of wills expresses itself in an hierachy of function. This is the essential nature of organization and constitutes its elementary form.

Great social organizations and institutions are not, however, to be found in this rudimentary form. What is ultimately responsible both for the proliferation of social organizations and for their internal complexity is the division of labor. The one great unalterable division of labor or of function in society is to be found in the family institution between the sexes. On this is superimposed the division of labor in the family in regard to obtaining the means of satisfaction of the family's wants. Of broader political scope and implication is the economic division of labor.[12] With the increase of man's knowledge and its application to the mastery of his environment, division of labor and specialization have grown apace.

Division of labor and consequent specialization increase the mutual interdependence of those affected, thereby creating a system of power where control eventuates not only as the result of man's quest for power but because of the need for integration. This principle is of the utmost importance in understanding not only the nature of administration but social and political evolution. Those whose functions are alike need not be associated together although they may do so to defend their interests through collective action. But those whose functions are dissimilar but contribute to a common end product have to be integrated or co-ordinated in order to make possible the achievement of the common purpose. Independent craftsmen, each producing a whole article, can work separately, but the minute division of labor occurs it makes necessary ultimately the closely integrated institution of modern industry and management.

The quest for power operating in conjunction with the need for integration results in the trend from diffusion to concentration or centralization of power. In the same organization the tendency is for one locus of authority to eliminate its rival. For that reason federalism is a transitory stage tending in the direction of the unitary form.[13]

The more differentiation of function there is—the result of division of labor—the greater the need for integration, which is effectuated through the establishment of power control within a power system. But the multiplication of the integrative decisional or supervisory functions increases the burden of those who issue orders. In these situations so-called bottlenecks or congestions of authority in the flow of organizational power are created. There simply is not enough time or energy available to the one in command to enable him to direct the multitudinous activities of a complex organization.

The remedy for this pathology in management is delegation and subdelegation of authority. Consequently, the greater the division of labor and differentiation of function the more numerous becomes the supervisory or directing cadre. But those who exercise delegated or subdelegated authority need of course to be co-ordinated or integrated by those above them. Complex organization, therefore, constitutes multilevel supervision which narrows as it ascends the scale, for in the nature of integration, those who co-ordinate are fewer than those who are co-ordinated. A complex, highly developed organization resembles a hierarchical pyramidal structure of power. The degree of control each individual in the pyramid exercises is roughly in proportion to the distance from the base of the pyramid or in reverse proportion to the distance from the top of the pyramid. Similarly, the amount of power each will exercise within the pyramid of power is in reverse ratio to the number of wills exercising the same degree of power. Those having more power are fewer in number than those having less, and as the amount of power exercised by each individual diminishes, the number of those exercising it increases. Every organization represents a class structure composed of a small upper class, a more numerous middle class, and a most numerous lower class. No clear demarcation between the classes is feasible, for the differences are graduated. The "iron law of oligarchy" is therefore inherent in the nature and structure of organization.[14] The analogy to the class structure of society is apparent.[15]

The tendencies of organizations to grow in size and in the scope of their functions lend fillip to the need for division of labor, differentiation, and integration. In fact, the pathology and degeneration of organization largely revolve around the problem of size, intensity, and complexity of organization.[16]

The tendency of organization to evolve from the simple to the complex may be viewed as a development from the amorphous to the crystallized or stratified. The system of power within which organization develops is completely amorphous. As organization develops and differentiation begins to take form as in an embryo, the uniform amorphousness begins to disappear and give way to ever greater crystallized distinctions. A fully developed complex organization is highly stratified in structure and highly specialized in function and status of its members. One characteristic of such an organization may be lack of flexibility in adjustment to changing conditions, a rigidity which may sometimes spell its demise. In terms of personnel, extreme stratification may mean a lack of what Pareto called "circulation of the elite"—and a consequent need for fresh blood.[17]

Still another important aspect of organizational development is the tendency for organizations to evolve from the unconscious to the intentional or planned. Most of the great social institutions have come into being in response not to articulated but to mute and unconscious purpose, and their early development is shrouded in custom, tradition, and planlessness. It is only with evolution that the traditional and unintended give way to the purposeful and the planned. The small primitive business entrepreneur had no definite plan for controlling the operations of the enterprise but a modern corporation has a budget. In fact, he could not have had a plan, for he lacked the necessary control over the power system in which he operated and was buffeted by the winds of fortune. The large corporation of today, relatively speaking, has greater power within its sphere and therefore can make plans for the future. Planning is power. Planning is impossible without the existence of power to carry out the plans. True integration of differentiation within an organization cannot take place unless a definite purpose or plan exists. Although there are vital distinctions in the type and degree of planning, it is the indispensable criterion of men's mastery over his environment. In the more rudimentary type of planning, adjustment is made to a sector of the environment over which no control can be exercised. This is exemplified by budgetary curtailment made by the individual businessman during or in anticipation of a depression. In the highly developed form of planning, the relevant sector of the environment itself is altered to conform to the purpose of the planner.

All these principles of organization and its development will be applied and receive further exposition in connection with the analysis of the nature, functions, and development of the state.

CHAPTER IV

Man and the State

1. THE NATURE OF THE STATE

The establishment of a control of wills within a sphere of power directed to achieving a certain purpose, in other words, organization, is a widespread phenomenon. Man is an organizational animal. To satisfy his wants he acts through organizations. This becomes more and more the case as society grows in complexity. Society is in fact the totality of man's relationships for the satisfaction of all his wants. When there is a configuration of these relationships in time and space we have a community, which may be either a village, a town, or a city.[1]

The state is the community organized as a whole and independently, in other words, the complete and ultimate power control integration of a total power system.[2] The government is the instrumentality or agency of the state for the performance of its functions. The state is the most complete and extensive power control yet established. This does not, of course, deny that states have relations with each other, which therefore may constitute a greater power sphere or system. But this sphere is not yet subject to control, which would be the case if a world government were established. Nor is every community a state. A village or city is a community but it is not a state, for though it may be organized it is not a self-sufficent independent power control system but is part of a state.[3] Identifying the state as an organization of the community is not the same as conceiving of it as an organism.[4]

It follows that wherever and whenever an independent community exists it constitutes a state. The corollary of the definition is that the state is as old as society itself, and just as it is impossible for man because of his nature to have lived outside of society, so has man never lived outside of the state.[5] As long as man lives in society, so long will he live within the confines of a state, whether a world state or one of more limited territory.

Throughout history the state exhibits a great variety of forms and character, both from the standpoint of scope, function, organs of government, form of power wielded and from that of distribution and basis of power. Special pleaders, because of their opposition to the policies of a particular type of state, have equated the whole concept and institution of the state with one form. The philosophical anarchists, opposed to the capitalist police state based on force and private property, declared abolition of the state as an objective.[6] The syndicalists rejected political means and relied on the economic weapon of the strike, and at least some like Sorrel apotheosized violence.[7] The Marxists, more realistic, hoped to capture the machinery of the state, promising the while that in the fullness of time the state would wither away, without furnishing any enlightenment on how this would occur.[8] The history of Soviet Russia could hardly furnish a text for a sermon on state atrophy.

The state as an institution transcends and cannot be equated with any of its forms. It is illogical to identify the state with the modern national state and deny its existence in feudal society or in the classical ancient world.[9] There is no historical foundation for Oppenheimer's position, elaborating on Gumplowitz, that the origin of the state as of social classes is due to conquest, originally of the husbandmen or agriculturists by the herdsmen.[10] Both the conquerors and the conquered lived in organized communities or states before the forcible coalescence occurred. There is no question that conquest and force played their important role in the formation of historical states and in influencing their evolution, but they do not account for the origin of the state as an institution which is inherent in and inseparable from society itself.[11]

Nor can property account for the origin of the state. Man was a member of a state when he was a huntsman, a herdsman, or an agriculturist. Territoriality is not a sine qua non element of statehood,[12] although it has become nearly that when society became in a sense attached to a fixed territory. The nomads, while migrating from land to land in response to vicissitudes in hunting and pasturing, and sweeping everything before them, were amorphous military formations akin to flying columns and constituted an organized social unit—a state. States have existed where property was feudal in ownership, privately owned, or collectively owned as in Russia.

The essential characteristic of all states in all stages of development is that each state, unlike other social organizations, constitutes a complete and self-sufficiently organized power system. The state as the controlling and integrative organization encompasses and determines the interrelationships and status of all individuals and associations composing the state. It is the state and the state alone among all types of associations that possesses the coercive power of enforcement. This does not mean that if in the future evolution of power coercion might conceivably be eliminated from social relations the state would disappear. The integrative function of the state would still be operative. Integrative control is quite compatible with diversity. For instance, in the United States freedom of religion is a constitutional principle. This means not that the state power of the United States does not apply to the religious realm but that in the religious realm the only control the state chooses to exercise is to guarantee the right to diversity. The American principle of religious freedom does not lend support to the pluralist doctrine of sovereignty, for it is the state that determines the status of the constituent organizations and is therefore superior to them in terms of power.[13]

States, then, differ among themselves in the type of control and integration they exercise in regard to various activities or phases of the total environment in which they find themselves. The type of integration that a state exercises is one of the chief distinguishing criteria among governments.[14]

What determines the type of integration, the policies of a state or its government at any particular time? This is a function of the supreme power or sovereignty within a state, which is the dominant resultant of the crosscurrents of all the forces and influences, not only that of government personnel, that go to make up an organized community and establish the power control system known as the state.[15]

Since the community organized as a whole, that is, the state, is the ultimate arbiter, all individual quests for power operating either as individuals or through groups and associations strive to control the state in order to obtain, defend, and increase their share of the total supply of means to satisfy wants—the aims of politics. Since man's quest for power is interminable and unequal as among individuals, as to both intensity and means of implementation, the contest of politics and the resultant supreme power in control of the state are constant and fluid. It is therefore more appropriate to speak of the process rather than the locus of sovereignty. Sovereignty may shift imperceptibly and be in fluid equilibrium, as in orderly times, or it may undergo violent and radical dislocation, as in revolutionary times, but it is always dynamic. Since man's quest for power operates through collective efforts of groups and organizations, as well as through individuals, the impact of the struggle of classes as well as of individuals for the control of the state becomes important.[16]

The given definition of sovereignty avoids the pitfall of advancing a teleological interpretation of the state, whether it conceives of the state as an instrument of exploitation in the hands of the dominant class[17] or as a means of achieving the common good.[18] Through the ages the state has been used even simultaneously to implement both purposes. The same capitalist state has been used to suppress labor unions and to sanction and protect them. What the state will do in any field at a particular time will depend on the reflection by the dominant influence of the manner and extent to which man's impulse to power has been politically socialized. The socialization of power constitutes the form of the state, democracy or dictatorship, for instance.[19] A better perspective on the nature of the state may be obtained by examining its growth and development.

2. THE ORIGIN OF THE STATE—THE FAMILY STATE

The history of the state parallels broadly the evolution of society. Similarly, primeval society would also constitute the rudimentary state. What is the primordial social community or institution? Perhaps a clue to the history of the race is afforded by the history of the individual, just as an embryo repeats the stages of evolution of the race.

A man is not born into the world but into a family and until he draws his last breath he never leaves it. It is the family that almost exclusively constitutes his world during the most formative period of his life. It is the image of his family that he carries within him when he leaves the parental fold to venture into the hostile world beyond. And this empty world he interprets in relation to and integrates in terms of his relationships within his family. Through the mechanism of transference man's larger society becomes peopled with the images of the family and is saturated with the hates and joys, aggressions and loves that the child was wont to receive and give to those about him. Man furnishes the world with his family furniture and populates it with his relatives.[20] The father image is displaced to political or economic authority. Even the revolutionary is not free from the hold of the family though Oedipus-like, is driven to his parricidal destiny. The father is dead; long live the father.[21]

The familial grip on the individual is a reflection of the aboriginal history of the race. It is the family that constitutes the irreducible community, sufficient to satisfy man's minimum biological and psychic needs. The family, therefore, could constitute the primordial human community, and the weight of anthropological authority points in that direction.[22] Sex promiscuity and group marriages are not considered as probable social antecedents of individual marriage, except in atypical circumstances.[23] Nor is the best evidence on the side of those who claim primacy for the matriarchate in primeval society.[24] Even in matrilineal societies, where the children followed in the line of the mother because maternity was a fact but paternity a presumption, the husband was the dominant member of the family. Because woman's biological function of childbearing and weaker muscular development handicapped her vis-à-vis her husband in the contest to control each other's will, it is not surprising that at least for historical society the patriarchate is generally accepted as the primordial antecedent.[25] For the suffragists at least the golden age is not in the past.

But if the patriarchal family was man's primeval society or social organization, could it also be considered as the aboriginal state? The answer must be in the affirmative.[26] The family was an independently organized community or power system which exhibited every characteristic and function of the state. Because of the smallness of the state unit and the consequent lack of a developed division of labor, the functions and organs of state were not yet crystallized but they existed in rudimentary form.[27] The property at the disposal of the family belonged to the family as a whole, just as territory is now at the disposal of the developed territorial state.[28] Within the insulated family unit there existed an intricate legal structure in the form of custom defining the interrelationship of its members. There was a class structure and a hierarchy of governors and governed biologically conditioned. The husband and father performed the functions of protector of the family lives and property against his aggressor neighbor. He acted as the magician, shaman, or priest in the family worship. He was legislator, executive, judge, jury, prosecutor, executioner, general, and priest.[29] To deny him the title of governor because in him the functions of government, which were later to be separated and specialized, were united is to deny the title of physician to the general practitioner because medicine is undergoing the process of specialization.

Unless we conceive of the family as the primordial state and not just a social unit we cannot fully comprehend the nature of the state. The family considered as a state affords a valuable clue to the evolution of the state.

Kinship was not only the basis of the original state but the initial determinant of its expansion. Multiplication of generations increased the number of families but the consciousness of common descent welded them into a unit presided over by the oldest patriarch. The family expanded into a sib, gens, clan, and tribe. Religion, which in the earliest period was essentially ancestor worship, was the ideological cement of the kinship state and made it more cohesive by providing the supernatural sanctions.[30] Religion was even flexible enough to sanction for adoption into the common descent of strangers to the blood when the expanding kinship group needed their inclusion.[31] The fiction of the common descent is not to be looked at, however, as a repudiation of the kinship principle but as its support, for by inclusion of strangers into the common fold the way was open through intermarriage to enlarge the kinship power system.

Nor is this process at an end. Modern nationalism is a derivative of the kinship principle, even though racial purity is a fiction. For consciousness of common descent, nationalism offers an awareness of common tradition; for common ancestors, the Founding Fathers; for the common blood and loyalties to the kinship group, the common culture and loyalty to fatherland and frequently common language and religion. By the element of propinquity within a common territory and consequent intermarriage, nationalism may serve to create a common blood bond.³² In any case, one of the cardinal errors of Marxism is its underestimation of the influence of the institution of nationalism. Russia has abundantly demonstrated that private ownership is not the basis of nationalism. Russia has reached its greatest nationalistic development under a collectivist economy and an ideology internationally oriented.³³

Nor is nationalism the only vestige of the kinship principle in the evolution of the state. In the Chinese state, and to a lesser extent in the Japanese state, the kinship principle has been interwoven with and embodied in the state.³⁴ In the West, a significant aspect of its social and political history may be characterized as the progressive breakup of the family state, in which process the family has been losing its political, legal, economic, and educational functions to the greater state that has been superseding it.

As the family was expanding into the greater kinship groupings of gens, clan, tribe, and ultimately into the territorial state, the family did not immediately lose its state functions and identity, which it would have done if it were only a social institution and not a state. The first government of the assembled clans or tribes was the patriarchs who participated as ambassadors or representatives of sovereign family states.³⁵ They came together to consult on matters of common interest such as defense against the common enemy or to secure internal peace, but this gerontocracy was not the government of a single state or power control but only the first step toward the creation of a unified state. Any decisions arrived at depended for ultimate sanction and enforcement on the will and action of the representatives of the participating family states. In the expanded state even at a late stage of evolution, which in some cases projected into kingship, the maintenance of internal order, the elementary police function of the state, was not the right or duty of the state but of the component family states.³⁶ This explains the institution of lex talionis, or self-help. When a breach of the peace took place, the injury to the individual was not a matter for the greater state to recognize but was considered within the peculiar province of the injured individual and his family, in other words, of the family state. The family state of the aggressor did not punish him, unless the delict in some way endangered the safety of the family state. The law of the expanded state in that stage of development was in all essentials the same as international law.³⁷ A breach of international law by a state or a member of that state is punished by the action of the injured state against the offending state, and only to the extent that its military power is superior.

It was not until after a long period of development, when the expanded state was well established and integrated, that it was able to afford a forum for compensation of damages to the injured and subsequently to provide a police system to prevent and punish the commission of breaches of the peace.[38] Then did it supplant the family state in internal security.

Similarly, the expanded state did not at first arrogate to itself the function of providing external security. Only in a relatively late stage of development does the expanded state monopolize the external security function by building up its own military forces, which replace the autonomous levies of the kinship groups.[39]

Even in regard to the civil and political rights and obligations of its members has the family state not yet fully and universally loosened its grip. That women's right to the political franchise has only in the twentieth century come to be recognized is due to the cultural lag anchored in the patriarchal family state in which the patriarch constituted the government. Similarly with respect to property rights of married women, a comparatively recent development.[40]

The influence of the family state on the evolution of the expanded state will appear also in other areas, as in the class structure of society, and in the form and organs of government.[41]

The original family community was a simple concentrated unicellular state. As the number of families multiplied through family division offshoots, new and more expanded power systems were established through the interrelationships of families and the ensuing struggle for supremacy, in which various forms of power, including personal qualities of leadership, property, force, and magic, played a part.[42]

This is not to say that states do not disintegrate. As a result of either conquest from without or disintegration from within, when the central authority, as among feudal states, is incapable of maintaining its power against the centrifugal tendencies of the component parts, states cease to exist.[43] History is the graveyard of states. But that does not deny the inner tendency of states to expand. Every acorn does not grow into an oak, for the soil and other circumstances may not be suitable. But little acorns do have a tendency to grow into big oaks.

Identifying the state with the independently organized community and the primordial state with the family would ascribe the nature and genesis of the state to a widespread, parallel, or independent development. Even in tracing the evolution of the state, similar circumstances would tend to evolve similar institutions. But, as intercommunication between peoples increases, there is no doubt that diffusion of culture plays its part in spreading state forms as well as other aspects of culture to neighboring countries, thus permitting the recipient countries to skip some aspects of stages of development. But we must guard against an extreme diffusionist position,[44] for no culture can duplicate another even though it may utilize the same idea or institution. The same idea may produce dissimilar consequences when the context of circumstances differs.[45] Capitalism in the United States and Great Britain has differed materially in its ramifications from its counterpart in Germany and Japan.[46]

CHAPTER V

The State in Precapitalist Economies

1. FAMILIAL, FEUDAL, TOWN AND MERCANTILIST ECONOMIES

Since the state is the independently organized community and man has never lived outside the state, it follows that property is not responsible for the formation of the state.[1] Similarly, property is not responsible for the class differentiation of society.[2] Economic determinism is false in giving methods of production a universal and invariable priority and causative influence on the prevailing social and cultural relations. True, there is some correspondence between the methods of production and the prevailing culture but one is not the active cause and the other the passive result. Nor is the political system made to order for methods of production. In our own time the assembly line has been operating successfully in democratic-capitalist Detroit, in Nazi Berlin, and in Communist Stalingrad. Methods of production and other aspects of a culture interact and are both cause and effect. It is the business of discerning inquiry to discriminate in which way the mutual influence expresses itself.[3]

Although property did not contain the genesis of the family state, it greatly strengthened it. Property was owned by the family. This must not be confused with communism, for the individual family members did not participate in the ownership that belonged to the family; its management belonged exclusively to the patriarch.[4] Property added the element of permanence to the relationship between husband and wife, bolstering up or even supplanting the capricious and often ephemeral sex attraction.[5] The family has gained immeasurably from mixing business with pleasure.

The cementing influence that property exercised on the family expressed itself also in regard to the children. As society passed through the stages of the hunter, the herdsman, and the agriculturist, and developed a "surplus" of goods in the form of cattle, grain, and land to be cultivated, it was advantageous to the patriarch to keep the sons in the household because of their usefulness as workers. Also, inheritance acquired a tangible advantage for the heirs and a strenghtened psychic advantage for the patriarch. Since property involves an extension of the ego, inheritance of property became a means to perpetuate the ego.[6] Inheritance of property fortified biologic immortality.

As the families multiplied and the family state expanded into the sibs, gens, clan, and tribe, the family remained the unit of ownership. There was no longer communal ownership until a later stage of development. After a protracted gradual evolution, the expanded state became first a kinship feudality and later a mixed feudality based on both kinship and nonkinship forms of power, such as territory, property, and conquest. Above all, the element of territoriality enters as a dominant factor influencing the development of the state when the agriculturist replaces the huntsman and the herdsman. Although the nomadic states roamed within a rather limited range, primitive conception of territory was inchoate. It was not until the transition to agriculture occurred that territoriality replaced kinship as a leading cohesive element of the state, both modifying and coalescing with kinship.[7] In the feudal state, which was a consolidated expanded state, the integrative function of the state in the economic order was complete. In exchange for military protection by the lord, the serf plowed the land of his lord. In the highly developed feudal state, whether of antiquity or the Middle Ages, there was a complete coalescence of political and economic power. The state had a monopoly of the property function as well as of external and internal security. The evolution of the expanded state in the economic order, as in the field of security, was from differentiation and diffusion among the component family units to control and integration in the expanded state.[8]

This evolution, it will be noted, was in regard to the agrarian economy or environment. A similiar if not parallel evolution took place in urban trade, handicraft, or commercial economy. There too the family remained the economic unit long after it was beginning to shed its other functions within the enclosure of the expanded state. It was with the growth of cities that a trade economy evolved. It was in the cities that nonagricultural industry or wealth was created and accumulated, and the money system of exchange developed.[9] Trade and commerce imply exchange, and since communication by sea was less difficult than by land, trading centers with some exceptions tended to be littoral. Some of these became maritime states containing a trading center and a small agricultural hinterland. Since trade and commerce have frequently gone hand in hand with conquest, it is not surprising that the first great empire in the West revolved around the Mediterranean basin and was centered in peninsular, maritime Rome. These maritime states even late in their development exhibited the kinship structure of families, gentes, and tribes, superimposed on a slave system based on property and conquest. Although ownership of commercial and craft enterprises was on a family basis, the cities minutely regulated their trade economies as to price, competition, and other aspects. There was a close correspondence between political and economic power.[10]

A similar development occurred in the medieval towns, with this difference—they did not become, with the exception of the Italian cities, city-states. As the trade centers grew in the Middle Ages and accumulated wealth, they represented a competing power to the feudal economy just as the central king or emperor represented a competing political power. To the traders of the cities the numerous feudalities were obstacles to free communication and trade on a broad geographical scale. To the central government the feudal barons were a check and diminution of authority. Even if the central authority through a series of wars managed to establish control over the feudalities, it was ephemeral, chiefly because the central authority had to delegate to the outlying barons the military power. In an agricultural economy the military could be supported only from agricultural produce on the spot.

Feudal economy and feudal military and political power were inseparable. Feudalism was a vicious circle of diffusion of power tending to become centralized by war and then decentralized and anarchic.[11] The growing wealth of the burghers offered the means of breaking up this cycle. Through taxation and credit offered by the cities, the central authority was able to build up and support standing armies. The application of gunpowder finished the job by dismounting the mailed knight in favor of the king's infantryman.[12] Only Don Quixote rides again.

The modern national state was born out of the union of the burgeoning burghers with the central kingship against the relatively few feudal barons. It represented a victory for those who wielded the political power of the larger power sphere against those who ruled the smaller and weaker power system. The integration of the pyramidal power system of the national state was effected through the alliance of the royal apex with the burgher base against the autonomous anarchic middle tiers of the feudalities. Whenever the many are suppressed by the few, they tend to be united by the one against the few.[13]

As the national state consolidated its power, the coalescence and interpenetration of the political with the new commercial power became embedded in the mercantilist state. Although ownership of property was private, its exercise in terms of ends and means became rigorously regulated by the state. The purposes were not solely or even chiefly economic but a mixture of the economic and the political. The overriding national idea was geopolitical, a self-sufficient, militarily powerful national state. Chief reliance for national defense was placed in economic autarchy. Its colonial expression called for discouragement of manufactures in the colonies, thereby making the colonies economically dependent on the mother country. Regulatory measures included price controls, import and export controls, and strict regulation of the employment relationship: encompassing control and regulation of free labor and indentured servitude; child labor and employment of women; maritime labor and conscription of labor; regulation of wages, hiring, dismissal, absenteeism, and regulation of concerted activities by trades and crafts, including restrictions on admission to a trade. These and other measures were designed to protect the labor market of the capitalists.[14]

2. THE DAWN OF THE MODERN WORLD

It would appear that here was the end of the evolution in the trend from diffusion to state integration and concentration in the realm of property. This state of affairs in fact lasted a few centuries. Then a reaction set in which in time swept away mercantilism and enthroned capitalistic laissez faire. The ensuing change embraced one of the most significant revolutions in the history of mankind in economics, politics, science, philosophy, and other aspects of culture and civilization.

What can be said about the underlying causes and influences? It is not enough to say that the methods of capitalist production could best be served by affording free reign to the individual entrepreneur. True or not, that still had to be proved. Then, how did the idea originate and gain currency? For the idea that property can best be managed by individual effort, free from communal or state control, was new and untried.

Mercantilist regulations proved hampering and burdensome to the economic entrepreneurs after the initial period when the national state consolidated internal peace and communication. The decomposition of the rural feudal economy had advanced far enough to furnish a steady stream of unemployed serfs flocking to join the ranks of the urban proletariat. The parvenus were as a rule in an inferior position, individually considered, as compared to royalty and the nobility in prestige, pomp, and circumstance, those intoxicating draughts of ego satisfaction. But why did not the burghers fight it out on the old battlefield of improvement and modification of state policy, instead of for the removal of the state from regulation of the economy?

The answer perhaps is that the West at that time faced the unfolding of a new world. Literally this was true in a global sense. Man discovered the planet on which he was precariously perched. For a millennium his feet were on the ground, but his ego was anchored in the heavens. The whole store of human knowledge and faith, buttressed by philosophy, socialized man's quest for power in ecclesiastical bonds.[15]

The explorations and navigations, the new astronomy and the new physics, the halting steps in engineering, proved too much for the shackles of the mind.[16] The Ptolemaic cosmology collapsed, and man discovered the earth beneath him and the stars above him. Even if the heavenly city[17] receded into the clouds, there was a whole globe to bounce around and to grab. The Reformation unhinged man's conscience from universal papal authority and ultimately enthroned individual relativism. Once started, ideas have their own dynamics and are carried by their momentum beyond the intent of the original progenitors. Protestantism did not aim to establish religious liberty, but, nevertheless it led to it. National churches gave way to religious freedom and toleration when long and bloody religious wars proved the futility of encasing a state into an ecclesiastic mold. Religion became a divisive, not a cohesive communal force. In economic and political activities intolerance ceased to pay. What did it matter after all what men's ideas about heaven and the godhead were as long as they worked hard, saved steadily, and fought the state's battles? Protestantism also swept away the moral and religious stigma that attached itself during the Middle Ages to usury, profit seeking, and other aspects of mobile wealth. Protestantism sanctioned the activities and motivations of the "economic man" and furnished one of the ideological motors to propel capitalistic individualism.[18] Man became atomized. The Ptolemaic geocentric, anthropomorphic world was cut from under him and he felt himself falling into the abyss of cosmic loneliness. The millennial security of a socialized quest for power was removed, and the ensuing insecurity sharpened the need for a new quest for security and power.[19] The world was fascinating, hostile, and menacing, and the old certitudes no longer worked. What is more, salvation was in the individual. The individual, however, was no longer powerless. The whole world was his oyster. He was acquiring the tools and weapons with which to conquer the new environment. What ultimately ensured the triumph of the new dispensation was that it worked and was useful in a thousand tangible ways. The new science and philosophy were not esoteric and only for the initiate few, for whom knowledge per se was most satisfying to the ego. It was pragmatic and helped one to navigate, to build, to produce, to kill more efficiently, and to gather wealth and power to gratify the ego. Truth triumphs when it is useful.

In the dawn of the modern era, man did not have to sit down with Alexander and weep because there were no more worlds to conquer. There was a whole expanding universe unclaimed, if only man's ego could keep apace. It was up to the individual and all bars were down. Is it any wonder that accent was on power, not on the tamed, passive, and indirect kind but on the wild, direct, ruthless, and amoral. The earth trembled from the unleashed dynamo of Renaissance Man's quest for power. All the arts and fields of human endeavor felt the impact of ruthlessness, deceit, fraud, violence, lust, and achievement.[20] And when Machiavelli held up the mirror to his generation, the vision frightened them, and he was blamed for what they beheld.[21] To destroy illusions is not the way to make friends.

That was the spirit of the times and all shared in it, princes and popes as well as the minor representatives of the elite. When the provincial Luther came to Rome he was shocked, but his subsequent career could serve to illustrate the Prince.[22]

The colonization process also was explosive of the political and economic statist supremacy. In a very real sense the colonist had to build a new world and community. Unlike the Spanish Conquistadores, the Puritans and those who followed them brought along the ethos and ideology of the burgeoning capitalism. The wilderness placed a premium on the acquisitive, the daring, and the ambitious. The rising colonial middle classes were dissatisfied with the crown because of the mercantilist strictures on manufacturers in the colonies in favor of those in the mother country. The American Revolution, in which the merchant and laboring groups played an active role, marked then not only a transfer of the locus of political sovereignty but a social revolution as well, whose full expression was not achieved for several decades.[23] The colonial independence movement was a process similar to the breaking off of distant feudalities from the central authority.

The countries where laissez faire saw greatest development were the colonizing countries or those with a colonial history. Equally trenchant is that capitalist individualism flourished most in England, which among the countries in Europe first entered the Industrial Revolution and achieved national unification. It was therefore to

England's advantage to remove the tariff barriers to international trade. It was also true that the mercantilist system of England and France, having been first to face the task of regulating the great new world economy, found it impossible to encompass. It had no precedents to guide it. By the time Germany reached the critical stage, the experience of England and France could be instructive. This may have been an operative cause why Germany, as it has been said, never had an eighteenth century. There capitalism never achieved the freedom from state interference that it enjoyed in England, France, and the United States.[24] By the time Russia reached the mercantilist stage on the eve of the revolution, her revolutionists no longer marched under the banner of individualism, but under Marxist collectivism which was designed as the successor to developed capitalism not to the infant capitalism of prerevolutionary Russia.[25] The process of cultural diffusion accelerates and telescopes cultural evolution. Different ideologies engrafted different economic and social systems on the same methods of production: economic determinism in reverse.

CHAPTER VI

The State in the Capitalist Economic Order

I. THE MECHANISM OF A SELF-REGULATED ECONOMY

In the new world of emerging liberal capitalism the slate appeared to be clean for a new decalogue of human motivations and social action which was to be consciously antistatist in orientation. Here, then, we have a crucial testing ground of the validity of our thesis, that the interplay of man's quest for power with the need for integration arising from social division of labor must eventuate into state integration of the ecenomy, for the state is the all-encompassing system of power. Let us observe how man's quest for power expressed itself in the capitalist economy, how luxuriant became the division of labor in modern technology; and what forms state integration or government regulation took and its imperatives for the future.

In the dawn of the Industrial Revolution mercantilist regulations, archaic in origin and inflexible in operation, could not possibly, in view of the available knowledge, encompass the need of the new world and were therefore swept away. As is natural in the course of human ideas, a specific nostrum is in time elevated to a panacea, particularly since the struggles for religious, political, and civil liberties were crystallized before economic liberalism. Adam Smith was preceded by Spinoza, Locke, and Milton—and Machiavelli too.[1]

In the realm of economics, the man of power became the "economic man." Liberated from restrictions on the manner of his employment of his energies and resources, his quest for power was to propel him to expanding acquisitiveness for the world's goods. Atomized man would be self-regarding in his lust for economic power. Hedonistic, responding to a pleasure-pain stimulus, and equipped with reasoned knowledge about what is economically most profitable, he set out in his covered wagon to conquer the economic wilderness.[2]

But what of the interests of society? How were the interests of society to be reconciled with those of the individual? The answer lay in making the interests of society dependent upon the interests of man. While medieval society sought to attain the fulfillment of the individual through the welfare of the group, liberal society attempted to advance the interests of the community through the self-regarding activities of the individual. The individual businessman was not conceived as the Rotarian symbol, actuated by an ungovernable passion for service to the community. He was kneaded more out of the substance of Machiavelli and Hobbes.[3] But out of his self-seeking drives was to result, despite his desires, society's good. The socialization of the businessman's drive for more and more was not in terms of modification of his desires or curbing them, but by the check of the counteracting power drives of his fellow businessmen. Competition was the magic formula that was to transmute the dross of selfishness into the gold of public welfare. In economic terms, competition expressed itself through the operation of the "natural law" of supply and demand within the price mechanism of a free market. If the stars above are held in their immutable courses by natural law, why should not the economic relations of men in society? If anthropomorphic God became deistic and fused with the universe in orderly pantheism, why should not man be subject to natural laws?

Absolute liberal capitalism was to operate automatically in somewhat the following oversimplified fashion under the functioning of the natural law of supply and demand. Under this aegis no one estimated the total demand and available supply. These were to be adjusted through the price equilibrium resulting from competition of actual and potential producers to supply an ever greater share of the total demand whatever that might be. If more was produced than the consumer would purchase, prices would drop. This would squeeze out the less efficient marginal producers. If this resulted ultimately in the total supply falling below the demand, prices would rise, and new producers and capital attracted by the higher prices would enter the field and bring up the supply where it would equal or surpass the demand. Supply and demand were supposed to move not in a circle but in fluctuating equilibrium in spiral form, like the Hegelian dialectic of history. The rising spiral was to represent the approximation of effective demand to ultimate potential demand. This approximation is important, for unless the economic system can come close to satisfying the total satisfactions of the community's material wants it fails to that extent in its goal.

Under this formula there were to be no permanent, excessive profits, for these would be eliminated by the attraction of new competing capital. For the same reason there was to be no monopoly, for the purpose of monopoly was to maintain prices above what the law of supply and demand would justify, and artificially high profits would attract new capital and producers, resulting in falling prices. Since workers among each other and employers among themselves would compete, the resultant wages also would be responsive to the law of supply and demand. There would be no unemployment, for under the equilibrium of supply and demand the full labor capacities of the community would be utilized. There would be no wild fluctuations or economic cycles, for the operation of supply and demand would reach over a long period a vibrating but nevertheless definite equilibrium.[4]

2. THE PATHOLOGIES OF AN UNCO-ORDINATED ECONOMY

The very enumeration of the phenomena that are not supposed to exist, but do nevertheless, under the hypothetical operation of liberal economics, constitutes the measure of the shortcomings of the laissez-faire system.

Short-term and long-term cycles of capitalist activity have become so pronounced a part of the economy that a cathartic function has been assigned to them by the devotees of the natural law of supply and demand. In other words, the law of supply and demand does not produce an equilibrium but a wave. High economic activity, investment, inflation, rising employment, and increasing consumption are characteristic of the peak of the wave, while economic stagnation, deflation, low investment, bankruptcies, and unemployment are experiences in the valley. There have been many adroit and technical explanations of business cycles, even to the extent of purporting to establish a connection between business cycles and sunspots.[5] Presumably that should furnish the ultimate justification for a do-nothing policy, but the validity of this theory should condemn laissez-faire capitalism, since a planned economy does not exhibit the same sensitivity to solar phenomena.

Nor is the pathology of capitalism limited to cyclical disturbances. Even in times of economic activity, unemployment has not been eliminated. In fact, unemployment has became the chronic disease of our peacetime economy, worsening with the years. In war unemployment has been eliminated but, as will be indicated, a war economy is a planned economy, while in peacetime our economy is not planned. A great undrained reservoir of unemployed means that the economy has not utilized its full manpower and plant capacities, and that the effective demand does not approximate the potential demand.[6]

Chronic and extensive peacetime unemployment aggravated by cyclical booms and busts constitutes the outstanding phenomenon of our economy, the repercussions of which are felt everywhere.

What is the explanation for this permanent and periodic breakdown of our economic order? Why has laissez-faire, absolute capitalism, not worked according to its theoretic hypothesis? The law of supply and demand is supposed to operate in a highly differentiated economy where the most intricate, increasingly intensive, division of labor and function exists. This is the basic fact from which any further analysis must proceed. This division of labor and function is technological, geographical, managerial, entrepreneurial, financial, and social, among others.

Because of the extreme division of labor and function characteristic of our economy, all its parts are interdependent and the whole cannot function properly unless all the interconnected parts dovetail or mesh and operate in unison. For this to take place there must be a co-ordinating, controlling mechanism which would integrate the whole system of power that is represented by the differentiated economy. This is unavoidable, for it is a demonstrable principle that there can be no differentiation of labor and function within a power system which is to operate as a whole without a controlling or integrating power. This is true of biologic organisms or of human and animal societies and organizations, industrial or otherwise. It is universal.[7] In laissez-faire capitalism the controlling mechanism was supposed to be competition, operating through the law of supply and demand and evidenced by the price index in a free market. For the mechanism to operate successfully, the whole system would have to be fluid and dynamic in all its parts, for if there is a breakdown in any part of the machinery the whole would slow down.

No such fluidity, however, obtained in practice. The free market economy was based on the proposition that no business enterprise should be so large that it alone, or in combination with others, could influence the equilibrium of prices. In point of fact, however, there is a steady and relentless trend toward the concentration of industrial control. While the Marxist thesis of concentration of ownership may or may not be true, there is no doubt about the accentuated trend toward concentration of economic control. The trend had its incipiency in time of peace. Every war, particularly World War II, accelerated the tendency.[8] The growth of corporations, mergers, trusts, interlocking directorates, holding companies, central financial control, price-fixing agreements, division of markets and restrictions of output cartels has transcended national lines. Monopoly or quasi monopoly governs our basic industries, which in turn set the tone for our whole economy.[9] Either through monopoly or through price and quota fixing of the leading producers, the automatic forces of competition through the law of supply and demand no longer determine prices or output in our basic industries. They are determined by a few men in control in each of the main industries. It is therefore clear that the issue is no longer whether we should or should not have price control. It is whether prices should be controlled by the government responsible to the people, and having the task of co-ordinating the whole economy, or whether prices should be controlled by those few in control of the monopoly corporations and trusts responsible not to the people but to no one.

Not even to their own stockholders. Through the medium of the modern corporation, ownership has undergone nuclear fission. The diffusion and dispersion of stockownership have divested property ownership of management control, because the management of the corporation can be appointed and controlled by a few of the principal stockholders whose total holdings may be only an insignificant fraction of the total number of shares.[10] This is an illustration of the principle that the greater the diffusion of power among an unorganized majority the easier it is for a small but disciplined and purposeful minority to obtain control.

To the lack of responsibility by corporate management to the body of stockholders must be added the lack of a substantial interest on their part in obtaining profits for the stockholders, for their share in that is insignificant. Nor is the profit motive effective in stimulating efficient operation of the business on the part of the stockholders, for they are no longer in control of the corporation. The drive for profits, the manifestation of man's quest for power in the economic field when ownership and management are united and the motive power of laissez-faire capitalism, is no longer operative in the promotion of efficiency and expansion of large corporate industry.[11] The quest for power of corporate finance and management finds chief expression in drives for monopoly. It may also be parenthetically remarked that those who rail against the irresponsibility of union officials to the membership would do well to be aware of the immeasurably greater irresponsibility of corporate management to stockholders. The great modern corporations have become public institutions whose existence and operation are independent of any laws of primitive laissez faire.

The concentration of wealth has exploded another atom of capitalist theory, namely, maintenance of equilibrium of savings and investment through the rate of interest. In the Keynesian analysis it has been pointed out that savings and investment are not made by the same people and are therefore not necessarily harmonious and mutually regulative. Savings do not necessarily result in investment. Where the income of the community is more evenly divided a greater amount of the savings will go into immediate or postponed consumption, and therefore investment. The savings represented by the profits of corporations and the accumulations of the very wealthy are the kind that figure in the causations of depressions, for these are not for present or future consumption. And whether they figure in investment is problematical, depending on whether opportunities exist for investment. According to J. M. Keynes, "in contemporary conditions the growth of wealth, so far from being dependent on the abstinence of the rich as is commonly supposed, is more likely to be impeded by it. One of the chief social justifications of great inequality of wealth is therefore removed."[12]

Competition, the law of supply and demand, free market determination of prices, the profit motive as an operative force, the harmony of savings and investment—one by one, these and other presumably automatic regulators of a laissez-faire economy have been found not to function properly or not to function at all. Is it any wonder that our economy in peacetime has been unable to throw off the creeping paralysis of severe unemployment intensified by cyclical fluctuation?

Since the automatic controls that were supposed to regularize the free market economy have been found not to be effectively operating, it should not be imagined that the highly differentiated economy has been functioning without any integrative process. As already indicated, no system of power can subsist long without a trend to the establishment of control through the conflict of individuals or groups competing for domination. It was therefore to be expected that the integrative process would manifest itself in our economy. In fact, the growth and concentration of economic power, which has loomed so significantly in capitalist society and has operated to destroy the effectiveness of the automatic controls, is a manifestation of the integrative process.

Competition, as the central premise of laissez-faire capitalism, could not continue automatically, for competition is self-destructive. Competition leads to monopoly, for man in his quest for power strives for monopoly and abhors competition.[13] The error of classical economics was the assumption that businessmen would be satisfied to abide by the decision of the efficiency umpire in the game of industrial competition. To the winners in efficiency would go the spoils and the least efficient marginal producers would politely bow out and leave the field, only to return when the reduced output should cause a rise in price sufficient to offer a profit to the marginal entrepreneur. However, since the stakes are high—economic survival, no less—the umpire is unceremoniously escorted from the field, and a free-for-all, no holds barred, begins to agitate the dust. At first the struggle for monopoly expresses itself in primitive terms, including mergers, cut-throat competition, and even violence. Then, as the surviving contestants get fewer and bigger, if no one of them establishes a complete monopoly, a situation is reached where no one is strong enough to destroy the other. In other words, a balance of power is attained which makes possible the establishment of a modus vivendi. Why engage in price competition, which would not be decisive and would only reduce profits, when everyone can fatten on higher profits resulting from jacked-up prices? This is the stage of cartelized agreements for fixed prices, production quotas, and division of markets.[14]

From the existence of severe unemployment it is evident that monopoly and concentration of industrial control are not a satisfactory instrument of integration. In the first place, industrial efficiency is not the guiding factor in the growth of monopoly. Technology and mass production facilitate the increase in the size of industrial enterprises but it is incontrovertible that monopoly control is not limited by optimum size. The "curse of bigness" is well known.[15] It can be shown that the largest corporations are not the most efficient producers. The holding company and other devices of financial control do not even relate to operating techniques. Such integration as does take place in our economy by reason of monopoly is guided simply by the interests of the monopolists and not by those of society as a whole. Similarly, the monopolies represent integrated control systems within the economy and cannot therefore serve as an adequate integration of the larger power system that is represented by our economy as a whole.

In our modern economy our great corporations and monopolies have been in a real sense duplicates of medieval feudalities. Each in its own time has been an integration of a partial section of power within a larger sphere or system of power. In the company town, the modern equivalent of the manor, there was even a high degree of coalescence between political and economic power. Coal and iron police and vigilantes were some of the manifestations of this phenomenon.[16]

3. GOVERNMENT REGULATION OF THE ECONOMY

The picture of industrial feudalism, descriptive of our economy, would not be complete without sketching in the role of the central authority which represents the larger power sphere encompassing all the economic feudalities. The idea of a self-regulated economy, free from state control, has given way to the realty of a complex economy regulated to an ever greater extent by the government. The world over, in one form or another, government is once again the arbiter of our economic destinies. Even in this country, the last outpost of private enterprise, government is called upon to intervene in the economic process.

The genesis of this phenomenon is not of recent vintage, though its full efflorescence is. Nor is state intervention the creature of the left. As a matter of fact, from the earliest days of liberal capitalism it was invoked by the capitalists themselves. Monopoly constitutes a resort to political power, that is, organizational means to protect and advance one's share in the community income. It is not surprising therefore that businessmen should not refrain from engaging the aid of the state to advance their economic interests. Subsidies, tariffs, and other government largess were never scorned by the business community. It was the businessmen who first demanded and received government aid, including loans after the 1929 crash. The progressive strengthening of the federal government at the expense of the states received its initial impetus at the hands of the business interests. Those who later clamored for "states' rights" did not refrain from pleading for federal injunctions against labor.[17] It was only after the federal government stepped in to protect the interests of labor that the National Association of Manufacturers began to find merit in decentralization. Those who are for removing of federal controls over business clamor for federal legislation to curb labor. When it has suited their immediate and particular purposes, businessmen have never objected to government intervention. That objection has been forthcoming only when a particular type of intervention happened to be considered unfavorable to business.

The occasions for such outcries on the part of business have been steady and numerous. As the capitalist economy failed to function satisfactorily, government action was invoked by those largely in opposition to the entrepreneur class. The industrial feudalities have found themselves in conflict with the urban lower and middle classes and with the agrarian interests. The entrepreneur employer group resorted to the organizational pattern of monopoly. The laboring groups similarly organized themselves in accordance with their economic interests into unions, bearing a strong analogy to the medieval guilds. Equalization of bargaining power with the employer through collective action has been the purpose. This has created a new feudality with significant implications on wage and price determinations, accentuating the imperative for government controls.[18] Farm groups too have organized to increase their share of the total income through collective action and government subsidies and controls.

Beyond the conflict on the economic level has been the no less significant contest on the political level for the control of state policies. Government intervention in our economy has not been in response to an over-all plan of control but to specific grievances. The extensive government economic intervention for the past hundred years in Great Britain and on the Continent and for half a century or so in the United States in the fields of labor legislation, public works, social security and welfare measures, antitrust laws, regulation of business and competitive practices, farm legislation—in a word, the whole gamut of the interpenetration of the political and economic processes has spread over too long a period over the whole globe to be dismissed merely as the conspiracy of mischievous theorists or misguided reformers.

This phenomenon does not conform with the classical economic hypothesis about human psychology, which assumed that man's quest for power would express itself in economic competition. The capitalists and entrepreneurs were the first to show the falsity of that assumption, for they resorted to the political means of combinations, restraints of trade, and government action. The same psychological behavior characterized also their victims. Farmers refused to accept the presumed workings of the law of supply and demand when this meant deflated prices. They demanded government credits and parity. Workers refused to resign themselves to substandard wages, dangerous working conditions, and chronic unemployment. They demanded a long list of government measures to remedy the grievances and relieve their lot. They refused to wait for prosperity to turn the corners. It may be inconsiderate and nasty of them, but businessmen, workers, and farmers do not happen to function the way Adam Smith, Hayek, and Hazlitt want them to behave.[19]

The all-pervasive government intervention in our economy is proof that the state could not, did not, shirk its responsibility, for the state is the organized community and reflects its collective will and power. The whole system of social legislation is a series of curbs on the privileges and abuses of the powerful few in favor of the underprivileged many. The Marxist claim that the state is the executive committee of the capitalist class is false when applied to the modern democratic state.[20] Economic power exercises a great and often predominant influence on state control and policies, but there is no complete control or exact correspondence between economic and political power. The right of opposition and the franchise have made the state an instrument of power which could be, and has been, used against the will of the wielders of economic power. As long as the state was passive, political democracy could be ignored by the industrial barons. But the increasing intervention of the central state into the economic order has confronted the economic feudalities with serious opposition.

The ever-expanding scope of state intervention in response to the grievances of the many against the abuses of the industrial feudalities indicates once more a union of the peak of the pyramid with its base against the middle. In the fascist state too the same power pattern of integrative control of the economy took place, even though the industrial feudalities attempted to bend the state to their dictation.[21] The Nazi bureaucracy had is own purposes and ambitions. We must, however, be careful to distinguish between the democratic administrative state and the one represented by fascism and communism, for in the latter two the integrative power of the central authority is not responsible to the base of the pyramid.

Whether the modern state is democratically oriented or not, the political and economic processes have there interpenetrated.

The modern state has more and more brought into control the new economic environment at the behest of multitudinous and often conflicting interests. Upon the state has devolved more and more the task of integrating the whole power system represented by our new industrial economy. Just as the feudal state was for its environment, the modern state for our economy becomes the ultimate co-ordinating mechanism.

The paramount need of our economic order is for co-ordination, integration, management, and administration as a unitary whole. Only the state can perform that function. This stage of development was reached in the feudal and mercantilist states, but the new industrial environment did not fit the agrarian mold. The evolutionary steps had to be repeated in the new economic environment: diffusion of power on a simple rudimentary level, differentiation of function, struggle for control, intermediate combination or organization, growing complexity, and ultimate state control or integration.[22]

If government intervention in our economy were not indigenous to our civilization, its tempo of development would not have been increased by the war—the classic accelerator of historical processes. War, involving the use of mass armies, particularly modern total war, is largely a function of the economy. Since success in war is the ultimate acid test of survival, it tends to bring to the surface the elements in our sociopolitical relationships best suited for the utilization of our technology. The mechanism for this is the tendency for the disappearance of opposition to wartime measures which in peacetime would be politically inconceivable short of some catastrophic event bordering on political and economic collapse. It is therefore a valid generalization that war is the laboratory of the future peace, that wartime controls of our economy reveal a glimpse of what the comparable peacetime techniques will ultimately be after an understandable time lag. World War I was a crucible for much of the labor legislation of the succeeding quarter of a century.

It should not, however, be assumed that the process of integration is complete or that it is invariable. It is neither wholly automatic nor wholly capricious. Its future course of development and our probable role in it will presently be examined.

CHAPTER VII

Proposed Approaches to Planning

1. THE EMPLOYMENT ACT OF 1946

In the United States we have finally recognized the government's legal responsibility for planning the economic order to produce "maximum employment."[1] Even in its diluted form the Employment Act of 1946 constitutes one of the landmarks of our history. It establishes a Council of Economic Advisers[2] which is empowered to make recommendations to the President as to what measures the government is to undertake so that the economy as a whole may provide maximum employment, and a Congressional Joint Committee to pass upon the President's Economic Report to Congress.[3]

However, the Council of Economic Advisers has no administrative, but only recommendatory powers and the Employment Act does not commit itself to any specific program of planning.[4] What should be the contents and incidence of economic planning? In importance this problem rivals the overriding issue of our civilization, whether we can avoid apocalyptic atomic warfare. What are the chief approaches to planning?

A few of the principal approaches to economic planning will be briefly analyzed. The criteria for their examination are whether they (1) sufficiently provide for government integration of the economy to hold out promise for success in achieving and maintaining an expanding economy of full employment, (2) are suitable to our economy of private enterprise, which is a going concern, and (3) are in accord with our democratic traditions.

2. THE RETURN TO ABSOLUTE CAPITALISM

The first type of planning approach to consider is the plan to end all government planning. It calls for an end of government intervention in our economy and a return to laissez-faire capitalism. Committing the egregious error of identifying planning with totalitarian dictatorship, whether of communism or of fascism, this school seeks to frighten the Western World into forsaking the primrose path of government controls for the joys of the Elysian fields of a free market economy. Aside from a few rudimentary social services, it calls in general terms for drastic decontrolling of government regulations of the economy. This school articulates the hopes and phobias of the reactionaries who have been opposed to the newer government regulations, which they find objectionable. It rationalizes policies calling for lowering of taxes in the upper brackets, for the elimination of price control, for the reduction to a minimum of all social security and of government spending for relief and public works, for lowering of wages and elimination of labor checks on management policies, and for freedom from government intervention to alleviate unemployment and cyclical fluctuations.[5]

In terms of idea structure, this resurrection of laissez faire calls for a return to the infancy of the race when presumably man was driven from Paradise because of sheer wickedness in tasting of the forbidden fruit.[6] In this instance the forbidden fruit is government aid in the economic process. The escapist character of this point of view becomes evident when the cry against government interference with business is transmuted from an afterdinner emotional sedative for capitalist gatherings to a concrete political program. The business community itself would protest vigorously against removing the myriad ways in which our economy has come to rely on government regulation. Is it realistic to expect that business, farmers, and labor would be content to sit idly by when severe depression comes and wait until the great spiral of deflation has run its course in bankruptcies, bank failures, and severe unemployment, without calling for government action? But this would have to happen in order to permit the functioning of the automatic economic forces of the price index.

Assuming, however, that by some political legerdemain the complete decontrol program, not only of the wartime controls, could be adopted and that the big monopolies and labor unions, which have rendered prices and wages rigid and not subject to competition, could be dissolved, would laissez faire be a workable solution? This island of absolute capitalism in the United States would have to operate in an ocean of governmentally controlled economies, thereby eliminating free international trade, the safety valve of a free economy. Even with this difficulty absent, absolute, unregulated capitalism would be doomed, for then the process, which in the past led the Western world from laissez faire to government intervention in the economy, would start all over again.

Those who call for a return to the "rugged individualism" of the 1920's have the responsibility of pointing out what there is about the newer laissez faire that immunizes it against the disaster that overtook the older variety. This is the basic question to be answered as the wage-price regulations are debated. It is economic Don Quixotism to call for withdrawal of the government from regulation of the economy. We can no more avoid a planned economy than business can operate without management and direction.

3. GOVERNMENT OWNERSHIP

At the opposite extreme of those calling for government nonintervention in our economy are the Socialists and Communists, who claim that public ownership of the means of production is the only road to the integration of our economy and that economic planning is incompatible with private property. Public ownership has been accepted by long tradition as the most direct systematic instrument for economic planning and is the one most widespread in the world today, principally through the expansion of Soviet Russia and the nationalization program now in process of establishment in England. Nevertheless, it is not true that public ownership is the only means to achieve a planned economy. We may eschew as we should their objectives and methods, but it is nevertheless a fact that Nazi Germany had a managed economy under a system of private property. Similiarly, the United States and Great Britain attained victory in war under a planned and governmentally managed economy. The tendency to dichotomize social systems on the basis of private or public ownership of the means of production is an anachronism. It stems from the nineteenth century when the great debate was between private ownership and laissez-faire capitalism, on the one hand, and public ownership and socialism, on the other hand.

Significant now are the social, economic, and political controls at the disposal of the government. These are now adequate to achieve a dynamically planned economy under our system of private ownership of the means of production for the overwhelming bulk of our economy, outside the exceptional fields of public utilities and power projects such as the Tennessee Valley Authority, atomic power projects, and military reservoirs of oil, and certain munitions factories, in which public ownership is indicated. In the United States a full-employment planned economy can be achieved more readily under private property than public ownership, and for an indefinite period would be more suitable to efficient operation and the maintenance of our traditional freedoms and democratic rights.[7] A democratically planned and managed economy is the only means to save the system of private ownership. Those who have vested interests in private ownership are confronted not with the choice between government regulation and no government regulation, but whether our economy should be privately owned and publicly planned or publicly owned and managed.

4. GOVERNMENT SPENDING

The most important approach to a planned economy which assumes the private ownership of the means of production stems directly or indirectly from the Keynes-Hansen analysis.[8] This school of economic analysis finds the cause for chronic severe unemployment in the lag between investment and savings, in the tendency of savings to outstrip investment. In order to close the fatal gap it is variously proposed that it is up to the government to spend in order to stimulate the need for investment, and likewise it is advocated to reduce interest rates and furnish other incentives, including reducing tax rates, to encourage private investment. Government spending is compatible with either a balanced budget, in which extensive government spending is balanced by sufficient tax income, or with an unbalanced budget, in which government spending is covered by government borrowing. Nevertheless, it is the latter application that has been decisive in the realm of practical politics. It was this phase which characterized New Deal recovery policies, particularly federal grants in aid to the states, public works, public relief expenditures, and loans to business.

The objection to this program, emanating from business circles, that government borrowing would lead to bankruptcy, is fallacious, for it considers government borrowing in the same light as individual indebtedness. As long as the debt is internal, as ours is, the community is not impoverished when it increases its debt. It owes to itself. Indeed, the amount of indebtedness is a good indicator of the rate of business activity in a community. As long as the current tax receipts are large enough to pay the interest, the public debt need not be a cause for concern. The drastic increase of the public debt during the war is proof that the dire prophecies often heard that imminent collapse would follow deficit spending in peacetime are not among the oracular verities that need be heeded.[9]

Government spending as a program for a planned economy is open to the more serious objection that it did not work in the United States or in Great Britain to wipe out unemployment in the 1930's. It is true, of course, that not enough government spending was done to serve as a stimulus to economic activity. But this condition may well prove a permanent feature in democracies, for paradoxically only when there is full employment is there a likelihood that sufficient appropriation would be provided for a public works program and other projects of public spending. If the past is any guide, during depressions enough would be appropriated only to serve as a stimulus to the consumers' goods industries and to ameliorate the privations incident to unemployment, but not to eliminate it. Pump priming cannot be a sustained long-term program.[10]

The fundamental objection to government spending as the nucleus of a program of economical planning is that it is insufficient as an integrative mechanism for our economy. Intentionally or otherwise, government spending, perhaps supplemented with a proficient tax program, has come to be looked upon as an open-sesame self-sufficient without other government controls to work the miracle of producing an economy of full employment.

Its advocates assume that once this type of government intervention is fully utilized, no other controls of substantial proportions would be necessary or even desirable. In a sense the Keynesian analysis has not liberated itself completely from the fallacy of classical economics in viewing the economic order as a machine capable of automatic operation. While during the nineteenth century the constant increase in population, territories, and foreign investments served as the expanding fuel that kept the machine in reasonably good operation, government spending would in the twentieth century serve the same purpose. All that is necessary is to keep dropping coins in the slot and the wheels would be set in motion, the gears into shifting and meshing, and out of the jukebox would come the dulcet tones of the sweet singer, with glad tidings for a waiting world—jobs for all.

However, our economic order is not and could not possibly be a self-operating automatic machine independent of human wills and purposes. The gaps between savings and investments, between production and purchasing power, or between supply and demand are not explanations of the root cause of our disequilibrated economy but rather its manifestations. The ultimate cause is the lack of integration of a power system which through its various divisions of labor has become interdependent and can operate successfully only as a co-ordinated whole. There is no panacea substitute for government regulation of the myriad aspects of our economy. Take, for instance, government controls over prices and wages. If government spending succeeds in achieving full employment, intervention would be necessary to avoid the spiral of rising prices and wages that causes disequilibrium of economic stability and cyclical fluctuation.[11] Neither is there anything in government spending that would make an antitrust program unnecessary. Shortages may appear at various levels of economic activity. We are now confronted with the task of insuring that the production of steel be large enough to service an expanding economy. Indeed, all the government controls associated with full employment, including production quotas, manpower, and materials allocation controls, may prove necessary whether the state of full employment is achieved through government spending or through some other method. There is no control scheme to end all government controls.

In scarcity economies, which exist virtually throughout the whole world, with the notable exception of the United States, economic planning has become a necessity in order best to conserve and utilize the existing resources. In an economy of abundance, which the United States is presently enjoying, planning of the economy is imperative to synchronize and mesh all the interdependent parts of the complex whole. Government spending is not enough by itself either to achieve full employment or to maintain it without the full gamut of government controls.

5. DISTRIBUTION SCHEMES

We now turn to the distribution approach to the problem of a full-employment economy.

The preoccupation of economics has been with the producer, not with the consumer, with production, not with demand. The individual entrepreneur has never been concerned with what the total demand was for his product, but only with what share he could capture for what he produced. Traditional economic theory, although vaguely aware that an optimum economic system must convert human needs into effective demand, never concerned itself with the problem of needs, but only of production. The road to economic utopia led through the well-being of the producer. If production is attended to, demand would take care of itself. All the ills and shortcomings of the economy were to be eliminated through measures which addressed themselves directly to the problems of the producer. Consumer demand and human needs were to be attended to, if at all, indirectly. Traditional economics concerned itself with the operation of the economic order rather than with economic goals and ways and means to achieve them.[12] Even the Keynes-Hansen analysis seeks to achieve full employment again chiefly through measures concerned with the producer, namely, through stimulus of investment.

The producercentric economics is quite understandable when we realize that even in the United States our economy up to very recently has been a scarcity economy in which the central problem was one of production. Even in Russia, where economic planning is crucial to the system, emphasis is still on production problems rather than on consumer needs, for the Russian economy is still in the infant capitalist state, not in the distributive stage of development attained by the American economy.[13]

Not the individual entrepreneur and traditional economic theory but the reformist movements, including labor, and the government became concerned with the problem of human needs. Out of this concern has emerged the system of social legislation whose purpose is to satisfy minimal needs through such provisions as minimum-wage standards, unemployment insurance, medical and hospital services, sickness insurance, and the rest of the program of social security. The social security system could not be the impetus to an economy of full employment, if for no other reason than that it was a minimal program and did not provide for the full satisfaction of the total needs. Proceeding from the premise that the way to full employment is through abundant purchasing power, a few marginal quasi-utopian schemes, which sought to solve the unemployment problem through distribution of a yearly income to each individual, have flourished and quickly perished. Aside from other objections that might be made to these distributive schemes, they are vulnerable in seeking to achieve the goal of a full-employment, stabilized economy through concern with only the needs aspect of the equation, ignoring the production side, just as traditional economies erred in being preoccupied with the producer interest. A viable program for a planned economy must encompass both sides of the total equation of production and needs.

CHAPTER VIII

A Planned Economy for Private Enterprise

1. PROGRAM FOR DIRECT PLANNING

What, then, should be done? What should be the program best calculated to achieve and maintain a dynamically planned economy of full employment?

The key to any effective planning of full employment is to be found in linking supply and demand.[1] Not indirectly and hypothetically, but directly and administratively. More particularly, it must convert human needs into effective demand by linking production to specific goals determined by total needs. This was done during the war, when capitalist economies, democratic and dictatorial, managed to achieve full employment.[2] Indeed, so successful has a planned war economy become in eliminating unemployment that the accumulated purchasing power, which could not be spent because so much of the industrial capacity was directed to war needs, has served for the immediate postwar period to convert the stagnant peace economy into an expanding type. As long as this pent-up purchasing power, sustained in part by the tremendous government outlays for military and other purposes, and supplemented by foreign exports, remains unspent, full employment will continue, creating peacetime all-time production records. Our goal is not a boom followed by inevitable bust deteriorating into chronic slough, but a stabilized economy running constantly on all cylinders. For that planning is essential.[3]

In seeking to devise a workable and practical plan for a full-employment economy we are not driven to untried hypotheses and radical innovations. The open-sesame is at our disposal, to be used for peace as it was successfully applied to winning the war. Our victorious industrial war effort brought about unprecedented industrial expansion and full utilization of our human and natural resources. Any plan for permanently stabilized full employment must envisage the continuation of these conditions. We must therefore address ourselves to the factors responsible for our industrial accomplishments during the war.

In wartime the government decided how many tanks, planes, and guns it needed and distributed the orders to private industry to fill under its supervision. Two basic phenomena which characterize our economic system during war are herein revealed. First, our productive demands were crystallized into specific goals which were reached in consequence of an over-all war plan. Second, the fulfillment of our production demands was carried out in the framework of our traditional private enterprise. If we maintain this combination we shall win the battle of production and employment in peace as we won it in war.

We must reform our economic thinking in terms of goals and ways of achieving them. When the government needed munitions, it did not set about looking for intricate devices to induce producers to manufacture them. It simply ordered them and planned the proper allocation of materials and manpower.

The same must be done in peacetime. We can ascertain the needs of the country in terms of housing, clothing, food, automobiles, refrigerators, electric appliances, etc. We can also take inventory of our natural resources, foreign imports, and industrial plants. We should be in a position to make accurate estimates of the desirable yearly production in each industry. The government would then assign a quota of production to each producer in the industry to fill, guaranteeing him against loss if he failed to sell the product. Since full employment would provide maximum purchasing power, the government would not be left with substantial quantities of unsold products, except for some small margins of error in the calculation of individual products. Errors would in time be largely eliminated as we acquired greater experience. Products left unsold would be included in the calculations for the coming year, thus further reducing the government's liability. The guarantee to the producer could be the average cost of production for the whole industry, plus a certain profit. Since application of the plan would make necessary the imposition of price controls, the average cost plus a certain profit could become the selling price. This formula has the advantage over the general wartime formula of cost plus of the individual producer, because it would reward the efficient producer and drive out the inefficient, making room for new entrepreneurs with initiative and new ideas. Since each producer would attempt to increase his profits by reducing his cost of production, the average cost of production for the industry generally would tend to diminish, reducing the commodity price. We would then have a price-control system which would operate as a check on industrial waste of manpower and as a spur to efficient operation.

It might not be necessary to apply the plan to every industry. Control of the key capital industries might suffice, at least initially.

2. PLANNING OF NEEDS

A planned economy involves three chief sectors of planning: (1) inventory and planning of needs; (2) inventory and planning of resources and production facilities; and (3) planning and supervision of production to satisfy the total needs.[4]

The rate of $203 billion yearly income in 1947 as compared with the $83-some billion in 1929, the highest previous peacetime year, is a clear indication that the day of the expanding economy is not past, even though the physical frontiers are closed, population growth is slackened, and foreign investments are no longer profitable. Since man's quest for power in terms of satisfaction of human needs is limitless, planning production for fulfillment of human wants creates the permanent condition for an ever-expanding economy of abundance and full employment. Even in the United States we need not yet worry about the limit to human wants. Our standard of living for the mass of the people is still low compared to even minimum requirements.[5]

In planning for our needs a social security system vastly extended and rationalized will assume its rightful place. If we assume that the best way to provide for full employment of our industrial plant and human and natural resources is to activate our demands and translate them from the potential to the actual by social planning, then a social security system falls into its proper sphere as a minimum determination of our individual needs. It also conserves our human resources. A well-conceived and well-executed social security system should apply universally to all individuals irrespective of their income or lack of it. This would eliminate any vestige of the anachronistic means test principle or any other condition precedent for the satisfaction of our minimum needs. The sins of an indolent father who refuses to work are not to be visited upon his wife and children. Even now this individual is no longer consigned to starvation.

The problems of sanctions and incentives to induce people to work will be of central import in an economy of abundance, but deprivation of minimal standards of life is not one of them.[6] One approach would be to raise the minimum take-home wages of those employed as much as possible above the minimum security provision. Another principle of social security is to provide for as many human needs as possible. For generations we have declared it to be an inalienable right of every American child to know Shakespeare. Why shouldn't he be entitled to bread and butter, good housing, adequate medical care and hospitalization? A health insurance program along the lines of the Wagner-Murray-Dingell bill is a minimum necessity. Medicine is one of our basic public utilities, and its regulation by government for the benefit of the community is indispensable to a planned economy within a free society. The training of physicians and other professionals should not be left to accident or to the decisions of the most puissant individuals or organizations within these professions, who are motivated not by the public interest but by the narrow self-regarding purpose of creating and maintaining scarcities. The government ought to plan for the building of medical and other schools for training of adequate numbers of physicians and other professionals to satisfy the professional needs of our society.

A satisfactory social security system should ultimately absorb private insurance schemes operated by labor and management, in order to promote efficiency of operation and to distribute the cost on a broader scale than the affected industry, whose financial position may not be sufficiently sound to sustain the concentrated burden.[7]

In taking inventory of our needs we should not neglect our military needs. War in an age of technology must be total war. Technological improvements will remove the immunity of our home front from attack. We shall not necessarily be vouchsafed a period of preparation after war has begun. We must preserve skills, skeleton plants, and raw materials which can be easily geared to war production. We must not again be caught without essential supplies. Such planning is no substitute for international organization for peace; it is one of its implementations.

3. RESOURCES PLANNING

In taking inventory of our total needs and planning for them, the guiding policy must be in the direction of constant expansion, but this should not be interpreted as utopian wish fulfillment without regard to the means at our disposal for satisfying our wants. Although the application of atomic energy to peaceful industrial uses as a fuel and the whole synthetic industry lift the curtain on unlimited horizons of abundance, at any given period the satisfaction of our needs will be limited by the available resources and plant.

If we are to achieve full employment by balancing our needs with our natural and human resources, we must keep an inventory of our natural resources and plan a long-range program of conservation. We would then be aware of the extent of our natural resources and the rate at which we could exploit them. Knowledge of impending exhaustion of resources would enable us to look for possible substitutes, natural or synthetic, and to supplement our resources by foreign imports.

Our technological skill and industrial plant[8] have placed us in an unrivaled position as far as satisfying our wants, but our position is not so favorable in natural resources. Our profligate waste of natural resources, both agriculture and mineral, in exploiting our continent and in serving as the world's arsenal during two world wars, have converted us to a near have-not nation in a number of critical materials. Although the development of the synthetic industry has opened up untapped vistas for substitute products, there is no doubt that we must think seriously in terms of replenishing and conserving our rapidly used-up natural resources. An intensive conservation program has become a national necessity. The federal Government ought to retain control over the tidelands oil. The 1946 act calling for the building up of stockpiles of critical materials is a step in the right direction but it defeats its purpose when it provides that preference be given to domestic products. The emphasis ought to be the other way. For both peace and military production we should give preference to foreign sources of raw materials whenever the domestic brand is threatened with impending exhaustion.

The waste and destruction of World War II will further accentuate the trend that made the United States an exporting nation. Unless we wish to continue to export our substance for worthless bonds or useless gold, we must import products which we cannot produce as efficiently as foreign countries and raw materials that we either lack or are about to exhaust.

Only an economy which is state controlled can profit from reparations from a defeated enemy. The United States, Great Britain, and France have not after World Wars I and II been in a position to collect reparations in kind and in manpower because of the opposition of business and labor in the areas where these would compete. The interests of the whole economy have been sacrificed to advance those of a part. But where full employment of men and enterprises is planned, the interests of the economy as a whole need not be dominated by the pressure of special interests in the realm of foreign commerce or reparations. Foreign commerce must properly be a function of domestic needs and also of political purposes. Our tariff must be revised to permit imports from countries with which it is to our interest to maintain close political and military liaison. Nations, like individuals, must live, and that means they must export.[9] It is therefore imperative for us by tariff revisions to make it possible for the countries of the world to trade with us through their exports as well as their imports, thereby precluding their being sucked into the vortex of a coalition bloc aimed against us. Economically too we shall gain from our exports only to the extent that they are balanced by imports. By cushioning the shifting of workers and producers from industries which must be displaced in part or in whole by necessary foreign imports, over-all planning will reduce the opposition of affected vested interests which now form the greatest obstacle to a rationalized foreign commerce.

In another respect too foreign commerce and business relations are pregnant with political and even military consequences. We are familiar with the international cartel agreements between American firms and Nazi-dominated enterprises which limited American production of critical war materials to the detriment of our war effort.[10] This was calculated Nazi military strategy. We are also familiar with American exports of scrap iron and oil to Japan when war with Japan was imminent, and with American investments in Germany, which together with British-German and Russo-German trade helped to rebuild Germany's war potential. This is not said to absolve those involved, who have to be responsible for the obvious consequences of their acts; but the point will be missed if we ignore the fundamental truth that the ultimate motivation of these acts is not large class interests or deep political calculations but the quest of business for profits.

Proof of that lies in the fact that American firms have not refused to do business with Russia. In fact, after World War II, Russia found no difficulty in purchasing important technological tools and other products useful for building up her war potential to be used ultimately against the same "monopoly capitalists." Business as usual is practiced as long as profits accrue. "Serve the paying customer," irrespective whether it is Japan, Nazi Germany, or Communist Russia. That is the business slogan, even though it may be opposed to the national interest. It is obviously up to the government to protect that interest. Foreign commerce must therefore be regulated to serve the interests of the economy as a whole and of its political and military objectives.[11]

Contributing both to the satisfaction of needs and to the conservation of resources is a public works program. That should be its overriding purpose, not the creation of jobs or the stimulation of investment. Used as a means to full employment, it has never achieved that purpose and has equally failed to satisfy community needs. For one, when used as a supplement to private enterprise, it has to be discontinued in times of high activity in order not to accelerate the inflationary spiral, but community needs cannot for that reason be left unsatisfied. Only when used within the framework of an over all plan can a public works program be directed to fulfill our communal needs which cannot be satisfied at all or as well by individual effort.

To the traditional category of public works, such as schools, roads, and parks, must be added other measures and projects which could contribute to betterment of our human resources and conservation of our natural and plant resources. Included must be government-controlled scientific research projects to co-ordinate private and communal research in various fields of the natural and social sciences. We have reaped the benefit of intensive nationally conducted research in atomic energy and other military problems. Modern science is too complex and too differentiated in labor and function to be handled by the unco-ordinated effort of isolated private enterprise. Fission of the atom is evidence of what calculated, intensive, governmentally integrated and sponsored research can accomplish. Why not mobilize comparable effort to eradicate cancer and other diseases that afflict mankind, and to tackle industrial problems which are too complex and costly for private firms to undertake? Neither should we neglect the social sciences. It is there that we must turn for guidance on how we can close the gap between the moral lag of humanity and the terrifying power for destruction that it wields. Great insight into the structure of the atom is not the same as knowledge of methods of social control of atomic energy or the political ability to organize such control.

Similar public projects must be organized for the arts. One of the enduring benefits of the much-ridiculed WPA have been the various art and writers' projects sponsored by it. Not only because it helped to nourish and preserve the talent that otherwise might have been lost, but also because of it many an American community has for the first time come to appreciate art forms other than the common run of community statuary. It is altogether possible that profit is not the sole or even the best criterion of merit either in the plastic or in the theatrical arts. If even one kernel is separated from the chaff, the total cost will have justified itself. It is not safe to assume that genius will always emerge triumphant, irrespective of obstacles. Our evidence on this score is of only one kind—only of those who have come to the surface. How many more never did? This is particularly appropos to the wage problem of musicians. The technological advances in that field have drastically reduced the number of musicians required to fill the world with music. Without defending the specific makework practices of the Musicians' Union or the strategy of its leaders, the problem of furnishing a livelihood to the musicians still remains. It may well be that the various industries that use music taken all together can well afford to provide a good living to the musicians. But if they cannot, then it is up to the government to see that this is done through either subsidies or other measures. In music, as in any other profession or art, if we want the ministration of the geniuses, we must make certain that the talented have the opportunity to earn a living.

4. PRODUCTION PLANNING

The chain of a planned economy of abundance is complete when the planned needs, modified and adjusted to the inventory of resources, both human and plant, are linked to planned production to satisfy the total needs. This is indeed more than an attempt to adjust or to conform to environment over which the individual business units have no control, and which has therefore in the past proved futile. Economic forecasting, true or false, and individual planning serve to intensify the swings in either direction. Planning for the economy as a whole modifies the economic environment to suit our needs. Through planning we become the masters of our economic destinies. The profit motive, which has proved inadequate as an automatic mechanism to achieve an economy of full employment, is supplanted by a conscious, deliberate policy of planning, although profit would still remain dominant among incentives.[12]

This completes the evolutionary development of economic organization from unconscious impersonal process to intended predetermined ends.[13] Those purposes include full employment of course, but full employment within an ever expanding framework of needs. Not a full employment at a yearly national income of $50, $70, or a $100 billion, but of $200 billion and more. This is of the utmost importance, for it places the emphasis where it belongs: on efficiency of production and availability of resources as the ultimate limit for the expansion of satisfied needs.

To achieve the objective of efficient production and full utilization of our economic capacities, government determination of the goal is not enough. There must be integration of our differentiated economy so that the interrelated parts would mesh and not stick. For that government regulation of our economic process is imperative. Price and wage controls would of course have to be maintained in order to avoid fluctuations and to maintain a stabilized economy. Since continuity of function is indispensable to modern industry, strikes for whatever purpose would have to be avoided.[14]

It would also be necessary to eliminate all obstacles to efficient production and full utilization of manpower. First on the agenda would be a revitalized antimonopoly enforcement campaign to eliminate restraints of trade and business monopolies and cartels. Despite decades of antitrust laws, it is doubtful whether these have appreciably impeded the trend toward monopoly and concentration. What are the reasons for expecting different results under the projected planned economy?

In the first place, the function of monopoly as an integrative mechanism will be done away with through the integration of over-all planning. Second, through the availability of government credit to new enterprises and government regulation of manpower and material priorities, it would be easier for new entrepreneurs to enter monopolistic fields. Similarly, by assigning specific goals to each producer and for certain industries, with price controls, restrictions on production, or price fixing for private gain would be swept aside. Pooling of patents would further liberate the competitive system. The small businessman would get a new lease on life. And the test of monopoly would not be size, but efficiency.[15] There may be a curse in bigness, but how big is big? Certain products can be maufactured most efficiently by large organizations. However, businesses which have surpassed their optimum operational size, and all types of combinations, such as holding company systems, which are grounded in financial control but not in operational need, would be broken up, a process similar to that envisaged in the Utilities Holding Company Act.

Indeed, under this system there would for the first time be effective supervision and evaluation of the operation of large corporations. For the first time, the large masses of American stockholders would have information from independent sources on the way corporate management performs its functions. The result would be salutary in increasing management responsibility to stockholders and to the public. Great corporations are less subject to democratic control by their stockholders than are great unions to control by their membership. But whether stockholder control can at best be more than nominal may be doubted. That is why government supervision of business operation through the system of antitrust and similar regulations is absolutely essential to the establishment of managerial responsibility.[16]

Anti trust enforcement promises to be more fruitful under a system of planned economy than under a planless dispensation because, under planning, monopoly would be deprived of its price-fixing and production-control devices. More important, the present system is the outmoded prosecution approach suitable at best to private litigation and not to regulating economic functions. In this case too the expert administrative technique, and not the archaic, occasional, and non-expert judicial method, is the one which promises most success in carrying on the day-to-day functions of economic regulation.[17] Business cannot be conducted by litigation, and neither can government. This system of antitrust enforcement envisages greater government regulation, but the result would be competitive free enterprise. It would not be the first time that government regulation of the right kind was emancipating. What is regimentation for the top dog is freedom for the underdog.[18]

Another set of restrictions on production and the use of manpower which ought to be eliminated emanates from labor's house divided against itself.[19]

It is in the context of a planned economy of full employment and full utilization of resources that elimination of business monopolies and cartels and of labor's restrictive practices becomes soluble.

Since the economic planning adumbrated provides for direct linking between needs and production, no central reliance is to be placed on taxation as an incentive leverage for investment. It may be used incidentally as a supplement to price and wage control for the purpose of avoiding inflationary tendencies by siphoning off excess savings. But the main purpose of taxation would be its elementary one to defray government outlay. Since under the plan outlined full employment would ensue, there would be no difficulty in balancing the budget. The plan does not contemplate deficit spending. The tax program should be centered around a graduated income tax system. This does not, however, weaken the profit motive, which, though it has proved inadequate as a regulator of our economy, nevertheless will flourish, not wither, in an expanding economy.

5. PLANNING TECHNIQUES AND AGENCIES

What should be the administrative techniques and agencies to be employed in executing this plan? Since this was the program that operated successfully during the war, the general conclusion should be ventured that the administrative techniques and agencies to be established should be patterned after their wartime prototypes. Nevertheless, it must be understood that those were improvised under pressure of emergency, and no blind tracing is indicated. There is great need for a thorough analysis of wartime administrative experience, which would afford us valuable illumination instead of happy hunches.

Until that knowledge is available, a few tentative and exploratory observations and suggestions are possible. The planning agencies should correspond to the different sectors of planning. A Public Requirements Board would ascertain the total needs. A Resources Inventory Board would keep an inventory of our resources and plan their use and conservation. A Production Planning Board would do the over-all planning and supervision of production. It is obvious that economic planning demands that the functions of these boards be integrated. This can be accomplished in one of two principal ways: (1)

by including their functions within an over-all board of which they would be merely subordinate bureaus or departments or (2) by making them independent of each other but responsible to the President, in which case any disagreement among them would be resolved by the President. In view of the importance of the planning function, there is danger that this over-all planning board might in time rival the Presidency and Cabinet. It would therefore appear desirable to have the President and his Cabinet produce the final plan based upon the well-articulated premises of independent officials rather than from the reports of one agency, which might be inclined to gloss over vital differences in policy.

Since these agencies would determine public policy, the board system is preferable to the single administrator, in order to afford a forum for differences of opinion.

How should the various interests be represented on these boards? Here again no categorical answer can be given. However, since these boards would be the ultimate agencies of co-ordination in their respective spheres, their members should not be appointed to represent any particular interest, industry, labor, or agrarian, but rather on their individual merit to represent the public interest. All these boards should have advisory committees composed of representatives of the various interests affected, labor, employer, farmer, and consumer. In the Production Planning Board there should be an administrative section for each industry with advisory representation by employer and employee organizations.

In the administrative part of the program we would need the equivalents of the Office of Price Administration and National War Labor Board to integrate the wage-price relationship. The task of co-ordinating our economy is colossal. But we have done it before and we can do it again. Chief responsibility for this job must devolve upon the President and his Cabinet. That is why the proposal is made that the Cabinet should be divested of administrative duties.[20]

6. THE MEANING OF THE ADMINISTRATIVE STATE

This is the plan that calls for a linking of supply and demand. It constitutes the ultimate conscious integration of our differentiated economy by the state. This plan is not untried, but proved a spectacular success during the war. Why not have it established as the industrial equivalent of war?

The miraculous accomplishments of American war production, which made possible the superimposition of a war economy on a substantial peacetime economy, was not the product of private enterprise but of private enterprise integrated by a democratic state. Our victory was won by a democratically planned economy. This generation has asserted its mastery over the economic environment by state action and democratic economic control. That is the greatest invention in social behavior since the evolution of the democratic form of government. We cannot afford to ignore it.

Even were it possible to conceive of dismantling our industrial machine or of some unforeseen scientific miracle which would abolish the intricate division of labor that obtains in our economy, that would hardly avoid ultimate state control, for even the much simpler agrarian economy was state integrated in the feudal form. The atom bomb, it is true, opens up infinite possibilities for destruction but its victims are likely to include not only the machines but those who tend them. Greater scientific knowledge and power would lead in the direction not of less but of more social controls. In fact the greater the amount of energy that science makes available to man the more intensive and complex will be the regulatory measures. Economic planning is unavoidable whether or not it can be free and democratic.

Since the first function of the modern laissez-faire capitalist state was of a purely police nature, that state could be referred to as a police state.[21] In that sphere was its first integrative operation performed. Now, since the economic life of the country will have to be integrated even in times of peace, it is the political agency of the state, the government, that will perform that vital function. It will not be in the police sphere; it will be in the realm of public administration that the main emphasis will be placed. We are on the threshold of what should be called the administrative state.[22]

BOOK TWO

Freedom and Democracy in the Administrative State

CHAPTER IX

Economic Freedom under Planning

1. THE CHOICE BEFORE US

We shall now consider whether the administrative state controlling an economy of active planning, whose evolution is inevitable, can be a free and democratic state.

The answer cannot affect the existence or nonexistence of an economy of planning, which is unavoidable.[1] In exploring the relationship of the administrative state to freedom and democracy it is necessary to make a number of vital distinctions. It is necessary to find out whether economic planning as such is incompatible with freedom and democracy. If it is, then our inquiry is at an end and we might as well launch ourselves on one last binge of license before the Stygian curtain of a new dark age descends on the twilight of freedom. However, if the inquiry reveals the glad tidings that freedom and democracy are not incompatible with planning, we should not therefore swing over to the opposite assumption: that planning is synonymous with freedom and democracy. We must then carefully investigate what types of planning are compatible with freedom and democracy and what conditions, safeguards, and social controls are necessary to make the administrative state free and democratic. Particular attention will be devoted to the type of economic planning outlined in this study. Conducive to clarity will be the reduction of general terms such as liberty and democracy to their elementary and specific meanings and observation of their application to concrete problems involved in economic planning.

Is economic planning incompatible with freedom and democracy? Those who reply in the affirmative invariably point to the example of the Russian and Nazi totalitarian dictatorships.[2] These dictatorships include planned economies within their systems, but all that this proves is that a planned economy may be dictatorial and autocratic. It does not demonstrate that this is necessarily so. The conscious and deliberate establishment of dictatorships by the Bolsheviks and Nazis was an integral part of their social philosophies. From this does not follow that a dynamically planned economy, which is established by those whose philosophy of government is democratic and libertarian, also must lead to a dictatorship. Nor is a planned economy the sine qua non condition of dictatorship. There is no invariable correspondence between economic systems and political systems.[3] The capitalistic system has existed in democracies and dictatorships, in republics and monarchies. Tyrannies and autocracies as well as democracies have crowded the pages of history since ancient times and under all forms of economic order. In our own day, Russia has instituted a planned economy through government ownership by dictatorial methods, while Great Britain continues her parliamentary democracy even during the critical formative period of a partial nationalization of industry. While there have been no democracy and freedom in the planned economies of present-day Russia and Nazi Germany, neither were they present in the capitalistic economies of these countries under the Czar and Kaiser, respectively. For the United States, whose cultural tradition is democratic and libertarian, the shadow of political things to come is not cast by what happened in Russia and Germany, whose traditions are autocratic and dictatorial.

In the matter of state economic integration we are in a position to exercise a collective volitional choice, and in what the ultimate choice is to be the cultural background of each state will play a decisive role. The importance of the individuality of cultures and of cultural influence cannot be overemphasized.[4]

We have had remarkable success in administering a democratically controlled planned war economy, and even during peace government regulation of our economy has been varied and broad in scope.

The administrative state is not necessarily the mausoleum of the idea of freedom despite the lamentations of those who assume to equate economic laissez faire with democracy. Democracy need not fear that fascism or communism has a monopoly on planning. Both in the objectives to be attained and in the methods of achieving them, the administrative state will admit of at least as great a variety of forms as its predecessors. The war has demonstrated that a planned economy is not incompatible with privately owned and operated industry as well as with an independent labor movement. The same can and should be true under the peacetime controls of the administrative state. This will be the American form molded in the tradition of our own culture.

2. THE MEANING OF FREEDOM

Freedom is the state or condition in which man can fulfill his capacities, his drives, and his appetites. Power is the totality of man's abilities to fulfill them. Freedom has come to refer to the condition; power, to the operating force. Thus freedom usually means freedom from restraints, "negative" freedom, though lately we have come to speak of freedom to do. In that sense "positive" freedom can be equated with power. The problem is one of semantics, not of essence. Power and freedom are two aspects of the same concept. They are synonymous. Absolute freedom can be enjoyed only by God. Man, because of the limitations of his organism and those arising out of his physical environment and of living within a society composed of other men with similar needs and wants, can have but limited freedom.[5] This does not of course underwrite the romantic concept that society is man's historic misfortune.[6]

Though society contributes to the fulfillment of man's wants it also limits them. But man is so constituted that he forever seeks the utmost expression of himself—absolute freedom.[7]

If we choose to refer to man's limitations—whether in himself, in the physical environment, or in his society—as fate, then the struggle for freedom is a struggle against man's fate. Man's struggle against his limitations or fate has hardly begun, especially outside the physical environment. We may therefore speak with justification of man's eternal struggle for liberty. This has apt application to the limitations inherent in the social realm in which man as a social animal must always have being. Man's history is the history of man's struggle for liberty.[8]

The mode of fulfillment of man's biological drives varies greatly.[9] Man's nature, within limits, is malleable. Individual and cultural mores show a variegated pattern. On the conscious level, intelligence plays an important place in the fulfillment of our needs. Man possesses the reality within limits of freedom of choice. In religion and philosophy, this has given rise to the problem of free will. In the natural, and particularly the social, sciences, to the issues of determination and causation.

Since society is dynamic and complex, man's social limitations are of the same character. Liberty too is therefore many faceted and ever changing in meaning and content, for liberty is the struggle against those limitations. The nature of the limitations at any particular time in society determines the character of the struggle for liberty directed against those limitations. This explains why the definition of liberty has varied with the specific struggles for freedom in all ages, lands, and realms of endeavor.[10]

3. FREEDOM AND SECURITY

In our age liberty has come to be inseparably connected with economic security. Freedom from want is basic in our Bill of Rights.

When the Founding Fathers foregathered to crystallize the American dream of liberty, their fight for freedom and their thinking were molded by the sociopolitical limitations they rebelled against. These were the restrictions of a decadent mercantilist society, enforced through the power of the state. Since the state was the author of the restrictions, the constitutional liberties at the founding of our Republic were of a political nature directed against action by the state.[11]

When the turn of this century was approaching, the American people became aware that the great aggregates of capital with their immense concentrations of economic power were imposing limitations upon the people in the fulfillment of their needs.[12] It was no longer the government as such that endangered the liberties of the people, but the great corporations. They therefore sought to protect their rights through regulatory statutes, both federal and state.

But much of this type of legislation failed to get the constitutional imprimatur. When the judges were construing the statutes, they read the federal and state constitutions between the lines and found with indelible, though invisible (to the uninitiate), ink inscribed the words of Smith and Spencer.[13] Laissez faire was no longer merely an economic doctrine, but a constitutional dogma. Constitutional restraints placed upon the government for the protection of the liberties of the people were converted into bonds to shackle the people and place them at the mercy of monopoly capitalism. What is liberty to one economic system is bondage to another. What was liberty for the Founding Fathers became bondage for their descendants. Social Darwinism was added to the Decalogue, and the law of the jungle became a part of the Constitution.

The Nazi nightmare has taught us not to take for granted nor to hold lightly our constitutional civil liberties. That we had come so to consider them before the advent of fascism cannot be denied. But the fault is not wholly in ourselves. Eternal vigilance is truly the price of liberty, but freedom's fate is being unfolded in many arenas. In our technological civilization the center one is occupied by the economic show. There all the economic giants, pygmies, and freaks disport themselves amid all the conflicts and contradictions of our society. There we witness the breath-taking dexterity and power of modern man as he leaps from one technical achievement to another, but there too we watch the crumpled bodies after they have come hurtling through the air from their precarious social perches.

Modern man is groping for the sociopolitical techniques to master his economic environment. And these techniques have to be of a sociopolitical, collective, character because man, the individual man, is himself helpless to hew out the rock of safety for himself. As our economic units increase in size and power over them becomes concentrated more and more into fewer hands, the mass of the people become less and less able to depend upon their individual selves for their economic well-being. Even in America, the frontier is gone.

The age of opportunities is not over. Unlimited horizons are ahead of us. But for the mass of people the opportunities must be collectively created and fostered: above all, employment opportunities. The "private initiative" of our tens of millions of factory workers has not and will not keep them employed. Hence, insecurity, which has been man's cosmic fate ever since he became aware that he is mortal, has become particularly accentuated in the present era. In consequence, man's drive for power has taken the form of a drive for security, one of the most emcompassing of contemporary forces and a characteristic phenomenon of our culture, including the political realm.[14] No wonder that our age has articulated a new freedom: freedom from fear. In Germany, because of the determining factor of the German military and racial cult, the escape from insecurity and fear culminated in nazism.[15] In Russia, because of the imperatives of its own Czarist past, the quest for security culminated in the Soviet dictatorship.[16]

The right to a job has become a fundamental human right whose satisfaction modern government can ignore only at its own peril. Since the individual in modern society is helpless to provide for himself the opportunities for a job, he looks to his government to provide it for him. In point of fact the world owes him a living, the opportunity for one. This is not surprising. Economic security is connected with the satisfaction of one of the most pressing biological and instinctual drives, that of hunger for food. Before man can appreciate freedom of speech he must eat. But economic security is more than assurance of three square meals a day. It is the assurance of full employment of his faculties, of having the feeling of being useful and wanted. If we want man to reach that degree of individuality and human dignity which is at the core of democratic values, we must provide him with the security, self-expression, and self-respect that a job affords.[17] Not only international peace but domestic liberty depends on freedom from want and freedom from fear.

Economic laissez faire has rationalized high profits as rewards for taking risks. This became inverted into the doctrine that economic liberty depends on the possibility of a high economic mortality. Soon this fallacy was restated out of its context into a universal maxim that liberty and security are mutually exclusive. Nothing could be further from the truth. Security is the basis of liberty and not its enemy. Security is the road to freedom. Security alone will not guarantee liberty but freedom without security cannot long endure, and we may be certain that in our quest for security our cultural pattern will assert itself as effectively as theirs have in the case of the German and the Russian. In the methods used to achieve the purposes we want we can exercise a wide area of choice within the broad and dynamic limits of the culture in which we operate. Therein is another good omen for the survival of the democratic way of life.

4. CONSUMER FREEDOM

The administrative state, democratically governed, will provide for economic security within a framework of liberty by achieving the full utilization of our manpower and economic resources. Liberty implies choice, and within an economy of abundance the area of selection will be great in the exercise of both the consuming and the producing function, not despite but because of economic planning.

For the consumer, a democratically planned economy would not be a regimented economy. Rationing is avoidable in a dynamically planned peacetime economy. It is a feature of a wartime economy because of shortages resulting from diversion of resources to military needs. In a planned society it might have to be resorted to only in unusual cases where the demand for a certain product has exceeded expectations. Rationing is not a denial of liberty, but the expression of complete democratic equality for the consumer in the satisfaction of his needs. Rationing is based on the worth of the individual, not on the size of his pocketbook. Rationing is not the cause of shortages but the means to equalize their incidence. Uniformity is not part of economic planning. Planning for diversity is implicit in our great industrial capacity. The consumer, to an unprecedented degree, would be in a position to gear his spending to his desires and tastes. It is illusory to imagine that in an unplanned economy, monopoly ridden and with partial utilization of resources and chronic unemployment, the consumer could be omnipotent. The doctrine of consumer sovereignty[18] is completely refuted by one sustained, straight-faced glance, if possible, at women's hats. In an economy where prices and production are determined in the basic industries by monopoly or semi-monopoly, the claim that the consumer determines production is far-fetched. What liberty of choice, indeed, do the unemployed and those with substandard incomes have in satisfying their wants? What liberty in choosing a physician is there for the mass of our people when medical care is dispensed not in response to need but to ability to pay? Where effective demand, or purchasing power, falls far short of human needs, liberty of choice in the satisfaction of wants is severely limited.

To the extent that the gap between effective demand and human wants is narrowed is this type of liberty augmented. Adequate purchasing power in the hands of the mass of the people is the basis of consumer democracy.

Economic planning, therefore, does imply certain consumer regulation or guidance within broad limits of the satisfaction of wants. A public works system geared to public needs rather than for make-work purposes is one requirement. Integration of the economy will also involve production planning to eliminate bottlenecks in the satisfaction of needs. For instance, it will be necessary to plan that sufficient housing be built for current needs. But in its total effect that is not a restraint but an enhancement of consumer liberty, for adequate housing is essential to the satisfaction of wants in regard to furniture, electrical appliances, and similar items. Because of our differentiated and complex technology we can aim at the maximum satisfaction of needs only through regulation, just as in our crowded communication arteries we can get where we want only through traffic regulation. Co-ordination is indispensable to living in a complex world.

5. FREE ENTERPRISE

Not only freedom of the consumer but the liberty of the entrepreneur will be enhanced in the democratic administrative state. There will be price and wage regulations, to be sure, but these will be the conditions and not the limitations of freedom of enterprise.

Assignment of production quotas should serve as a challenge and not a constraint on business opportunities, for there would be no compulsion to engage in business. With the war pressure for speed in production lifted and with the possibility open for long-range planning, necessary production would be attained through profit incentives rather than compulsion.[19]

An assured market for current output as well as guaranteed average cost plus profit would not eliminate all risk of business failure, but would serve as a stimulus to business acumen and enterprise. Freed of the constraints of monopolistic practices and armed with sufficient access to materials and manpower, big and little businessmen would be faced with a constantly expanding market for their ideas and energies. The claim that business risk is a stimulus to enterprise must be revised in the light of our wartime experience of unprecedented production in an era devoid of business failures. Fear of failure may be paralyzing instead of a fillip to activity. Desire for greater profits may be even more effective than the wish to avoid losses. The profit motive will have received its emancipation in a planned economy. In a constantly expanding planned economy, enterprise will have greater opportunities and therefore greater freedom to fulfill its functions than it has had in a planless, stagnant, and contracting economy.

A similar enhancement of economic freedom will be the lot of the workers in a democratically planned economy.[20]

CHAPTER X

Cultural and Political Liberties under Planning

---

1. CULTURAL FREEDOM

A democratically regulated economy dynamically planned is favorable to our economic liberties. It is indeed the basis for their full flowering. But what is the relationship between economic planning and cultural freedom? Are we destined to sacrifice at the altar of economic security our cherished freedoms of religion, inquiry, and artistic expression as well as our civil and political liberties of speech, press, and assembly? Are economic planning and cultural and civil freedom incompatible?

An economy being planned does not necessarily involve a planned culture. While in the economic and political realms uniformity of regulation and application is a sine qua non condition, no such uniformity is necessary in the matter of religion, art, or ideals.[1] Our economy as planned during the war was operated efficiently without benefit of regimenting the beliefs of Catholics, Protestants, Jews, and atheists. Why should this be necessary in time of peace? In order to set goals for employment, it is not necessary to dictate what plays to produce, what novels to publish, what churches to attend or not to attend.

Indeed, economic and political activities can best be organized by the state when the state withdraws from dictation in the cultural realm. It was not until the end of the religious wars, when man eschewed the medieval fallacy that the correct concept about his heavenly fate is essential to the security of the state, that the nationalist state acquired stability.[2] That Russian and Nazi totalitarianisms have regimented culture is due not to their economies being planned but to their totalitarian creeds. Because economic and political activities are not necessarily decisive of the cultural realm, instances may be cited in history of political tyranny being superimposed on certain aspects of cultural freedom. Art in the Italian Renaissance cities is an example. However, because of the great ramifications of our differentiated economic order, some claim might be made that a planned economy dictatorially controlled must be totalitarian, that is, must involve regimentation and government control of every aspect of human activity. From this it does not follow, however, that a planned economy necessarily involves totalitarian control. On the contrary, a planned economy democratically oriented presupposes cultural freedom as an essential policy and condition of development of culture.

The upheaval of revolution is not conducive to the mood of creative work. Even so, the sterility of Bolshevik literature and art even in the forms in which Russia has excelled is due in most part to the regimentation of all creative impulses to serve narrow political ends and the shifting dictates of the party line.[3] Spontaneity is the prime requisite of cultural creativeness, and there is no spontaneity without freedom. Love and creativeness cannot be supplied on order. Only outward compliance, not the spontaneous essence. Art can be propaganda when it is a spontaneous distillation of the artist, not when it is custom made to fit the current edict. In the latter case it may serve as propaganda but it will lack the quality of real art. Totalitarian dictatorship is incompatible not only with the dignity of man but with cultural fecundity as well. This is not surprising, for cultural creativeness is the individual self-expression of the artist—his sublimated quest for power.

Diversity of expression is therefore indispensable to creativeness. On the international scale, and within each community, cultural diversity must be held up as an objective of policy. Any government project, such as the WPA artists' and writers' projects which afforded opportunity for more diversified artistic expression, not straightjacketed by the profit criterion, serves a useful communal purpose if no attempt is made to dictate what the product should be. Government subsidies ought to be forthcoming to permit research in "pure" science undirected and unrestrained in order to replenish our severely exhausted stock of abstract principles. This applies even more to the social than to the natural sciences.

Another opportunity for increasing diversity is in the educational field, where the federal government is called upon more and more for financial assistance. Freedom in education is one of the bases of the democratic administrative state but this means freedom not only from government restraints but from the dictates of private economic and other interests. The constitutional principle of the separation of church and state is as applicable to a planned as to an unplanned economy. This principle is violated when a church seeks to use government authority or group pressure to impose its sectarian views of manners and morals not on its communicants only but on the citizenry generally. If we are to preserve our liberties we must never forget that our freedoms have been acquired through long, arduous, and agonizing struggle against the straight-jacket monopoly of clericalism. Not only freedom of speech and of the press but even freedom of worship has been won in the face of church opposition.[4] We must be particularly on guard against the slow erosion of the American doctrine of the separation of church and state.

Freedom of cultural pursuits and organization is predicated on voluntary adherence and compliance. When this is replaced by organizational compulsions, cultural freedom is no less violated than if the state committed the repressing act. When a church becomes identified with a political and social order, it shares with that order the latter's enemies and ultimate fate. Much of the antagonism of Russian revolutionaries to the Russian Orthodox Church was due to the latter's having been identified as the religious bulwark of the Czarist regime. The recently reorganized church under the Bolsheviks would appear to be as much an instrument of government policy as it was under the old regime, or as the labor unions are now.[5]

2. CIVIL LIBERTIES

If economic planning does not necessarily involve cultural regimentation, neither does it lead to the abolition of the related civil liberties, such as freedom of speech, press, and assembly. Although freedom in certain cultural realms of art and religion has existed in some instances under a dictatorship, no civil liberties are compatible with autocracy irrespective of economic planning. The presence or absence of civil liberties is the ultimate proof whether a system is democratic or dictatorial, for on civil liberties depends the right of opposition, the distinguishing mark of democracy. The absence of civil liberties in the Nazi and Communist totalitarianisms is due therefore not to economic planning but to the dictatorial elements in their systems.

On the other hand, if a planned economy is to be democratically controlled, free speech and a free press are indispensable, for economic planning involves great issues of public policy on which the fullest informative light needs to be focused.

There are two aspects to free communication of ideas: the right to articulate and the right to receive information. Both of these must be realized in actuality for democracy to function properly. In dictatorships freedom of communication of ideas is prevented by prohibiting the free utterance of thought, but the ultimate aim of that policy is to maintain a monopoly by relentless control of the minds of the people. This is betrayed by the frantic attempts of the Nazis and Bolsheviks to insulate their subjects within hermetically sealed encampments against the infiltration of ideas by radio, travel, and literature from the world outside their sway. Is this one of the conditioning factors in the psychopathic suspicions and fears of foreign systems, characteristic of the totalitarians? As long as there are ideas abroad which are not controlled by them they cannot feel safe at home. Is this why totalitarianism, whether of the right or of the left, is driven to world domination?

In democracies early emphasis was focused on the right to articulate ideas, for the restrictions on freedom of speech and the press were those of government. This is why our constitutional liberties are guarantees against state action. But the center of the stage has been taken over by freedom to receive ideas. The right to see, to listen, and to read is receiving our greater attention as the foundation on which is predicated the ability to exercise a choice, the nexus of democracy, industrial as well as political.[6] But choice involves information on alternatives, and becomes limited to the extent that the sources of information available to the electorate are monopolized. Freedom of communication is justified, according to Justice Holmes, because "the ultimate good desired is better reached by free trade in ideas—that the best test of truth is the power of the thought to get itself accepted in the competition of the market."[7] This democratic faith is predicated on the existence of a free competitive market for ideas. It cannot operate where competition is replaced by monopoly or quasi monopoly. But just as competition in economic goods has fallen victim to technology and combinations in restraint of trade, so has the free market of ideas.

Radio networks, chain newspapers, decreasing number of newspapers despite increase in population, combined ownership of both newspapers and radio stations—all these and other manifestations of concentration spell monopoly or quasi monopoly in the control over media of communication and dissemination of information.[8] It is not enough that Americans get more truthful and more diversified press and radio information than any other people in the world. We must constantly strive for greater democratization, and monopoly of information is incompatible with diversification of views essential to intelligent choice among the complex issues of our time. Concentration of control over the media of information has been weighted heavily against liberalism, despite the trend toward liberal legislation.[9] The conservative and reactionary position, propagated day in and day out by the overwhelming portion of the press, becomes undermined only in times of great crisis when severe unemployment brings home to the electorate that they have been led astray by false prophets. Press monopoly contributes to crisis government and deprives the American system of the advantages of gradualist long-range adjustment.[10]

It is no answer to declare that liberal and labor organizations have the right to publish daily newspapers. It is an indication of the lack of enlightment on the part of organized labor in the field of public relations that the powerful American labor movement, which increasingly participates in politics, cannot boast of one metropolitan newspaper. But this does not alter the fact that the right to diversified information is infringed by monopoly or quasi monopoly, and the result is the same whether the source of the infringement is the government or private interests. Nor is it wise to rely on the forbearance and enlightenment of private monopoly. Power without responsibility corrupts private monopolies no less than government dictatorship.

3. A PROGRAM FOR FREEDOM OF INFORMATION

What to do? Here, again, the state as the integrative agency of the community has been called upon by the people to protect their rights by regulatory measures. Because of the mechanical imperatives for control, radio communication has come under extensive regulation by the Federal Communications Commission. Breaking up of network control over programs of individual stations, dissolution of ownership and control over stations in certain circumstances, and reviews of programs to obtain balancing of opinions in the presentation of controversial issues have been among the measures adopted by the Commission to obtain diversity of information. In this case government regulation has proved an instrument not for censorship but for the diminution of regimentation of information.[11]

Why not a similar program for the daily press? Forcible decentralization of ownership and control may or may not be advisable, but it would not be adequate and is unnecessary in order to achieve diversity of information for the public. The following program is preferable and promises to be more effective in achieving the indicated objective:

Under auspices of the government a Board of Dissemination of Information should be established. This should be composed of representations of various interests, such as labor, capital, agriculture, consumers, publishers, government, political parties, racial, religious, and cultural groups. In order to avoid suspicion of packing, the representatives should be chosen by the various interested organizations. This board should appoint and supervise a staff of experts in various fields whose function would be twofold. They would collate and review the pertinent facts and opposing views on important current events and controversial issues as these gain the center of public attention. Articles of reasonable length containing these reviews of the opposing sides would be issued daily to the press of the country for printing in a prominent place in the newspapers. Likewise each radio station would broadcast this feature of information on a favored time. In addition to this regular feature, distributed in the manner of the services of the great newsgathering agencies, the board would send occasional replies to unanswered articles or editorials of particular newspapers. These replies would have to be published by the affected newspaper in the same space as the original news article or editorial. For this purpose the board might enlist the co-operation of citizens' committees of similarly representative character and organized in each locality, whose function would be to observe and report on the condition of diversity of information in their communities and to apply the general plan to local issues.

This plan simply regularizes the principle of the town hall forum and the political debates of the Lincoln-Douglas type, and adapts it to the exigencies of modern technology and media of information, in order to provide for the American electorate a greater measure of diversity of opinion and factual information. This plan carries with it several advantages. It does not involve any drastic treatment of the problem of ownership and control. It does not establish government censorship. It leaves the operation and control of the plan to the affected interests in our society, including newspaper publishers. It brings diversity of information to the readers of every newspaper, instead of relying on the conjectural hope that readers might be exposed to more than one newspaper. Publishers would still have the right to print or not to print anything they wanted, to distort, falsify, and unjustly attack. But their monopoly on the eyes and ears of America would have been broken. The very fact that a publisher would know that any misstatements of fact, intentional or otherwise, would be brought to the attention of his readers would serve as a restraining influence on reckless, irresponsible journalism and would contribute to making the American press more factual and better informed.

The right to reply is the new form of the right to freedom of speech. It is the right of all interests not represented by those exercising a monopoly or quasi monopoly over the media of information. That monopoly must be broken if democracy is to function in the modern world. There is no greater issue before the American public, and no amount of calumny or vituperation which is being poured by those affected about the heads of those who call attention to this problem will avoid its ultimate solution. That solution lies not in government censorship but in regulation to achieve diversity of information. Public media of information such as the press and radio have become public utilities impressed with a public interest. The press and the radio are entitled to no greater immunity from government regulation than are other forms of business or labor. It is all a question whether the objectives and methods of such regulation are democratic.

The attention that is frequently focused upon the conduct of public opinion polls is all to the good. The relationship of such polls to the functioning of our democracy is close, direct, and even crucial.

The public opinion polls influence our lawmakers by placing at their disposal a mirror of the electorate on the issues of the day by which to guide their voting in the legislative halls. Whether we believe that the function of the legislator is to lead and mold public opinion or merely automatically to record public opinion in voting on legislation, we cannot deny that the results of the polls leave their impress on our representatives. Indeed, it is only on the issues on which he feels a deep and abiding conviction that the legislator would dare consistently to swim against the current.

Although their avowed function is to measure and ascertain public opinion, the public opinion polls also of necessity help to create it.

This is derived from the natural human tendency to conform to the cultural pattern common to an environment. Whether the preference is in regard to a candidate or an issue, the desire to climb on the band wagon is generally recognized and exploited. Hence, we find editorials on opposite sides of a question each declaring that the American people want so and so . . . The objective is phrased as a fact so that as an assumption it may transmute itself into a fact through the process of emulation and conformity. This is true whether or not the particular editorial writer is under the illusion that he is peculiarly sensitized to the voice of the people.

The public opinion polls have became public utilities in whose proper operation there resides a definite public interest.

The discussions and investigations occasioned by the inaccuracy of certain polls in underestimating Roosevelt's strength in the 1944 presidential election have concerned themselves chiefly with the problem of the reliability of techniques used by the polls in measuring public preference for candidates. This is of the utmost importance. But it is regrettable that the controversy about this aspect of the operation of the polls has blotted out a no less significant phase of the polls' functioning—the measuring of public opinion in regard to issues.

This is the more regrettable because this phase of the polls' work is most influential in its consequences on the climate of opinion and government. No government in power in a democracy can for long proceed with a program which is being opposed consistently by the people. Moreover, in measuring public opinion on issues, the polls are under no check inherent in their work, as is true in the case of ascertaining preference as to candidates. In the latter instance the elections show up the polls' shortcomings. Generally, no such check and consequent restraint obtains in measuring public opinion on issues. There are no public referenda conducted by the federal government in the United States to serve as a check on the accuracy of polls. Hence the temptation to negligence, incompetence, political and social bias, or even to possible dishonesty is infinitely greater than in candidate polls.

We need not linger on the possibility of error and mischief relating to the technique of sampling, evaluation, and interpretation, which is applicable to measuring preferences for candidates as well as issues. Peculiar to the latter function, however, is the problem of phrasing the question to which a reply is sought. On first thought it may appear that formulating a question is a routine ministerial act involving no discretion or skill and is devoid of importance. But in reality this task is fundamental. It should have the objective of phrasing the question so as to avoid indicating what kind of reply is desired and expected by the interrogator. We are familiar how in ordinary conversation or in formal examination in courts it is almost impossible for the interrogator not to betray even by the tone of voice what answer he wishes to get. On paper too, the opinion of the interrogator on the issue may come through from the wording of the question. This is true even if the one who formulates the question consciously attempts to be objective and to strip the wordage of all layers of emotionalism and bias. But that such an intent is universal on the part of the polls one cannot always be persuaded.

No legitimate defense can be made of the practice of using the question not as a means of eliciting but of creating public opinion. If a question is prefaced by some information for the guidance of the poll voter, the conflicting issues should be presented fairly and impartially. The loaded question has no place in public opinion polls.

How should the desideratum of complete fairness and adroit skill in formulating questions be achieved?

More emphasis on this aspect of the work will help, of course. So will greater competence in the staff. Contributing to the same end will be a firm resolve to prosecute the task with favor toward none. But all these will prove inadequate. They will not materially help in eliminating the imperceptible unconscious molding of questions in the image of one's inarticulate and therefore decisive premises. What is necessary is that even the subconscious bias should be cast off in the crucible of indepedent examination by the various interests and experts related to the subject matter of the particular question. This problem exists without impugning the integrity or competence of the public opinion polls as a whole.

It is therefore proposed that within the Board for Dissemination of Information there be established a panel or board of question editors representing the affected interests.

The method of decision on each question is best left to experience to determine. It would not be desirable to keep the panel in an advisory capacity only and for the polls to retain the ultimate decision. The decision should be left to the panel itself. However, it is not anticipated that intransigeance will develop and irreconcilable disagreements will ensue. The ultimate product will only rarely be the result of divided decision. The very existence of an agency of criticism will tend to the objectivization of phraseology even in the first formulation of the question by the polls themselves.

Perhaps the establishment of a similar board or panel may be found advisable in relation to the other functions and workings of public opinion polls. Only if the polls are above suspicion will they be able to give the full measure of their public service, which impinges on the functioning of our democratic system.

4. LIBERTY AND ANTIDEMOCRATIC FORCES

The problem of civil liberties in the administrative state involves the issue of the extent of tolerance that a democracy ought to accord to antidemocratic forces. The issue is not new and is in no way dependent on whether the economy is planned or unplanned. It has, however, become of critical importance in the modern state because of the refined fifth column techniques of undermining democratic states which have been developed by the Fascist and Communist parties. In claiming civil rights for themselves in democracies, these antidemocratic forces are essentially in the position of wanting for themselves those rights which democrats, because of their democratic philosophy, must accord them, but which they, the Fascist and Communists, are compelled by their own ideology when in power to deny to the democrats.

There are important implications in domestic policy. There is no democratic principle that compels a democratic state to accord freedom of speech, press, and assembly to representatives of foreign countries. It is a violation of international law for the representative of one country to intervene in the domestic affairs of another country.[12] This is no less the case where the representatives are citizens of the country whose sovereignty is violated. Enjoyment of civil liberties is based on the premise of loyalty to the country irrespective of what views may be held concerning the policies and heads of government. No such loyalty can be imputed to those in America whose views about American policy is determined by the dictates and interests of another state. It would therefore be no violation of democratic philosophy for the United States to outlaw the Communist party. This action would be predicated not on advocacy of the overthrow of the government by force but on control of the party by a foreign government.

As to the desirability or expediency of this course, grave doubt may be expressed. The antics of the Dies, Rankin, and Thomas committees in pinning the Communist label on anyone to the left of the United States Chamber of Commerce without the elementary protection of procedural due process is a warning that must be heeded. Yet the United States government may sooner or later have to deal in earnest with the Communist fifth column as it had to do in the past with the Nazi brand and will have to continue to deal with the native Fascists.

Ill-advised is the relevant provision of the Taft-Hartley Act of 1947 which denies to a union access to the procedures of the NLRB unless each of its officers and those of its national or international affiliates file an affidavit that he is not a member of the Communist party and "does not believe in and is not a member of or supports any organization that believes in or teaches the overthrow of the United States Government by force or by any illegal or unconstitutional methods." This provision would not aid in the elimination of Communists from the labor movement. It would drive them underground, where it would be more difficult to detect them.

In those cases in which subterfuge would be impossible, the Communist-controlled unions would forgo the peaceful processes of the board rather than surrender power. The members of the outlaw union, who are the innocent victims of the Communists, would be penalized by being deprived of the protection of the law, although they are endowed with no greater power to escape from Communist tentacles. Barred from recourse to the peaceful procedures of the law, the union would have to resort to strikes as a measure of self-help to gain its ends. The ensuing strife, bitterness, and confusion would furnish the fruitful soil for the flourishing of Communist disruptive tactics.

The provision is also objectionable in that it unjustifiably addresses itself to the labor movement exclusively. The cartel agreements between American businessmen and their German counterparts, which frequently limited American production of critical materials to the detriment of our war effort, should be a grave warning that subversive elements such as Fascists in management as in Congress can be at least as dangerous to the safety of our Republic as Communists in the labor movement. If the real target is the subversive elements and not the labor movement, why single out unions for special attention?

Perhaps the best approach to the problem of antidemocratic forces, in addition to the necessary check on sabotage and espionage, is disclosure and publicity. Since Communist strength derives from covert infiltration leading to control, particularly in labor unions and liberal organizations, prime responsibility for eliminating Communists and fellow travelers resides in the organizations and leaders affected. Even Republicans have been known to enter into alliance with Communists when it suited their short-range purposes. Helpful, but not without danger to liberty, would be an overall government program of disclosure which would require all organizations to publish their membership rolls and an accounting of their income and outlay. Public disclosure of the business connections of public officials would be salutary in avoiding public suspicion of the innocent.

Feasible too is the broad application of the right of immediate reply to antisocial propaganda. The disclosures of the Canadian communist spy trials and the communist-led political strikes in France and Italy in 1947 must be a warning to those who would ignore the problem of national security. The task will not be easy but it must be performed: to evolve empirically effective devices for dealing with the infiltrational, conspiratorial techniques of modern antidemocratic forces, which would be equally responsive to the dictates of national security and civil liberties.

Above all, however, the safety of the democratic state must rest on the development of an enlightened public opinion devoted to the democratic faith. To achieve this objective it is necessary to keep the channels of public information clear of monopolistic restraints and to provide the people with opportunity for economic security. Liberty and security are inseparable twins in the democratic administrative state. So are liberty and law, whether in the economic field or in the political. The state must intervene to regulate and integrate the highly differentiated technology and social structure in order that the people may enjoy their liberties. Freedom can no longer be left to chance. Of course there is danger of abuse of power but our problems are too overwhelming not to demand great application of power to their solution. Whether that power is wisely and beneficially exercised will depend on the kinds of democratic social controls we employ—on whether or not the administrative state will be democratic.[13]

CHAPTER XI

Power Distribution and Political Systems

1. INQUIRY INTO THE DISTRIBUTION OF POWER

Ever since Plato and Aristotle democracy has occupied the center ring of political philosophy and conflict.[1] Democracy needs clarification and restatement. This was the Greeks' word for it, but the social and political system to which the Greeks applied it would hardly be consonant with our conception of democracy. What the Greeks called a democratic polis excluded from participation in the affairs of the state a large slave class and those alien to the city's kindred.[2] In our own day, not only Stalin but Hitler, Franco, and Mussolini claimed upon occasion that their systems of government were real democracies. Through the ages the term "democracy" has become too complex and vague to serve as a frame of reference.[3]

Beyond the question of good or evil of democracy as a system of society, is democracy possible at all? Is democracy just a myth, an ideology, Plato's "royal lie" to keep the masses in subjection by casting before them the artificial pearls of illusion? Or is democracy the promised land to which we may set sail with assurance that we may land on its shores if we quicken our efforts and are knowledgeable in navigation?

Ever since the Greeks named it, democracy has come to refer to government by the people.[4] In the more analytical definition phrased by Lincoln but nevertheless encompassed by the basic Greek concept, democracy identified a form of government "of the people, by the people, and for the people."[5]

Democracy as a form of society refers to a specific power relationship within the state or to a form of distribution within the state of power which controls the state. Democracy differs from other forms of government in the distribution of sovereign power—in the power that controls the personnel and policies of the government.[6] What is involved is not the "right" to govern but the power to govern, not the formal and nominal but the actual. This does not gainsay the important democratic institution of universal suffrage and eligibility to office, but because of these constitutional provisions we must not conclude that they necessarily correspond to the reality of government by the people. When we study the distribution of income among the population we are not foreclosed by the legal right of every citizen to be a millionnaire; neither should we be content to limit our inquiry to formal concepts in studying the distribution of power.

If the distribution of all forms of power controlling the state corresponded with the theory of democracy, it would be on an equal basis among the adult individuals composing the state, for then power would be coextensive with democratic political rights, which are characterized by equality. It is therefore not surprising that equalitarianism is the basic tenet of the democratic faith.[7] Attempting to justify democratic self-government, the Declaration of Independence commits itself to the biological assumption that all men are created equal, which at a later period was restated in extreme behaviorism.[8] Basic to our inquiry is therefore the question whether each individual shares or can share equally in the distribution of power controlling the state. This inquiry must be conducted along two main lines: factors present in the general environment and those connected with the individual.

2. LEADERSHIP AND SOCIAL STRUCTURE

A universal phenomenon of human society, and perhaps of the higher animal societies as well, is leadership.[9] This characteristic is not the fortuitous consequence of historical evolution which can be cast off once the historical process takes a different turn, as in the case of the replacement of private with public ownership of the means of production. Leadership is as integral a part of the Soviet system as of the capitalistic countries.

Leadership is indispensable because of the nature of man and society. Political power is the result of man's quest for mastery of his social environment, that is, the wills of others. As soon as a control of wills is established within a power system organization is born. Leadership can be identified with the superordinated will and the following with the subordinated will in an organization.[10]

In rudimentary form leadership expresses itself in a psychological hierarchy of wills between the rulers and the ruled. Proliferation of division of labor and of function within an organization contributes to the complexity of organization and the need for integration, and to the need for an officer class to administer the affairs of the organization. This officer class has the signal advantage of controlling the instruments of information, publicity, finance, the whole administrative apparatus. The general membership is too preoccupied with their own daily lives to be able to keep track fully of organizational matters. Leadership is a full-time job. Only in small organizations is it possible to get the whole membership, or even any substantial portion of it, into one meeting place. In consequence, the mass of the people in any organization are on the periphery of power which resides in the hands of the representatives to whom the power is delegated. Result is that every organization constitutes a hierarchical pyramid structure of power.[11] Since society is a conglomerate of organizations headed by the state, society is by its nature hierarchical in structure, composed of leadership and following.

Dovetailing with the organizational basis of leadership is the psychological imperative. If all men were equal in native endowment and had the identical social and natural environment, no organization would be possible, for no one can establish a system of control where the power of each individual is equal to that of any of the others. But no two individuals have the same native equipment or general environment. All men quest for power to satisfy their wants but men differ among themselves in the intensity of their drives for power, in their love of ego power, in their quest for political power, which is control over the wills of others. Particularly, it is in the intensity of the drive for political power that leadership excels.

This is not to say that all those in position of leadership have this or the other qualities associated with leadership, but that the psychological equipment of leadership includes a particularly intense and active drive to control the wills of others. Not only does society by reason of organization provide positions of leadership but it has a reservoir of men psychologically driven to leadership.

Society in its manifold activities could not exist without leaders. Ideas originate not in the mass but in the minds of individuals. For these ideas to spread and to become accepted they must be transmitted from the conceiving individual to others and then perhaps from the minority to the majority.[12] For that process initiative in organization is necessary, which is another quality of leadership. No wonder, then, that any cause is shorn of success to the extent that it is deprived of its leadership. In order to stifle union organization, employers have frequently found it unnecessary to eliminate all union members but only the leaders.[13] The history of the world is a drama of leadership within the dynamism of social forces.[14]

The initiative and drive of leadership in any cause and organization are made more effective by general apathy and passivity. Only relatively small minorities attend meetings and are active in organizations. A disciplined, purposeful minority, even though numerically small, can dominate and control a mass of unorganized wills, for an organized minority is more powerful than the individual. Even in direct democracy leadership is unavoidable. When to this is added the concentrated control that resides in the chosen representatives by reason of division of functions we can appreciate how powerful organized minorities can become. This is ultimately the reason for the phenomenal success of the Communist minority in acquiring control of any organization which they are allowed to infiltrate. Communist strength cannot be measured by their numbers but by their control over the instruments of power.

Since leadership is inherent in the nature of man and society, its traces should be found in the earliest society and state. In the family state leadership was patriarchal. As the family state began to break up and expand into sib, gens, and tribe, leadership was asserted among assemblies of patriarchs by those possessing one or more of various forms of power: psychological assertiveness, military ability, or magic manipulation.[15] Out of this leadership there evolved kingship and a blood nobility which contrasted with the commoners. Thus the rudiments of social stratification began as the result of leadership inherent in society. The unequal accumulation of property, which resulted from skill, accident, or conquest, further accentuated class differentiation. Slavery, which replaced cannibalism as the spoils of victory, also contributed in the same direction.[16] As economic functional differentiation and division of labor progressed it carried class division still further. But we must reject the Marxist concept that class divisions are due to property relations.[17] Rather, property relations are due to class divisions, which in turn are due to the division of society into leaders and followers. Property contributed greatly to the development of social classes through impetus to the phenomenon of the division of labor. It has also served as a means of exercising political power, but even here priority is not always with property. Thus military power, magic power, control of the state machinery, and power of propaganda have frequently served as steppingstones to economic power and to leadership. Power is continuously transmuted from one form into another.[18]

That private accumulation of property is not the ultimate cause of a class society is proved by the existence of a leadership-follower division in society before the element of property exercised its influence, when kinship was the chief bond of cohesion of the state. In India there is no necessary correlation between the caste system and the amount of property owned. Although private ownership of the means of production has been replaced in Russia by public ownership, the result has not been a classless society, as it should have been if the Marxist assumption, that private property is the basis of economic classes, was not fallacious.

Rather, class and economic differentiation follows the leadership principle and demarcation of a society. This is implicit in the nature of leadership and the purpose of political power to obtain the greatest satisfaction of man's wants. Since the leaders are the ones who occupy the position of superordination in a control of wills, it is they who obtain proportionately the greatest satisfaction of their wants and who exercise relatively the most control of their society. Those who are on top get the best and the most of whatever is valued in the particular society: economic goods, prestige, or choice of mates. The leadership of any society can be identified by the possession of control over the instruments of power and a relatively high standard of living and economic security. It is no wonder that the leaders of the state do possess those advantages. The Soviet hierarchy of power corresponds rather closely with the gradations in the standard of living.[19]

Within any complex society, however, there are not one but a number of forms of power—agricultural, industrial, priestly, scientific, military, managerial, propagandistic, financial, and bureaucratic —and the tangible returns flowing to the leadership of each are not the same. The class structure of society is a composite of the class structure of all the pyramids in each field of power. The upper class is composed of the few who are to be found on the apex of each of the pyramids. The middle class is made up of the more numerous individuals to be found along the middle tiers of the various pyramids, and the lower class encompasses all those who are at the base of the pyramids. In any complex society there is no clear demarcation between leaders and followers but rather a graduated difference between classes. Nor is there any uniform leadership, but a conglomerate of many leaderships. The frequent purges that have occurred in totalitarian states give the lie to the claim that their societies and leaderships are monolythic.

The inquiry into the distribution of power within a state has thus far disclosed an unequal division of power among many individuals depending on whether they are leaders or followers. This dichotomy is responsible for the composite pyramidal class structure of society both in terms of control and in the enjoyment of the world's goods. The class structure of society, however, is not permanently static, for the reason that human society, unlike the society of insects, is never static. Leadership too depends on the uncontrollable combination of various individual factors with a changeable social and natural environment. The psychological basis of leadership, the intensive drive for power, may or may not go together with a proportionate amount of intelligence or of other qualities desirable for leadership in a particular form of society. Also leadership does not depend solely or even principally on the personal qualities of leadership, but on the possession of the instruments of power in the particular society or one's position in the social hierarchy.

In the ideal world leadership would be determined on the basis of perfect, infallible tests of personal qualities, but this does not bear any correspondence to the actual world. Whom you know, runs the common saying, is more important than what you know, and more important than that is the foresight to be born in the right family. This is due in part, and in minor part to boot, to heredity and more to environment. The son is more certain to inherit wealth than ability. A similarly greater assurance applies to the inheritance of lack of wealth than lack of ability. Throughout history incompetence has not been found wanting in the seats of the mighty or high ability in the hovels of the poor. Despite genealogical pretensions of those who have arrived economically, if not socially, the most complex, powerful, and in many respects, the greatest civilization in the history of the world has been built up by the descendants of those of humble origin in the countries of their birth.

This is not to belittle the importance of heredity, but the distribution of leadership abilities cannot necessarily be superimposed on the class structure of a society. As Plato expressed it, those who have power may lack wisdom and those who do possess wisdom may lack power.[20]

However, those possessing personal qualities of leadership, who find themselves in the lower tiers of the social pyramid, constantly press upward toward the apex, driven on by their intense striving for power. Those on top naturally defend their preferred positions. There is also the conflict between the leaderships of the various forms of power. Other forms of leadership conflict are among the natural leaders themselves and among those possessing positions of leadership. Involved in these interleadership conflicts are the fortunes and conflicts of the masses. This is of the essence of the class struggle.[21]

In the contest for leadership, those endowed with personal qualities of leadership, innate or acquired, have a better chance to emerge victorious where the environmental factors are more equally balanced. This is more likely to be the case in new societies or in times when new economic vistas of the environment are opened up. That the United States is a relatively new society, that the frontier and immigration have continued past the turn of the century, that technological and industrial changes have been more intense here than elsewhere, all serve to explain why there has been greater circulation from one class to another in America than in the older and therefore more stratified and static English society, although the government machinery of the latter is more responsive to the will of the people than is ours.

Similarly, great social revolutions, violent or peaceful, have the effect of raising from the people a new leadership to replenish or supplant the old. This is true whether the revolution is democratic or dictatorial in character. The rise of capitalism caused the emergence of a new bourgeois elite to rival the old nobility, both in England, where the change was relatively peaceful, and in France, through the French Revolution. Both Nazi and Russian revolutions brought forth to the seats of supreme power elites from the bowels of the pyramidal hierarchy.

Once the new leadership has established itself and has consolidated its power, however, the trend sets in to convert the leadership into a closed unit and for society to become increasingly stratified and rigid in its class structure.[22] A number of factors contribute to this social tendency. The pressure from below is for a time relaxed. The very creation of the new leadership drained the people of individuals with the most activated leadership qualities and power, and it takes time biologically and environmentally for a new potential elite to arise. It was pointed out that in the past two centuries an ever-decreasing proportion of the leaders in Great Britain come from the lower classes. Eugenicists may point to that as an exhaustion of talent in the lower classes.[23] Significant as the biological factor is, this phenomenon in Great Britain may be due in greater degree to the fact that the children of the British leaders have greater educational and other opportunities than those of the masses. As society becomes stabilized it becomes more and more difficult to break through class demarcations. It is easier to reach the top rung of the ladder when it is unoccupied than when it involves dislodging someone already on top. In a stratified society potential leadership must strive for an opening to ascend to the seats of power through some form of power other than that monopolized by the established leadership. The vitality of the British Labor party and trade unions is due not in small measure to these being virtually the sole avenues for advancement open to leaders of humble origin.

As a social system becomes stabilized, the striving of the established elite for monopoly of privileges tends to close entrance to its ranks by winning control of the instruments of power and access to them through the acquisition of the necessary skills and opportunities. These are denied to those outside the leadership and are made available only to the descendants of the elite. This is reinforced by the kinship principle operating through the institution of nobility, under which with few exceptions only those born to the preferred class are eligible to the offices and privileges of the particular society. Where the sources of power depend on the possession of certain training and skills, confining of the opportunities to acquire these skills and training to the descendants of the ruling class leads to the perpetuation of the growing elite.[24]

But no leadership is eternal and no social structure unchanging. What are the forces contributing to social metamorphosis and to the decline and fall of established leaderships? One important factor is heredity and inheritance, already mentioned. The primordial institu-

but society itself. Excluded from the control of the established medium of power, the new potential leadership turns its energies to the new form of power. The triumph of the new leadership means also the ascendancy of a new social system. The supplanting of feudalism by the capitalist society is one example, and the outstanding political expression of the transition was the French Revolution. The Russian Revolution is another instance of a cataclysmic social change wrought by the fusion of a leadership conflict with fundamental economic changes.

It is in the great social revolutions that the deterioration of the established leadership is most apparent. The chief factor in the success of a political revolution is not the strength of the revolutionists but the weakness of the established government. The loss of faith in the existing social order does not merely, or even chiefly, express itself in the disillusionment of the masses, but in the loss of self-confidence by the established leadership, a void which is filled by skepticism and leads to creeping paralysis. Emptied of faith, hope, and charity, they flounder about in helpless rage before they founder on the rocks of their own ineffectualness.[29] Without detracting from the rare revolutionary genius of that miraculous combination of Lenin and Trotsky, neither the Bolshevik Revolution nor the preceding one, which overthrew the Czarist regime, would have succeeded had not the government in power in each instance been devoid of resolution and ability to use the vast actual and symbolic power at its command. The vast Russian mass of illiterate peasants were completely out of the revolutionary picture. The outbreaks in Petrograd in the March Revolution would have fizzled against a determined and activated government leadership. No more substantial was the Bolshevik challenge, but the deterioration and paralysis carried over from the Czarist regime to the provisional government. The structure was feebly pushed and to the amazement of the world the house of cards toppled over. So is history made.[30]

Thus are great changes in leadership effected and the composition of social classes changed. But revolutions do not change the fundamental pyramidal social structure of society, for they cannot alter the interaction of the nature of organization with man's varying drive for power, which renders leadership unavoidable. No equality is possible where men are unequal in their aspirations. Of course, the masses are involved. They do most of the dying for both sides of any conflict.

They hear themselves proclaimed as the sole beneficiary of and reason for the upheaval. Beyond the hill of revolutionary triumph, the proletariat, or by whatever name the masses are known in the ideology of the current fashion, will enter Eldorado. There the chains will be broken and man will be set free. There men who are born equal will live in equality. There the class-ridden unjust social order will give way to a just and classless society. All this is not from the utopian wishing well but according to eternal unalterable principles of scientific socialism.[31] However, after the carnage and agony of revolution have given way to the quiet despair of everyday existence, the masses find themselves again at the bottom of the pyramid waiting for crumbs to fall from the heavy-laden tables of the few masters at the top. And then the cycle of permanent struggle begins all over.[32] This is not as it should be but as it is, as it has always been, and in fundamental contours, as it always will be as long as man and society remain unaltered in their fundamental natures.

3. SOURCES OF LEADERSHIP

If in all societies at all times the pyramidal class structure is unavoidable, is there no difference between systems of government? If society is impossible without leadership, have the masses no interest or part in the kind of social and political system that prevails? Has the struggle for democracy throughout the ages signified nothing, and is our opposition to totalitarianism and dictatorship folly born of ignorance? Is democracy a myth, an ideology, or is it or can it be a way of life?

Accepting the indispensability of leadership and the pyramidal structure of power in society, there are yet great and vital values in democracy that can be realized, and these stamp democracy as the best form of government. Fundamentally, these stem from the proposition that if in the life of society leadership plays a great and indispensable role it is in the interest of the people and of society as a whole that the leaders should be vigorous, able, skilled, and just rather than lax, incompetent, inefficient, and unjust; that they should perform their tasks and functions well rather than badly. Society, therefore, has a vital interest that its leadership cadre should correspond as much as possible to the prevalence of personal qualities of leadership among the population; that its actual leadership should be based on personal qualities rather than on possession of advantageous positions of leadership; that those who can, rather than those who have, should lead.

In the first instance, this involves the problem of the source of leadership. From this standpoint all forms of government may be ranged according to the degree to which they incorporate the democratic doctrine, based on the proposition that government should be of the people, that leadership should be derived from all social classes wherever it can be found. Aristocratic society, ideologically based on the proposition that government should be by those having ability, relies on heredity and inheritance for the mechanism of transmission of the ruling authority.[33] In actual practice no system of government is, from the standpoint of the source of leadership, either purely democratic or purely aristocratic. All governments contain mixtures of both but are nevertheless sufficiently distinct in their composition to be divided into two clearly differentiated systems.

Those in which the aristocratic principle predominates have been known in history as monarchies, aristocracies, obligarchies, autocracies, despotisms, tyrannies, and dictatorships. All these have one feature in common. They strive to perpetuate their leaderships through descent and to exclude outsiders from entrance into their ranks. In monarchies and aristocracies, the principle of transmission of power by descent and kinship as the test of authority is openly incorporated. It is therefore not surprising that these forms of government were the most prevalent in the infancy of society and of the state when the patriarchal family state began to expand beyond the gens and the tribe, when kinship was yet the greatest if not the only cohesive force and basis of the state.[34] It is not surprising that kinship as the basis of authority was ideologically rationalized and sanctified by the doctrine of divine right of kingship before genetics and eugenics could offer supporting scientific data. Ideologically this doctrine is a derivative of the universal primitive myth that our rulers are descendants from heavenly poobahs.[35] The Mikado is or was the son of the sun-goddess.

The aristocratic doctrine of descent as a means of transmission of power is predominant in the modern dictatorships, of the right or the left, in all systems, in fact, in which the leadership is not chosen by the people. Not being subject to the check of popular choice, leaderships in dictatorships are not accountable to the people, and therefore can indulge without restraint the tendency of all leaderships to perpetuate their monopoly of power through descent. Therefore, no matter how popularly recruited is leadership in a new dictatorship, it nevertheless ends up as a closed static hereditary aristocracy if the dictatorship continues in power long enough.

The effect of heredity and other influences on the deterioration of static and closed aristocracies has already been considered. Aristotle noted this when he deemed oligarchy, or government by the wealthy, as a pathological corruption of aristocracy.[36] In democracies, direct or representative, the danger of leadership deterioration is met in part by the democratic technique of recruiting leadership from every class of society as a permanent, continuing mechanism of replenishment and renewal. This is not the same as the democratically deleterious Jacksonian doctrine of rotation in office,[37] but is a principle of broad application to the recruitment of every type of leadership in society as a whole. Fluidity of social structure and free circulation from one class to another would tend to make leadership conform to ability rather than to accident of birth or to luck, the latter a much underrated element in a man's fortunes.[38] But this is obviously a democratic goal rather than a mirror of reality.

Since, through fluidity of social structure, positions of leadership tend to be filled by those who possess the qualities of leadership, we arrive at the paradox that the more democratic a society is in its sources for the recruitment of leadership the more aristocratic it is in the classic meaning of the term: government by ability.

4. RECRUITMENT AND CONTROL OF LEADERSHIP

Inseparable from the problem of the sources from which leadership is recruited is the method of recruitment. On this issue, as on the former proposition, there is a dichotomy between systems of government and the alignment is virtually the same. Those societies which are aristocratic also incorporate predominantly the dictatorial doctrine in the recruitment of leadership, while democratic societies employ to a decisive degree the democratic method of recruitment. As in the problem of the sources of leadership so in the methods of recruitment, actual governmental forms are not pure specimens of either, but are mixed examples which are, nevertheless, sufficiently distinctive in composition to be capable of classification as belonging to the one category or the other. In governments characterized by the dictatorial method, the leadership is or tends to be self-perpetuating and therefore monopolizes control over the policies of the state. In democracies, the political leadership is chosen by the people or mass of followers, who therefore share to a greater or lesser degree in the control over the policies of the state.[39]

In examining the operation of the opposing techniques in the recruitment and control of leadership, the inquiry is shifted from social structure and leadership to state, government, or political leadership proper. In the dictatorial systems this is not as important as in the democratic forms. In autocracies of whatever form, particularly in the totalitarian dictatorship, the social structure pyramid corresponds closely to the power structure of the state hierarchy itself. The pyramid may or may not be truncated, depending more on accident of personality and occasion than on form. Even in absolute monarchies the power of the king varies with the personality of the monarch. This is true also with dictatorships. Exigencies of administrative devolution or war and peace likewise influence the concentration or decentralization of authority.[40] But in autocracies in any event power resides in the elite which controls the state. This does not mean that the bureaucracy is identical with the ruling class. Particularly in the lower levels of the administrative personnel there is a wide gap between the two. In autocracies, however, those at the top of the pyramid of class structure likewise control the state. This derives from the psychological nature of power, that those who monopolize the sources of power will likewise seek to monopolize its benefits.

In democracies the power relationship is more complex by reason of the democratic principle of equality of individuals as applied to selection of the political leadership. Equality of individuals in regard to eligibility to office and political franchise cannot be equated with actual equality of power even in political matters. What is established by the democratic principle of equality of political rights is that the state leadership, or political governing class, is chosen by the people—what the Declaration of Independence meant by government by the consent of the governed. While in autocracies the leadership enjoys a monopoly of power as against the mass of the followers, in democracies the political leadership does not command a monopoly of power as against the mass of the electorate. Directly or indirectly they are accountable to the voters, who have the right of selection. This is made possible by the democratic principle of the right of opposition and the consequent civil and political rights, particularly freedom of speech and of the press.[41]

The right of opposition regularizes leadership competition and makes the mass of the people the umpires in that contest. The competing leaderships must curry the favor of the electorate in order to emerge successfully in the contest. The weapons of the arena are propaganda mechanisms for influencing the minds of the people. Each one of the competing leaderships attempts to convince the people that their welfare would be better served if they elected into office a particular party. This propaganda is carried on on several levels. Most widespread is the appeal to the mass ego. No democratic ideology in the arena of conflict omits reference to the omnipotence of the people as rulers and the statement that the public welfare is the sole aim and purpose of at least one of the contestants. It is noteworthy that even dictators use this rationale for their power. The broader the suffrage, however, the more sycophantic and demagogic is campaign oratory likely to be.[42] The democratic competition of leadership for the favor of the voters ultimately brings to the latter, in addition to the right to choose leaders, the right to select among competing policies of the state. This is not to minimize the power of demagogues, phonies, and frauds, but where the right of opposition also involves the opportunity of opposition, then in the long run the majority of the people will not be forever fooled. Much more important than words are deeds as propaganda. In our complex society, it is futile to expect that the mass of the people would be able to judge expertly of the intricate methods and means to achieve desirable ends, but they are in a position to judge of results that affect their own lives.

Given the opportunity, leaderships will always compete with each other, and over a period of time the scepter of power will be placed by the people in the hands of a leadership which will execute policies called for by the economic and social compulsives. Free competition of leadership is conducive to government for the people.

In dictatorships too, as in all societies, there is competition among the leaders, which seethes behind the false monolithic façade until it bursts forth in purges or revolutions. However, not the people but brutal force is the arbiter of that contest. Even under dictatorships there is no absolute monopoly of power. It is tempered by assassination and limited by what the people can stand. Long famine and complete disorganization of life will break the bonds of obedience, despite fear of dire reprisals. But the level of tolerance of adverse conditions by people in dictatorships is much higher than in democracies. Because of government monopoly of information, what the Russian people will tolerate is enhanced by tales in their press about the plight of the people in the United States and other lands. In dictatorships, the people are the material for the entrenched elite to work upon and fashion, material which has its limitations which a wise craftsman must consider, but material nevertheless. In democracies, through their right to choose their leaders and their policies, the people become participants in the process of government. The people can demand more and are more likely to get it where leaderships have to compete than in societies where leaderships enjoy a monopoly.

What the people think is the end result of a process originating with a minority, for ideas do not have spontaneous mass origin. However, since in a democracy no leadership enjoys a monopoly in the formation of public opinion, no leadership in or out of power can afford to be permanently opposed by public opinion. Therefore, public opinion, always a composite rather than a monolithic structure, is a constant check on the competing leaderships.[43] Since in dictatorships public opinion is the creature of a monopolistic leadership, it is not an effective check on the elite.

The operation of democracy has not meant that the democratic way of life has been realized. Far from it, democracy is not static. It is a process, a goal, a direction, and any democratic society should be judged by how much it incorporates of the component democratic principles and by the direction and pace of its development. Its progress is dependent on the extent and level of the general education and rational maturity of the people and on the mechanisms of democratic controls. It is essential that there should be no monopoly in the channels of information and that civil liberties be jealously preserved and expanded. Liberty is both a condition and a consequence of democracy.[44]

If democracy is a process, it is yet fundamentally different from dictatorships in the vital social values it propagates. The difference between the democratic and autocratic principles in the choice of leadership is not a distinction in inconsequential mechanics. The substitution of ballots for bullets is as great a step in social evolution as the creation of a new species in the biological counterpart. This is true in its effect on the mass of the people, on the leadership and on the stability of the state.

Since the right of opposition and dissent is outlawed in dictatorships, opposition to the government becomes treason and is driven underground to plot and conspire for the overthrow of the government, which relies on force and secret police to maintain itself. The nature of the government determines the character of its change. Rulers who lean upon the sword are likely to perish by it. A government based on violence always operates under the threat of violent revolution. Our contemporary dictatorships, Communist or Fascist, have periodically undergone violent purges. Brute force, terror, and physical coercion are inherent in dictatorships. Hence, leaders in a dictatorship must excel in these qualities and forms of power in order to attain and retain power. All leaders are characterized by a certain resoluteness or ruthlessness of ambition, purpose, or will to power.[45] But in dictatorships leaders deal in the primitive forms of power, including economic coercion, and monopoly control over the minds of men, and in all this they are unrestrained. In democracies, leaders have to deal, because of competition, in the higher form of power—peaceful persuasion.

It is true that modern dictatorships rely a great deal on propaganda to mold the mass mind and have achieved seemingly spectacular success, but that is not persuasion. It cannot be unless there is an opposition propaganda. Monopoly of propaganda in the dictatorships leads to the enthrallment of man's mind and to the debasement of his nature. In democratic countries, competition in ideas leads to skepticism and some measure of immunity to pressure propaganda. The efficacy of propaganda even in a dictatorship may be doubted. There is no doubt that the Germans and the Russians have voiced their approval of their respective dictators but that is not equivalent to acceptance based on persuasion. It is an artificial demonstration of morale for propaganda purposes in which the dictators themselves have no confidence. If they did they would not continue to rely on suppression of opposition by the secret police, slave labor, and the firing squad.

There is no need to underestimate the great genius for leadership of masses demonstrated by Mussolini, Hitler, and Stalin, but that is of a primitive and inferior nature in the light of the incomparable democratic statesmanship of Franklin D. Roosevelt. He led the people out of economic collapse and in the direction of mastery over their economic environment. He removed the isolationist blind from the vision of the people and made them see that their destiny was tied to that of the world. He fused the diverse elements of a peaceful and complex society into the greatest military power the world has ever seen. And all this through persuasion in the face of the most virulent opposition of the overwhelming output of the channels of information. That is democratic statesmanship of human society at its best, in comparison with which the great dictators pale into leaders of herds.

The difference in statesmanship is reflected in the people. To the extent that the element of persuasion increases and fear of compulsion diminishes in democracies, maturity is likely to prevail over infantilism.[46] The dignity and worth of the individual are incompatible with purges and with the degradation involved in periodic public "confessions." These values can flourish only in a democratic society, where leadership must face open competition.

Individuals are unequal in their capacities, but the democratic doctrine of equality, superimposed on leadership competition, has important ramifications. It tends to restrain the leaders and elevate the self-respect and stature of the people. The title of general was good enough for Washington and is good enough for Marshall and Eisenhower. Compare this with the extravagant military titles and medals of the army of the proletariat. The General Patton soldier-slapping incident is no reflection either on the American Army or on the great field leader. In what other army in the world would a great war leader be made to apologize publicly for slapping a soldier? There is no doubt that we ought to strive for the elimination of the caste system in our armed forces, but the American Army is more democratic than its counterpart in Russia. There the trend has been in the opposite direction after the revolution: from a classless beginning to a highly stratified and aristocratic organization in the tradition of the Czarist regime.

The democratic values and techniques have a close connection with the problem of efficiency of social systems. The record of the United States particularly in World War II explodes a fallacy that has masqueraded as a truism from Plato to Hitler—that democracy is less competent and efficient than dictatorship. It is significant that preference for dictatorship has always gone hand in hand with preference for a particular type of dictatorship, custom made in the image of one's wishes and definitions. Utopia can always be made to appear more attractive than reality. But a realistic political philosophy must be based on the proposition that actual government invariably falls short of the ideal.

The lot of the dissenter in dictatorships is not to be envied. The instrument of the purge when applied to political, racial, or religious minorities is harmful even to the leadership and society wielding it. The great contribution made by Jews and other exiles from Nazi-dominated Europe to the development of atomic energy in the United States should serve as a warning that intolerance is practiced at a prohibitive cost to a social system. Intolerance does not pay.

In more primitive societies, where work was backbreaking but simple, coercion was an effective method of control. But in the highly complex technology of today even industrial efficiency is incompatible with industrial absolutism.[47] Liberty and democracy, far from being incompatible with efficiency and security, are the very conditions of their fullest realization.

Patriotism too is on a firmer foundation in democracies than in dictatorships, for in democracies there is more widespread consciousness of state, and loyalty to country is independent of fidelity to a particular political system. In dictatorships dissenters are compelled to become traitors.

In democracies the problem of government succession is solved through the operation of the representative or elective principle. In autocracies characterized by monarchic rule, the problem of government succession is also determined by orderly process although with less certainty than in democracies. Throughout history the Achilles heel of dictatorships has been their failure to provide for a regularized and accepted mode of government succession. They have been for that reason the least stable of governmental forms and most subject to violence and revolution. This would apply equally to the modern so-called party dictatorships of the right and left. Although the Communist and Fascist parties are supposed to provide the vehicle for the choice of leaders, they are in actuality the instruments, not the masters of the dictatorships. The one party system is no guaranty against inevitable internal divisions. The Nazi party purges are well known. It took Stalin fifteen years after Lenin's death of continuous purges of opponents in the Communist party to establish and consolidate his power. How long will it take Stalin's successor to do likewise? Stalin's death will result in an extended scramble for power in Russia which will further unsettle the world situation. It may for a time relax Russian pressure on its perimeter by inverting the energies of its elite to the internal struggle, but it may also eventuate in an outright foreign aggressive venture as a means of consolidating the home front behind the ascendant victors.

By leaving the door to leadership open to the competition of talent from all social classes, democracy's leadership is better equipped by natural endowment and training than that of societies in which the leadership is a closed unit and static. The wisest of men is not infallible and the vision of the most farsighted is limited. Even dictators make mistakes despite claims to infallibility. In democracies, because of competition of leaders, it is possible to rectify errors through change of leaderships and policies. Ideas are tested in the crucible of competition. In dictatorships, although there may be changes in the lower rungs of the hierarchy, a change in the upper reaches takes place only through violence. As a result, a dictatorship is less likely than a democracy to get the benefit of harmony between policies and sympathetic administrators. Even sophisticated men become the victims of their own propaganda. Vanity in the leader and sycophancy in the followers tend to eliminate from the circle of the mighty those with courage to disagree with the voice of authority.[48] In dictatorships this danger is multiplied by the element of fear, which haunts all dissenters. In consequence, dictators are likely to receive only information which is in line with the fundamental policies of the system. Dictators increasingly lose touch with the world about them, and their policies become sharpened, canalized, and inexorable. How else can one explain Hitler's repetition of the Kaiser's fatal error of arraigning a united coalition against himself? Hitler severely criticized the Kaiser for fighting a two-front war and was on the road to triumph as long as he kept his enemies divided. But then with the fatality of a Greek tragedy the myth of the German superman took hold once more, and before England was finished Russia was attacked, and then in the morass of indecisive conflict the decisive technology and manpower of America were provoked and attacked.

Although Moscow's agents, the fifth column Communist parties in the countries of the West, are much more competent than Hitler's agents, they are likely to send reports about America which feed, not abate, the flames of global ambitions, for that is what the recipients want to hear. There lies the danger to world peace and civilization if the Hitler tragedy is any guide.

CHAPTER XII

Democracy in a Planned Economy

---

1. CONDITIONS OF DEMOCRATIC VIABILITY

Democracy, then, is a system of the state wherein the sovereign power mirrors the pyramidal structure of society, leadership is recruited from all social strata, and the free competition of leaderships and state policies by means of persuasion is decided by the consent of the people, the governed. Dictatorship is a closed, oligarchic monopoly based on coercion.

How will the democratic system of government be affected by a planned economy and how will it fare in the administrative state?

Even in democratic societies, established leaderships tend to perpetuate their power through descent by transmission of opportunities for acquiring the necessary skills and positions of power. This cannot be entirely eliminated but it can be minimized within the framework of the democratic administrative state. The key to the problem is in the opportunities for advancement afforded to talent of humble origin, in creating and maintaining competition for the well placed. In the United States, although the ranks of the very rich may be closing to newcomers because of the high income taxes, the sources of power are undergoing some diffusion. In private industry, the separation of the management function from ownership opens avenues for influential and profitable careers to the trained. Similar opportunities are increasing in government service for the educated and ambitious who may not come from the socially elite. An economy which employs planning will greatly increase the administrative personnel of the government, thus affording a broad highway for talent, which in private industry is handicapped by racial, religious, and class prejudices. The enormous vitality of the New Deal, which carried over its momentum into the war effort, is in no small measure due to its having enlisted great skills, dynamic aspirations, and humanitarian impulses which found themselves blocked or retarded in private business. The businessman's values are not the only ones that should have their place in the mosaic that is America. It is well that the "professor" and the expert have added their voices to the symphony of leadership talents that is indispensable to the functioning of modern society.[1]

But the universal legal right to hold elective or appointive political office or to climb the ladder of the industrial hierarchy is not enough. There must be actual opportunities for this right to become realized. We must increase the opportunities for higher education for those of humble means and remove by legal enactment all discrimination in educational institutions as well as in industry. By eliminating unemployment and by increasing the income of families, gifted and ambitious children of the lower income groups will be freer to fufill themselves. Government subsidies and scholarships should not be limited to veterans, but should be open to all of talent. The science of measurement of human talents, psychological traits, and occupational aptitudes is yet in its infancy. In time it should make a contribution to the adjustment of man's talents to his social environment. These measures are not utopian, but are practical policies implicit in full employment and abundance. We can afford them—in fact we cannot afford not to adopt them.

All this and anything else that might be suggested would not alter the pyramidal structure of society in terms of leadership and power, which is unavoidable, but it will contribute to making our leadership to an ever greater degree one of talent and skill rather than one of position. The democratic doctrine of equality means equality of opportunity to fulfill one's talents to the utmost. Though man's innate differences are real, they are not as great or as significant as the inequalities in status and wealth prevalent throughout history would lead us to believe. Our diversified civilization and culture, fructified by the principle of equality of opportunity, would afford ever-increasing outlets for expression of man's varied talents and capacity for leadership. The broader avenues for expression of the talents of the people would serve as a catharsis for man's drive for power.[2] With wider opportunities for leadership qualities and abilities to come to the surface in a democratically planned economy, America would be a better governed and led society. It is in the administrative state that the democratic doctrine of government of the people would find fertile soil for further development.

Increase in economic opportunities would be of particular democratic significance in shoring up the economic foundations of the middle class. It is the middle class that furnishes the dynamics of any society.[3] Those on the base of the pyramid have been throughout history too preoccupied with grubbing toil to have much left over for power drives for higher places in the social pyramid. Those at the apex of the pyramid have arrived and thus virtually expended their drive for quantitative power and become quiescent. It is the middle classes on the fringes of power and in contact with the instruments of power whose power appetite and drives are whetted and sharpened to dynamic proportions. It is the middle class that will furnish the top leaders of the future as it has furnished the leaders for the nationalist and revolutionary movements of the world.

If the middle classes are prosperous and their ambitions have established outlets for top leadership, the society is stable and the social foundation exists for an enduring democracy. But if the middle class is impoverished and frustrated it becomes receptive to Fascist ideas and adventures. On the economic plight of the middle class fascism flourished in Europe. The small independent entrepreneur is losing out to big business. The great urban middle class is becoming assimulated into the industrial machine and hierarchy. Atomized, without organization, the industrial middle class finds itself between the Scylla of the corporate employer and the Charybdis of organized rank-and-file employees. The only road to economic salvation for the industrial middle class is through unionization, including unionization of the supervisory hierarchy.[4] Only thus will they be in position to close the dangerous gulf between a rich and powerful upper class and a weak and frustrated proletariat, a gulf which destroys the consensus basis of society and explodes in revolution and dictatorship.

Consensus among the various classes, which is the cohesive basis of democratic society, is strengthened by the fact that the class conflict of society is not solely along horizontal lines but is crisscrossed with divisions along perpendicular alignments. This is so because the social pyramid is not monolithic, but a complex composite of pyramids of power in each form or field of power which are in dynamic relationship to each other and in flux of conflict and change.

The Marxist conception of the class struggle as solely along horizontal lines, principally between capitalists and the proletariat, does not correspond with a complex society in which there are many forms of economic diversification.[5] It may have accorded with a simple agricultural economy, where the chief social division was between lords and serfs, or with the early capitalist economy, where the class division was between small employers and workers. It does not accord with the highly complex society of today where conflict is constantly current between industry and agriculture and among industries as well as between employers and employees. This multilateral conflict is reflected in the political arena. Traditionally, organized labor and the industrial magnates have been allied in support of the tariff at the expense of the agrarian interests. The economic conflict of society may take a distinctly regional and violent form, which at one time threatened the very existence of the United States. Regional conflict is still very much a dominant pattern in American politics.

The Marxist concept of a class interest as a distinct entity is at variance with the actualities. There is no organized class interest that is separate and distinct from the interests of those composing it. Individuals do not think of the interests of their class but only of their own, and the two may as often as not collide. It is a fallacy to conceive of organized labor as a distinct uniform interest. There is internal bitter conflict not only between the C.I.O. and the A.F.L. but among unions within each federation.[6]

The crux of the problem is contained in Socrates's denial of Thrasymachus's claim that justice is the interest of the strongest, since the strongest may not know where their best interests lie.[7] As society gains in complexity, the number of ways in which an interest may be served is infinitely multiplied. It is the multiplicity of opinion that is possible on any problem that makes it unlikely that absent coercion parties could remain uniform and unchanging in their policies over a period of years. That is the ultimate proof of the fact that Communist parties outside Russia are dominated by the Kremlin. Otherwise they could not remain tied to Russian policies throughout all the gyrations of the party line.

That social conflict is not rigid but fluid, is not static along permanent lines but dynamic and in ever-changing combinations, is not lamentable but salutary because it avoids irrepressible conflicts destructive of social cohesiveness and contributes to compromise and consensus.

This is evidenced in our political parties, which are federations of interests reflecting regional and class divisions rather than those of any one dominant class.

The dynamics and fractionalization of interests implicit in our composite pyramidal social structure are basic to the maintenance of democracy, for they sustain the competition of social forces and are inimical to the evolution of monopoly of power, which constitutes dictatorship. It is the struggle of social forces that is the chief safeguard of democracy, not the checks and balance system in the government structure.[8] Majorities can be, have been known to be, tyrannous, but they can never be as bad or as durable as despotisms of minorities, for majorities are divided and composed of minorities which are in mutual conflict and in constant change.

The democratic administrative state would not measurably alter the existing complex relationship of power. Full employment of labor and government regulation of wages and prices would contribute to more uniform national levels of incomes in the various levels of the economic hierarchy, but competition among various pyramids of power would remain. In fact, the administrative state will accelerate the coming of age of the administrative class, the government personnel charged with executing the integrative function of the state in the planned economy. Their allegiance will not be to labor, to management, or to any other social or economic interest. Since their skills, talents, and ambitions—their quest for power—will express themselves in co-ordinating our economy, the public interest will be advanced through their ambitions and talents.

It need not, however, be feared that the administrative class will become the omnipotent dictatorial class. As in every other broad class or form of power, there would be internal pyramids of power within it in the form of agencies in constant competition with each other. Has the fact that the army and navy are both subdivisions of the government precluded them from being long-standing, bitter rivals? A similar situation exists in the case of civilian bureaus. The problem is not how to create rivalry but how to mitigate it and to effect co-operation for common purposes. Above all, government administration is and will remain under the supervision and control of Congress, the Judiciary, and the Executive.[9]

In the mosaic of pyramids of power, it is hazardous to predict who will be most prominent. It is a distorted oversimplification at variance with reality to state that the "managerial revolution" will lead to the dominance of the managerial class because this class will be in control of the instruments of production.[10] The Marxist doctrine, that those who control the instruments of production achieve control of the state, is not true as a statement of universal priorities. In history frequently those commanding military power have acquired control of the instruments of production. In Soviet Russia those who acquired the state power mechanism achieved control of the instruments of production. However, if the Marxist dictum means no more than that the instruments of production are in the hands of the leadership of the state, it is no longer meaningful as a statement of economic determinism. The phrase "instruments of production" has a deceptive simplicity about it. In a highly differentiated and complex economy like ours the instruments of production expand in scope until they cover virtually every form of power including managerial, economic, engineering, propaganda, skills and the professions. Even the managerial function is a composite.[11]

It is therefore not certain and predictable which elite in which form of power emerges to the top in the fluid and ever-changing contours of the struggle. What is important is that the administrative state will further accentuate the rise of the intelligentsia, the men of skill, talent, training, and expertness in every form of power. This trend in leadership has been apparent for some decades and is inherent in the complexity of our civilization, which places a premium not on rudimentary but on expert application of power.[12] While it is true that political leadership and labor officialdom will play a greater role than they have in the past, they too will be divided, and the multiple leaderships of business and other sectors of power will remain significant and enduring. The menace of atomic warfare will enhance the power and prestige of the military but not to the extent that it is feared.

Though the contest of leaderships will not be materially altered, the democratic controls will expand from the political into other realms as the laissez-faire state gives way to the administrative state in which our economy is regulated. The people will have a greater voice in the determination of their destinies as the government expands its functions. Unionism is one way which in part has replaced industrial absolutism with industrial democracy.[13] State expansion will give even greater impetus to this movement.

Would not this tend to destroy all class and power inequalities? Definitely not. As already demonstrated, the oligarchic leadership principle applies to all human organizations, including political and labor. Plato's "royal lie," the ideology of all societies, which makes the people acquiesce in according greater advantages to leadership will prevail. But extreme economic inequalities will tend to disappear in our democratic administrative state. Equalitarianism in opportunities as a goal for which we must constantly aim will be strengthened.[14] The relative fluidity and dynamism of our class structure must be forever accentuated. The manifestations of restiveness and drive in the individual American are all to the good, though the contents of the grail could stand some sweetening. Our leadership and class lines should never become closed and rigid if America is to avoid violent social revolution. Social stability depends on opportunities for orderly circulation from one class to another. This is the American, not the Trotsky, version of permanent revolution.

2. THE PROBLEM OF TRANSITION

A fear based on an assumption has been current for the past few decades, that as the entrenched economic interests become confronted with the necessity of sharing or surrendering power to an encroaching democratic state they would resort to violent overthrow of political democracy. The examples of Mussolini's Italy, Hitler's Germany, and Franco's Spain were cited as irrefutable proof.[15] A corollary of this proposition was that a planned economy could be established only by revolutionary violence. The Russian experience was supposed to eliminate any doubt on this score.

Political democracy was possible, so the claim ran, because it did not matter much what decisions were made since a laissez-faire state did not affect the fundamentals of the social system. The people in democracies could afford to disagree on the trivialities since they agreed on the fundamentals.[16] This view of democracy does not stand analysis. What fundamentals and whose? To the contenders for political power there is nothing more important or fundamental than the outcome of the contest. Yet in democracies that issue is decided by ballots, not bullets.

The National Labor Relations Act and the other measures of the New Deal have involved fundamental changes in the distribution of power and have aroused bitter and intransigeant opposition on the part of the entrenched interests, and yet there was no revolution. The policies of the republics in Italy, Germany, and Spain were not more drastic when they gave way to Fascist aggression. In Britain we are now witnessing nationalization of the instruments of production and the establishment of socialism by peaceful and orderly means, and yet the Tories are far from mobilizing the armed forces to protect their interests. Surely the change is a fundamental one. Democracy does not rest on a lack of importance of the issues it decides. The only consensus that is fundamental in a democracy is agreement to abide by the decision of the electorate. That is why it is no violation of democratic principles for a democracy to outlaw from the body politic organizations which would establish a dictatorship once they are in power. Democracy must be a continuing process.

The historical experience in government of Great Britain and the United States is fundamentally different from those of Germany, Italy, and Spain, where the democratic tradition had no deep roots. It cannot be overemphasized that democracy as a form of government and way of life is not imprisoned in economic systems but is conditioned by cultural influences and experience. In terms of governmental and social systems, the Russians and the Germans are primitives alongside us. They have to look to us, not we to them, for guidance.

The transition from one economic system to another need not be violent. It is equally true that it is the part of statemanship to aim and work for peaceful change. Gradualness of rate of change is important in this respect, for it lessens the resistance of those entrenched, since it permits them and their descendants to adjust themselves to the new system and become assimilated into the emerging leadership of power. This saves the talents and skills that are lost through purges. The chaos and upheaval accompanying revolutions and the need to replace the old leadership may more than neutralize the value of revolutionary dynamics.

The value of gradualness should not be converted into an argument for standpattism, for the longer necessary changes are postponed the more violent is the cumulative change.[17] To the impatient actors involved, revolution is a short cut to progress, and to successful revolutionists their revolution is per se an achievement. In great social revolutions, the blueprints of ideology create the impression of fundamental alterations in society. But viewed over a long period of time, it is doubtful whether countries which travel the route of revolution get further than those which remain on the rails of orderly progress. In some aspects of economic institutions and in membership of elites, revolutions may effect rapid changes, but in the whole complex of mass and leadership attitudes, mores, culture, and social relationships which affect the economic realm, gradualness of change is virtually inevitable.[18]

CHAPTER XIII

Property and the Social Order

1. PROPERTY AND SOCIAL STATUS

The democratic administrative state relies on a planned economy based in the main on private ownership of the means of production while the planned economy of Russia, most of the European continent, and to an increasing extent that of Great Britain rely on public ownership. This calls once more for a restatement, and if possible for a resolution of the great issue of private versus public ownership.

In the nineteenth century the great debate was between private ownership and capitalism, on the one hand, and public ownership and socialism, on the other. All the ills of mankind then existing—war, imperialism, class domination and conflict, and economic exploitation—were considered by the Socialists, Communists, and Anarchists as the consequence of the system of private ownership.[1] All that was necessary therefore to bring peace on earth and prosperity to man was to abolish private property and institute public ownership. It was a neat trick in ideological warfare, for the Marxist thesis was proved by definition and could not be checked against actual conditions. The ideological conflict then was between the gray realities of laissez-faire capitalism and the rosy assumptions of Marxist theory. At present we have the advantage of comparing actual political and social systems.

In the international field the organization of society on the basis of public ownership of instruments of production instead of private ownership has failed to exercise the expected influence for the elimination of nationalist and imperialist rivalries. What of other fields of activity or relationships of society? Has public ownership brought with it a classless society? There is nothing in the program or activities of the Labor Government to justify such an expectation in England. What of the Russian experience?

The old concept of property can no longer serve as a frame of reference, because it is too complex and vague for specific analysis and comparative study of social systems. To appreciate the trend and direction of politics we must therefore break down the compound social concept into its component parts.[2]

Ownership of property involves, among other aspects and rights, one's standard of living, economic security, power over the economy, and transmission of these rights to the next generation. What influence has public ownership exercised over these concepts and privileges?

When the red flag was unfurled over the Kremlin the spirit of the new society was epitomized by the traditional Socialist slogan, "From each according to his ability, to each according to his needs."[3] One could of course observe that acknowledgment that the needs of men differ offered a new sanction and rationale for class differentiations and privileges. Accent was nevertheless on equality. The corresponding slogan of the new Soviet Constitution, "From each according to his capacity, to each according to his work," obviously eschewed completely the doctrine of equalitarianism. The new direction on this cardinal point was begun under Lenin. Differences in real income and therefore standard of living are basic in Russian society, and these differentials correspond to one's position in the industrial, agricultural, bureaucratic, and professional hierarchy. By eliminating the private capitalist, the Communists have not abolished social classes. They have merely substituted a new elite for the old aristocracy. Soviet society is a pyramidal hierarchy judged in terms of standard of living.[4]

An attempt has been made to distinguish the Russian intelligentsia from the ruling classes in other lands on the ground that the Russian elite is not a leisure class. It must work. Yet this is not a peculiar function of the system but is true of all elites during the period of acquisition and consolidation of power. The first generation of the rich are not the idle rich. It is those who come after them who drop from their hands the reins of management. Ford and Carnegie and the others who made their fortunes could not be accused of love of idleness. The formative generations of aristocracies are not leisure ridden. Nor need the succeeding generations fall prey to the virus. The British upper classes have built up a tradition of public service. Although he has never met a payroll, Churchill could hardly be called an idle man.

In Russia the ruling class depend not on capital accumulations but on their status for economic and social security. The deification of its leaders and the luxury of the caviar-covered festive boards indicate that the Russian elite is not immune to corrupting afflictions. The needs of the son and grandson of the commissar will be greater than those of the parent. A grateful fatherland will not refrain from rewarding the descendants of the founding fathers.

That Russian society is class ridden is even more apparent when we examine the significant factor of control over the economy. When the Bolsheviks first came into power, the management of the factories was taken over by Workers' Committees.[5] This power came to be shared with an appointed manager of the enterprise who had technical knowledge and with representatives of the Communist party. Under Lenin's guidance the Workers' Committees were progressively stripped of their powers of management, which were transferred to the manager. The early rivalry and conflict between the technical managers and the Communist party were eliminated as new expert managers were trained who were virtually all members of the party. One-man management is the accepted form in industry. A similar developmental tendency is characteristic of the kolkhoz, the agricultural unit of production. Collective bargaining agreements have been abolished in industry. Employee representatives have no powers whatever in regard to hiring, discharge, wages, and working conditions. All these are within the sole control of the manager of the enterprise under the supervision and direction of the administrative hierarchy connected with industrial planning and administration. Despite the fact that Russia's trade unions are controlled by the Communist party, they are completely devoid of even the rudimentary functions associated with labor unions. Their only industrial function is to serve as agencies of management to stimulate production, not to protect the interests of the workers in regard to terms and conditions of employment. Their possible American analogue would be the labor-management committees which mushroomed during the war to increase productivity, not American labor unions.

The complete impotence of the Russian trade unions should be contrasted with the growing power of the American labor movement, politically and industrially.[6]

It is fair to state that ownership of property in the United States affords less power over the means of production than does status in the ruling elite of Russia. There is no check by the workers upon the power of management in Russia, while this check does exist in the United States through the power of labor unions.

But, it might be observed, while the Russian ruling class has greater control over the instruments of production than its American counterpart, it does not have the latter's power to transmit its control to the next generation—the right to perpetuate itself. While no right of inheritance to publicly owned property exists, this does not mean that the Russian elite is without means to perpetuate its power. This will become apparent when we examine Russian society from the standpoint of democratic doctrine.

Since no right of opposition exists in Russia, the democratic provisions of the Soviet Constitution are a dead letter. In the sense of the consent of the governed there is no democracy in Russia. More complicated is the problem of the source and methods of recruitment of leadership. In Russia the revolution brought forth a new leadership. The upper echelons of the Old Bolsheviks were mostly intellectuals of the middle class with some admixture of the lower nobility. The lower ranks of the Communist party after the revolution were manned chiefly by those of proletarian and peasant origin. Humble origin was of distinct advantage in obtaining educational and other preferments for years after the revolution. The need to replenish the old political leadership and recruit a new industrial leadership opened the gates of the secondary schools and colleges to the able and ambitious sons and daughters of the people. By the middle thirties, however, the leadership vacuum was nearly filled and the educational doors were swinging shut to the children of the proletariat and the peasants. Workers were no longer being promoted extensively to administrative positions. Self-made men gave way to trained specialists. Educational and entrance requirements were being raised, giving an advantage to the children of the intelligentsia. Tuition fees were reinstated for secondary schools and higher institutions which only those with high salaries could pay. Extensive recruitment by scholarships was discontinued. The sons and daughters of manual workers and peasants have had to be satisfied with specially designed trade schools. All this was reflected in the rising proportion in the colleges of children of the high salaried. So much so that the "lower-salaried appear to have lost the opportunity to give their children a higher education."[7]

By limiting the opportunities to acquire skills and training to the descendants of the ruling class, the Russian elite is perpetuating itself. When to this is added the lack of political and economic accountability by the ruling class to the masses, we have in Russia the makings of an hereditary aristocracy of a rather static and closed character.

2. STAGES OF ECONOMIC DEVELOPMENT

Since dialectical materialism pointed to socialism as the inevitable successor to capitalism, Russian communism has come to be accepted by the devout as being an advance stage of our political and economic evolution. Even opponents have come to accept uncritically this thesis, pointing to the "managerial revolution" in Russia as the most advanced outpost on the road on which we are embarked.[8]

To the extent that Russia illustrates the universal tendency to more and more government intervention in the economic realm this is true. But there the parallel ends. From the standpoint of economic development, Russia is at the beginning and not at the end of capitalist development. It is a curious phenomenon that Communists should first acquire power in Russia, where capitalist development was in its infancy, instead of in America and Britain, where capitalist development has been at its highest. What happened in Russia of course was not inevitable. Russian revolutionaries being schooled in the Socialist theories of the West sought to mold the Russian Revolution in the image of a theory designed for societies of high capitalist development. Russian revolutionaries justified the attempts to establish their system by resorting to the doctrine of the possibility of skipping economic systems. This in reality played havoc with Marxist inevitability of historical development and economic determinism, for if leaders could through the exercise of will and political power institute the system they desired, then economic determinism of property relationships is not the arbiter of history.

It may be, however, that revolutions and economic development have their own logic, which may not be subject to the will of the revolutionaries. All that the Russian revolutionists proved after all is that Communists triumphed, not communism. It may well be that the capitalist stage of economic development could not be skipped in Russia after all. The economic techniques and structure in Russia bear a more than accidental resemblance to those of the capitalist West. The problems of prices, profits, inflation, subsidies, taxes, money, currency devaluation, credit, banks, and other capitalist devices are well known to Russian administrators. Even black markets are part of the Russian landscape, operated of course by the government.

Even more revealing is the emphasis of Russian industrial policy on the building up of an industrial machine or capital for the production of goods at the expense of the living standards of the masses. This is what occurred in England during the Industrial Revolution, when capitalism was in its infancy. Russian managers behave much like early capitalists, the robber barons. You find the same economic exploitation of the masses, the same callousness to human suffering, the same emphasis on piecework, cheap labor, and glorification of the speed-up system, Stakhanovism, the same restrictions on the mobility of labor, and an identical opposition to the independent organization of labor which might thwart the will of the industrial overseer. Conditions of labor under seventeenth- and eighteenth-century mercantilism bear a strong resemblance to those in Russia under the dictatorship of the proletariat.[9] While later laissez-faire capitalists freed themselves from the restrictions of the mercantilist state by limiting the state's functions mainly to policing duties, the new Russian industrialists went them one better by capturing the apparatus of the state completely, thereby removing all possibility of opposition.

Even more illuminating evidence that Russia is in the infant capitalist stage is furnished by an examination of the Russian mind functioning through its ideology, myth, and intangible incentives. Reference has already been made to the wide differentials in income among the Russians. We are apologetic for the inequalities existing in our civilization. Significantly not so the Bolsheviks. Equalitarianism is looked upon as utopian and contempt is reserved for "bourgeois leveling." Emphasis is not on the virtues of co-operation and mutuality but on competition and individual aggrandizement. Ruthless effort, economic ladder climbing, and personal success are worshiped in Russia as in the early capitalist communities. Russia is an acquisitive society with all that this implies in terms of emphasis on work, thrift, and austere puritanic morality. The "economic man" of classical economics is the recipient of the Order of Lenin. Concepts of the good life of Russian managers are not very different from those of the National Association of Manufacturers. Of course, the hedonistic ethic is rationalized by a guilt-removing assurance that all this enlightened self-interest is the basis of the public welfare. But you will find the same sermon preached by the "service" clubs of America. The voice is that of Karl Marx but the hands are those of Adam Smith.[10]

It is when we realize that Russia has a scarcity economy in which production is the first and main task that we can appreciate some of its social phenomena. The United States has passed the production stage of economic development. We are in the distributive era of economic evolution, in which the main problem is integration of distribution to avoid maladjustment resulting in unemployment.

For that purpose the experience of Russia is illuminating but not decisive. Being in the infant, rapidly expanding stage of capitalist development, it was to be expected that Russia would not be faced with the problem of unemployment, irrespective of its collectivist economy. Full employment was equally true of early capitalism in England and in early America. Similarly, in an expanding economy geared to war demands neither Germany nor the United States faced unemployment.[11]

Owing to the destruction of World War II, Western Europe, including England, has been placed again in an era resembling infant capitalism with the consequent need to build up capital goods at the expense of the living standards of the people. Therefore, England and the rest of Europe will be driven to labor compulsives which are not inherent in planning and need not be repeated in our economy, which has a highly developed industrial plant.

3. PROPERTY AND POLITICAL SYSTEMS

Nor need we be frightened off democratic planning by the haunting example of Russian dictatorship. Forms of government are influenced but not determined by economic systems. What matters in this respect is national tradition. Russia, like Germany, has never had an eighteenth century and hardly a nineteenth. Force, violence, is a primitive form of power. For us, in political system as in economic development, Russia is not the wave of the future but the backwash of the past.

In a country with a democratic culture, public ownership would not spell the end of democracy, for competition of leadership would not be obliterated by the coalescence of political and economic power. What is decisive is not coalescence of the forms of power but whether the total power is concentrated or diffused. Government functionaries divide and compete like any other leadership. The need for devolution for management purposes would in time create pyramids of power based on various industries, skills, and talents. As long as the democratic controls would be maintained, public ownership would not lead to dictatorship.

Nevertheless, in private ownership the devolution of power and competition of leadership is an accomplished fact. The advantage of a planned economy based on private ownership is that the planning only is integrated, while operationally the economy is decentralized into autonomous units in which private acumen, ambition, talent, and initiative have their freest rein. In public ownership of the whole economy there is less likelihood of operational autonomy, at least at the beginning. It would appear therefore that in the United States a planned economy based on private ownership of the means of production is the optimum system. Lloyd's, however, does not insure social systems, including one based on private ownership. It is not inconceivable that private ownership may be doomed. One cannot be certain about this. One may note, for instance, that even in Russia there are sectors in the economy where private trading is permitted, as in agricultural produce, and private ownership and inheritance of personal fortunes is growing. In the United States at least, private ownership is a going concern which has shown itself capable of developing the highest stage of productive capacity. It should not be scrapped. For an indefinite future it has a great role to perform, for it is capable of evoking the greatest capacities and energies for productive purposes, if its distributive shortcomings are eliminated through integration by a planned economy. But it will not endure if the economy is not planned.

The overwhelming problems of the modern world demand great concentrations of power for their solution. Our task is to see that this power is democratically controlled and used. The democratic administrative state is the answer. The need for leadership and for evolving adequate democratic controls increases as science and technology place ever more powerful weapons in our hands. Up to now the weapons in the hands of the dictators were rather crude and could have no effect on the basic material of human nature. Now we are entering a period of scientific development in which fundamental human traits and character might not be beyond the reach of human tampering and planning. Transplantation of human organs is showing great promise. It is not unlikely that atomic energy in some form may be used to change fundamentally the human species. What such a weapon might mean in the hands of a dictatorial leadership, the human abattoirs maintained by the German beasts for genocidal purposes have demonstrated. What of the future? Is it any wonder that our very survival demands that our administrative state, which is inevitable, should be democratic![12]

BOOK THREE

Labor Relations in the Administrative State

CHAPTER XIV

Compulsives in Labor Relations

1. GOVERNMENT INTERVENTION IN POSTWAR STRIKES

So crucial has become the role of labor in our society that no analysis of the modern state can be considered complete without fathoming the manifold relationships of labor to the state. Since organized labor is based on the association of wage earners for the protection of their common economic interests, it has come to be peculiarly characteristic of the capitalist era of economic development.[1] Nevertheless, it has recognizable precursors in history—the medieval guilds, for one.

Though in its crystallized form organized labor is of relatively recent historical evolution, it is in its varied forms universal. Moreover, it surpasses all other social organizations, with the exception of the state itself, in its social, economic, and political ramifications both as an active force and as a reflector of the influence of other social forces abroad. Organized labor is indeed the microcosm of our society.

In the emergence of the administrative state, organized labor has played a decisive role in creating compulsives in labor relations for a planned economy.[2]

It is no secret that organized labor was eager to cast off wartime governmental controls in the field of labor relations. At least the observer was justified in arriving at this conclusion from the loud protestations of labor leaders in convention addresses and in postprandial dissertations.

The chief wartime restrictions from which deliverance was sought were strike taboos and wage ceilings. This desire of organized labor to return to the status quo ante in collective bargaining paralleled an even more articulated nostalgia of business for the golden age of laissez faire, "free enterprise."

With the coming of V-J day, business and organized labor breathed a sigh of relief at the prospect of the government's withdrawing from its role of compulsory arbitrator of disputes concerning wages and other provisions of the collective agreement. The President's Labor-

Management Conference meeting in the fall of 1945 rejected compulsory arbitration as a method of settling labor disputes arising in the negotiations of contracts, and relied instead on the traditional methods of mediation and voluntary arbitration.[3] The Administration too placed chief reliance upon autonomous collective bargaining and proceeded to decontrol its wartime regulations of wages and power to decide deadlocked contract negotiations. The National War Labor Board was disbanded, and its successor, the National Wage Stabilization Board, was given only interim skeleton powers of veto over raises which entailed a rise in prices.

But no sooner were the decontrol plans set in motion than any hopes entertained for an immediate diminution of government intervention in labor disputes had to be discarded. The General Motors strike appeared as an ominous cloud on the horizon of voluntarism. The Administration was still committed to the doctrine of letting labor disputes run their course and the auto industry was not considered a key industry like transportation. The General Motors strike was therefore permitted to run for over three months. But the government actively intervened even in this dispute. A Fact-Finding Board was appointed which recommended an 18½ cents an hour increase. This wage increase was recommended in substance by other fact-finding boards and it soon became the standard pattern of wage increases—in sum, a governmentally determined national wage policy. This wage increase was above that settled for by labor up to that time. Although C.I.O.'s President Murray and other labor leaders attacked the Truman proposal for a "cooling-off" period and fact-finding boards as tending to enslave labor, it did not deter them from demanding that the White Father intervene in their disputes with employers. While the General Motors strike lasted for several weeks after the Fact-Finding Board brought in its recommendation, the steel strike was permitted to last only a few days and the settlement was on terms dictated by the White House. The paralytic impact of the steel strike was apparent at once.

With coal inventories high, the coal strike in the spring of 1946 was permitted to continue until the cumulative effect began to be felt. Then the strike was settled by the Administration through agreement with John L. Lewis but without the consent of the coal operators. Because of the then greater need for fuel, the government moved to obtain a labor injunction as soon as the coal strike impended in November of 1946. The telephone strike of 1947 was permitted to run its course because the weakness of the union combined with the dial system to render the strike ineffective as a serious interruption of critical service.

With the reconversion process well on its way, the pressure of business for lifting of price ceilings by resorting to producer strikes as in meat caused the collapse of price controls by the end of 1946 and with it the lifting of wage controls as well.

Was government regulation of the wage-price relationship peculiar to the war and reconversion economy, or is it to return as a permanent peacetime policy after an interlude of autonomous collective bargaining?

The irreversible trend toward monopolization of industry on a national scale and its cartelization in the international field has been conditioned by the division of labor, by mass production, and by the drive for power in the economic realm. These factors pyramiding up to monopoly render necessary the positive participation of government in the economic process if our industrial machine is to be run at anywhere near full capacity.[4]

Is the same trend manifest in the actualities of labor relations?

2. THE GROWING STRENGTH OF LABOR

An analysis of the labor situation must begin with the size and growth of labor organization as a point of departure. When Roosevelt took the oath of office in 1933, the membership of organized labor was down to about 3 millions and the curve was still pointing downward.[5] Organized labor as a factor in our society, both economic and political, was approaching the vanishing point. By the end of the war the membership of organized labor approximated 15 millions. If we compare these figures with the total working population of the country engaged in industry and commerce, organized labor blankets about 33 per cent.[6] Though these figures mount to an impressive picture of labor strength, even when viewed in and by themselves, they do not convey sufficiently the full dynamic contours. The details of the silhouette are even more imposing. Railroads, bus lines, telephone, telegraph, radio, steel, autos, aircraft, mining, shipbuilding, and many other industries are operating under collective bargaining agreements with unions. Stated differently, the operation of our basic industries and of our communication system is necessarily conditioned and greatly influenced by the economic and ultimately political policies of organized labor. Hence the nuclear character of organized labor's position in our economy.

Nor is it realistic to look toward the postwar period for a substantial and permanent diminution in labor strength and influence. Peace might ultimately bring about the elimination of many women and older workers from industry with consequent loss in union membership. It is true, of course, that unemployment will be a factor as it has been in the past, to reduce union membership. In a period of widespread unemployment the returning veterans have been looked upon as a fertile source for antiunion mobilization by certain unreconstructed elements in industrial circles who have not yet reconciled themselves to the reality that collective bargaining is here to stay. Similarly, the increase of union membership during the war is not due altogether to intensive honest-to-goodness organizing campaigns. Much of labor's mushrooming has been due to the blanketing character of union security contracts that labor has been able to obtain under the pressure of wartime production. It would be surprising indeed if multitudes of union members did not look upon their union only as an agency for the collection of dues. Union officials have for the most part done little in the direction of educating their members as to the reason for existence and the benefits of unions. The internecine conflict in labor chiefly between the C.I.O. and A.F.L., with the accouplement of John L. Lewis, tends to reduce the influence of labor because of the inversion of its energies. This was demonstrated in the ineffectiveness of labor's opposition to the Taft-Hartley Act.

Despite these factors, whose potency is not being minimized, union strength viewed over a period of several years rather than for the immediate postwar interval will undergo accretion. For the following reasons: Unemployment will not accomplish the elimination of organized labor. It will accelerate, however, the process of that which the irreconcilables fear most—government intervention. If there is one assertion worthy of generalization into a maxim of modern politics it is that no government, irrespective of party affiliation or ideological fidelity, will be suffered by the people to stand by for long and permit unemployment to "run its course." It will be expected to provide not only relief but also employment, or lose not only its right but its power to govern. The doctrine of states' rights does not fill the breadbasket, and it is only on full stomachs that democratic liberties have a chance to survive in modern society.

The veteran out of a job might be told that his salvation lies in taking a job away from a member of the union. But in case of widespread unemployment and shutdown plants this will hardly sound convincing. The veteran might, of course, fall victim of at least para-Fascist propaganda, but it has been shown at least thus far that, having returned to the civilian environment, the veteran has been grafted to the same social roots which are responsible for the growth of unions. It has been noted that veterans have frequently been found among the leaders or at least participants of even wartime strikes.

The veterans, like the rest of industrial America, are finding that it is organized labor that can be most relied upon to exert even political pressure to have the government provide jobs or create the conditions for jobs. Curiously, in the conviction that organized labor is an effective pressure group which can deliver the goods, the masses of workers have been substantially assisted by the daily press. Every time one read a tirade against a labor leader or some union for striking to bring pressure on the government to raise wages, there was of course a resentment against this action which during the war interfered with the war effort. But there was also a residue of sentiment hardly articulate, because it is patriotically taboo, that a union is effective in getting a raise.

That the example of organized labor is not without its effect on the minds of the unorganized is indicated by the fact that organization is permeating the middle class and aristocracy of industrial and white-collar workers and the professions.[7]

There is no reason to believe that organized labor will cease to exert its pressure, direct or indirect, on the consciousness of the unorganized. Of course, the energies and aspirations of labor leadership are an exceedingly important factor. The tendency of labor leaders is in time to lose the drive and push characteristic of their youth, particularly when there are enough honors and emoluments to go around.

But there is in labor a factor which would tend to counteract the lethargies of union organizers. Labor's house divided against itself is adding wings. The rivalry of the A.F.L. and the C.I.O. for supremacy serves as an impetus to organizing campaigns on both sides. The contest for jurisdiction is a fillip to stake out and to work claims. Imperialism is a power phenomenon and therefore has its counterpart in labor's competitive milieu. If labor is to heal its breach, it will have to find the organizing equivalent of labor's civil war. The need to organize the unorganized in order to avoid their undermining the standards of the unionized will continue to operate as a stimulus to organizing drives.

The Taft-Hartley Act will not substantially and durably diminish labor's strength. The elimination of the closed shop and the automatic checkoff will not cause a stampede of dues-payers to leave the fold. Those who hug to their breasts the comforting delusion that the growth of unions is due to "coercion" should have been forewarned by the experience of the National War Labor Board with the "escape period" during which union members could get out before union security became operative. Only an insignificant fraction of 1 per cent availed themselves of the opportunity. The Taft-Hartley Act undoubtedly imposes considerable legal restrictions on unions' organizing activities. However, it has so jolted labor from its complacency to a realization of the dangers it faces that labor's organizing drives, as well as its political activities, are bound to be galvanized into action for some time to come.

The socioeconomic forces point to a long-range increase in labor's organizational power.

3. THE IMPACT OF STRIKES ON A MODERN ECONOMY

What are the implications and consequences of this strength in regard to government regulation of our economy?

Labor's cumulative power will have a decisive influence on labor's exercise of its right to strike in the postwar period.

Despite newspaper headlines, labor's strike record during the war was remarkably good, much better in fact than it was in World War I, and compares favorably with that in England even though American labor did not work under the psychological imperatives operating in the midst of a war theater.[8] But strikes increased toward the end of the war. Labor was restless and the restiveness welled from the rank and file and communicated itself to the leaders. In the immediate postwar period, under pressure of inflationary forces, strikes of epidemic proportions have been taking place. The experience of 1919 was to some extent recapitulated.[9] If the strike lull, induced by employer ability to raise prices to compensate for wage raises, is followed by a rash of strikes, it may well result in permanent legislation drastically curbing labor's right to strike.

But independent of antistrike legislation and unconditioned by strike figures in the immediate postwar period, the strike is becoming obsolescent as labor's economic weapon even in time of peace. In our key industries, labor has lost the right to strike. This is the blunt and unpalatable truth. Labor's power operating against the background of modern technology is responsible for this. The reasons are endemic in labor's strength.

The general strike is no longer to be found in labor's arsenal. It is not a weapon calculated to achieve economic results when directed against the employer class. Even if its avowed purposes are economic and the objectives limited to the usual trade-union variety and though it addresses its conscious pressure against employer groups, the general strike is a political and indeed a revolutionary weapon aimed in fact if not in intent against the government. The reason lies in the very impact of the general strike upon society—and that impact is paralyzing. The effective general strike stops the services and functions necessary for the maintenance of the life of the community whether this is on a local or a national scale. This is particularly true of modern urban society, whose life is so dependent on a continuous maintenance of services. Since the elementary and primary function of government is to sustain and protect the life of the community or state, no government can expect to remain in power unless it causes the immediate discontinuance of the general strike. It can encompass this purpose by granting the demands of the strikers, by effecting a compromise on the issues involved, or by refusing all demands and breaking the strike.

But whatever method the government uses it cannot, whatever its sympathy in regard to the contestants may be, sit idly by and twiddle its collective thumb, the while permitting the strike to run its course. It must intervene promptly and effectively to stop the strike. The life of the community must go on. This is the reason why general strikes have traditionally been avowedly of a political or revolutionary character. And even where this has not been the case, it was treated as such, as in the general strike in England in 1926, which was unsuccessful and resulted in antilabor legislation in 1927.

The general strike is not an economic weapon which can be used by labor to attain economic ends without government intervention because of the colossal effect of the use of the weapon on the community. The conclusion is warranted, then, that whenever any other type of strike will approximate in effect the proportions of a general strike, it too will in time cease to be wielded by labor, for it too will bring about government action for its discontinuance and ultimately its prevention.

And because of the organization of modern industry and the growth of labor organization, strategic industrial and communication strikes will tend to approximate the effect of general strikes on the community. Corporate organization of industry in large units increases the range of the employer's voice in the determination of labor policy. Employer associations along industrial and interindustry lines further accentuate the trend toward uniformity and extensiveness of employer influence.

This development is paralleled in the labor movement. The radius of the union's reach in the making of labor policy is lengthening with the unionization of the workers. The industrial form of labor organization as contrasted with the craft type is a contributing factor of development in the same direction. Industry-wide collective bargaining, such as is found in coal and the needle trades, is the ultimate development thus far in the direction of extending the direct effect of employer-union decision. But even without the formalization of industry-wide bargaining a substantially similar result is obtained, due to the already indicated large-scale employer organization characteristic of our basic industries and the industrial form of labor organization. The association of labor unions into large federations such as the A.F.L. and the C.I.O. further enhances the impact of a decision in labor relations by increasing the incidence of sympathetic strikes.

The factors of employer and labor organization on an industry-wide basis tend to prolong any deadlock which may result in a strike. The effectiveness of any strike threat against a single employer resides in his fear that he might lose his trade to his competitors during the threatened strike. But when a strike envelops a whole industry, the fear of competition is removed from the brow of the employer negotiators. Likewise, in large-scale corporate organization, loss of immediate profits due to idle plants does not loom so large in consideration as with the small individual entrepreneur. With the individual employer and the representative of the local union, the mediator may ply the tricks of his trade with greater success than is true when industry-wide impasses develop where the decisions to be made are great in their effect. Big Corporation versus Big Union-Stalemate.

An industry-wide strike immediately withdraws the purchasing power in the communities directly affected, thus increasing the social and political tensions of the mercantile, professional, and farm groups of the population whose livelihood is dependent on the factory payroll. But the effect of such strikes transcends the immediate communities involved. Other industries which utilize the products of the industry affected may have to shut down when the strike is of any substantial duration. The effect of a coal, steel, or railroad strike cannot be insulated. An industry-wide strike in any of the basic production or communication industries is of national import in its consequences.

Such a strike does equal in catastrophic effect a general strike in peacetime or an extensive strike in wartime. In an economy, such as ours is, which places so great a premium on full and continuous employment, large-scale strikes are not a phenomenon which government can observe without positive intervention to do away with and render unnecessary.

The category of key industries is ever expanding. It now includes land and maritime communication, and electric power, for in these a strike has an immediate effect on industry and the life of the community. Steel and coal also are on the list. Theoretically it is possible for industry to build up large inventories of them, but practically this is unlikely in an economy of full production and constant demand. Storage problems also are formidable. Not only in key industries but in key trades as well are strikes catastrophic. A strike in 1945 of elevator operators in the business buildings of New York virtually brought to a standstill for a few days the business life of the metropolis. As industry-wide collective bargaining spreads, more and more industries will be added to those in which strikes could not be tolerated because of the economic disequilibration of work stoppage.

The future in regard to strikes has already cast its shadow on at least two of our basic industries—the railroads and coal—and the reference is not to wartime conditions. With more praise than understanding the Railway Labor Act[10] applicable to the railroad industry is pointed to as a model for industry generally to avoid strikes by means of mediation and voluntary arbitration. Particularly endearing has become the so-called "cooling-off" period provided for in the statute during which no strike or lockout may occur while the healing poultices are being applied to the collective bargaining process.

For one, the "cooling-off" period has really proved to be under the War Labor Disputes Act, which provided for it in regard to war contractors a "heating-up" period.[11] Even where no strike was intended the machinery provided for was utilized to demonstrate that a strike was in preparation. Of course, this was resorted to frequently as a ceremonial ritual for the effect it would have on the public, employers, and government officials. But it may well be that the war dance developed psychological drives for release in actual war in the participants themselves. The James-Lange theory is not without its application in mass movements.

More significant, it may be surprising but even in peacetime there has not been any independent, private, collective bargaining on the railroads on the vital issues that can and have caused impasses. The reason for that is that even in peacetime the government could not tolerate the exercise of the right to strike on a large scale on the railroads, whose continuous operation is so vital to the nation. Great strikes have failed to occur not because the cooling-off period afforded opportunity for wiser heads to work the miracles of voluntarism and that blessed word "mediation." Great strikes have been prevented because on the vital issues on which the parties would really be expected to lock horns, ad hoc Emergency Boards have been appointed by the government, which decided them for the parties.[12] That the awards of these boards are only recommendations in form, which the parties are free to ignore after a cooling-off interval, does not in any way alter their actual mandatory character backed by the power of the government. The parties have understood that and have acted accordingly. In the one case in 1946 when the railroad unions availed themselves of the right to strike afforded by the act, the President broke the strike within hours after it began. How can we speak of the right to strike in the railroad industry when its exercise, though sanctioned by the Railway Labor Act, brings with it swift retaliation?

How can we realistically speak of the right to strike and of autonomous bargaining in the coal industry? In the spring and summer of 1946 John L. Lewis did his eloquent and sonorous best to remove government controls over prices and wages. However, in November of 1946 this great foe of government intervention, wishing to catch up with runaway prices, refused to deal with the coal operators and insisted on dealing only with the government. The coal operators too were unwilling to negotiate and were content to leave the determination of wages to the government, although they continued to derive profits while their industry was under government operation. Similarly, the Administration, which had just washed its hands of the wage-price relationship and told labor and management that collective bargaining—like marriage—was a private affair, jumped into the breach as soon as a strike was imminent and proceeded to obtain a labor injunction which broke the strike.[13] This is not said in criticism of the determination of the Administration to take a hand. Beyond the personalities involved there emerges the actuality that we must face, however unpalatable it may be, that there is no longer the right to strike in the coal industry.

It is not unlikely that the strike weapon, which was suitable as a labor counterpoise in a small-scale capitalistic economy, is becoming obsolescent in a modern economy in which institutional continuity of operation is of the essence. In the fullness of time it may take its place with the barricades among other memorabilia of the capitalistic class struggle. Of course, it will continue to receive the kudos of the pious as among the sacred inalienable rights, but it will have as much relevance to the actualities of the situation as the eighteenth-century formulated right of revolution that is found in our politico-legal heritage. What has been said is not an argument to outlaw strikes. This has been proved rather futile, particularly as a means of avoiding the explosive wildcat variety.[14] The latter type of strike has deep emotional roots in industrial psychology and can be reduced, if not altogether eliminated, through the application of scientific management methods within the framework of mature collective bargaining—a slow process at best. This analysis deals with strikes over the terms of employment, and this cause is not psychological but primarily economic and incapable of solution except on an economy-wide basis.[15] The analysis, however, points strongly in the direction of increasing intervention by the government in peacetime too to decide the terms of the labor contract as a means of avoiding strikes in the organized basic industries. What sanctions and incentives are to be used to make government compulsory arbitration effective in avoiding strikes is a subject demanding separate analysis.[16]

If the government is impelled to avoid strikes it must intervene to determine at least the vital issues, such as wages, of the employer-employee relationship. In its ultimate essentials collective bargaining is a contest between the economic power of labor and that of management. Labor's economic weapon is the strike: that of the employer is to refuse to accede to the union's demands, to replace economic strikers, and the lockout. Even where the strike is not resorted to, the possibility of such an occurrence is the unexorcisable spirit of the conference room. The ultimate agreement is an estimate by both sides of the conference table of what the result would be if an actual trial of strength took place.

When labor is without its right to strike, genuine private collective bargaining is no longer possible, for the agreement is then a product of unilateral voluntary decision—that of the employer. Unless labor, then, is to become completely impotent vis-à-vis the employer, decision must be left to a third party. That is why even in peacetime, whenever labor consents to a no-strike provision in a contract, the logic of the situation calls for the appointment of an impartial arbitrator to administer the contract and decide disputes arising during the contract. That is why when labor gave its no-strike pledge for the duration, the government, through the National War Labor Board, had to decide in dispute cases not only wages but other issues of the collective agreement such as union security.[17] Hence NWLB was being forced to rule on more and more issues of the collective agreement despite recurrent pleas of its members that labor and management learn to settle their own differences without invoking government intervention. As long as labor was without the right to strike such pleas were futile however well intentioned they were.

Of course some might be in favor of depriving labor of its right to strike and leave the employer the complete freedom to determine the terms of the contract, but obviously no government with any pretense to democratic principles could afford to do that. More significant, not even under fascism, where labor has no right to strike, have employers been left with a free hand in the employer-employee relationship. The reason lies in the nature of our economy. To the extent that labor loses its power to strike, government intervention to determine the terms and conditions of employment will become imperative.

4. THE WAGE-PRICE RELATIONSHIP

Government compulsory arbitration to decide issues between employers and unions is indicated not solely or even primarily by the necessity of avoiding crippling strikes. That objective aside, increasing government regulation of the employer-employee relationship even in regard to the terms and conditions of employment, will be brought about by the need to resolve conflicting social interests and to maintain economic equilibrium.

To the evolution of this need as to the imperative of preventing strikes, the growth and structure of organized labor as well as the large-scale organization of employers are prime contributors.

It is elementary that wages in any industry do have a relationship to the price structure of that industry. Wages are frequently the chief factor affecting costs, but in any case they are among the most important components of production costs.[18] Thus, a wage award of the National War Labor Board became effective when the Office of Price Administration decided that no price increase would result, but if price ceiling revisions became necessary, wage increases were subject to the approval of the Stabilization Director.[19] A numerically small labor movement organized along craft lines does not influence substantially the costs of the industry in which it is only a small part of the total labor force, however militant the craft union is in behalf of its own members. Raises in wages obtained by the few craft members can in ordinary times be absorbed without causing a rise in costs, through a speed-up of production, an increase in the time worked, or a wage reduction of the unorganized many. Craft unionism tends therefore to become exclusive, conservative, and opposed to mass organization of labor, particularly on industrial lines. These characteristics have been associated with the history of labor's aristocracy in the United States.

When labor becomes numerous and organized along industrial lines, when a union blankets all or even most of the workers in an industry, any upward revision of wages tends to have a constantly more pronounced and immediate effect on costs.[20] There are few, if any, unorganized to absorb the wage increases. Neither can profits be depended upon to be adequate for the absorption even if employer opposition can be overcome. While the few can profit at the expense of the many, the converse is not true. Prices, too, cannot always be relied on to absorb the rise in labor costs. A price rise may result in the reduction of the number of purchases, thus causing reduction of force. Frequently, moreover, no price rise is possible without affecting adversely the competitive position of the industry. Thus, ordinarily the price of coal cannot be indefinitely raised without causing more widespread use of oil and other fuels.

But even where the organized industry is not limited by the prices of competitive products, its price level cannot be freely raised without effecting severe dislocation in the economy and causing social conflicts. Of prime importance as a dislocating factor in a great and prolonged depression is not the deflationary nature of the price level, though that in itself is significant, because it increases the debt burden of society and thereby improves the position of the creditor class vis-à-vis the rest of the population. Even of greater import is that even within the movement of prices there are great variations. While some prices, in monopolistic industries, such as steel, for instance, remain rigid, others, more subject to competition, as in agriculture, show a more precipitate and deeper decline.

What workers as producers gain in padded take-homes they more than lose as consumers in the market place, for wages lag behind rising prices.[21] Nevertheless, the interunion rivalry among labor leaders has been so keen that pressure of organized labor has been and will for an indefinite period continue for higher and still higher wages. In an economy of full employment and expanding consumer demand there is no automatic check visible on the horizon which would avoid a spiraling of wages and prices. It is futilitarian to rely on the self-restraint of labor leaders or of businessmen to prevent a spiraling of wages and prices in an economy of full employment. Even a reservoir of unemployed would not act as an effective brake on demands of organized labor for higher wages since the competition of the unemployed will be deflected to the unorganized trades. Nor can reliance be placed on expected increase in production efficiency to outstrip increases in wages.

Only the government is in a position to exercise some control over the upward pressure of wages on prices, imperfectly as it has done that during the war and the reconversion period. Nor is it feasible to have government control over wages and prices to avoid strikes in the key industries without correlative controls over the wage-price equation in industry generally. As the unorganized middle classes begin to feel the squeeze of the wage-price catch-as-catch-can they too will clamor for government controls.

If labor through mass industrial organization would continuously succeed in raising labor costs and thereby the price level, is there any doubt that this would arouse the opposition of the farm population and of the unorganized urban groups? But even within labor's organized family conflict will become hydra-headed. A rise in steel prices due to raises in wages may prevent an increase in wages of other industries in whose products steel is an important ingredient.

In the light of these social conflicts[22] is it not reasonable to assume that the cry for "parity" will become more persistent and widespread and will emanate from many quarters including groups within labor? Where labor is unorganized, it is possible to maintain so-called traditional interindustry differentials in wages even in the same locality but not in the face of spreading labor organization. Despite government reluctance, the trend has been during the war in the direction of eliminating intra- and interindustry inequalities, particularly at the substandard level.[23] Of course, the chief operative forces have been manpower requirements and union pressure, but what may be termed the politico-moral factor should not be ignored: that in a democracy it is difficult indefinitely to defend with success the maintenance of particularly severe mass inequalities, once public opinion is persistently focused upon them and social forces are favorable for their elimination. The effect of still more widespread organization of labor will be to accentuate the drive, already advanced during the war, toward the equalization of the wage structure of industry, at least on the lower and middle levels.

The wage structure of the country will then be determined by the trial of strength among gigantic combinations of industry and labor in each industry and as between industries. The situation in regard to wages will parallel that obtaining in prices in many basic industries where monopoly is the determining agent.[24] Indeed, the effect of wages so determined will be to reinforce the monopoly influence on price by removing competition in labor costs.

An economy so constituted that wages and prices are monopolistically determined could hardly be referred to as a market economy, in which prices and wages are fixed in response to "automatic" economic forces operating through competition. Where the economic units are so small that no one unit or moderate combination of them is powerful enough to influence prices or wages, it is perhaps understandable why the competitive interplay of forces can be called automatic but to call decisions reached in a conference room automatic is inexcusable even though one is blinded by the smoke on the premises.[25]

5. THE INTEGRATING ROLE OF GOVERNMENT

Even if unions and employers in each industry were actuated by the best of goodwill and public spirit as well as wisdom, they could not avoid the necessity of co-ordinating their decisions in regard to wages and perhaps prices with those made in other industries. It is this lack of provision for co-ordination that is one of the chief fallacies of anarcho-syndicalism or any other socioeconomic doctrine from the right or the left that seeks to avoid government intervention.[26] To argue that management and labor should organize to treat of the problems of their particular industries under the supervision but not the domination of government is to indulge in semantic juggling. Even were there no disputes between labor and management, government would have to hold the power of decision both as a means of protecting the "parity" claims of interests other than the immediate producing interest and to co-ordinate and interrelate the various industrial plans and decisions. Such co-ordination of planning is rendered necessary by a program for full employment which accentuates requirements for interdependence and equilibrium among various parts of our economy.

The cry for self-government for industry involves a conceptual fallacy. Even if society could be prevailed upon to leave capital and labor outside the pale of government intervention, their decisions would not be effective if they depended solely on voluntarism. But if councils composed of representatives of capital and labor were granted enforcement powers, they would become part of the government, for the state is ultimately that agency of society which possesses the power of enforcement. Nor is it feasible to exclude the political agencies of the government from the industrial field. When the cries for parity are made, they are addressed to the government.

Labor's political pressure will affect but will not render impossible the government's integrative function in the wage-price relationship. Competition among unions will continue for favorable decisions, but ultimately it will become accepted that the people as a whole, including labor, cannot stand to gain if the economy is constantly disequilibrated by a spiraling of wages and prices. Organized labor will come to support the government's stabilization policies.

Public ownership per se will not solve the strike problem. In democratically oriented Socialist economies in which a free labor movement existed, the same conflicting forces would operate to necessitate a stabilized economy. A Socialist government, as any other kind, would be confronted with the necessity of saying no to certain demands from labor unions. In labor relations, as well as in other fields, public ownership is not a short cut to utopia. In problems of economics as well as in industrial psychology the task of management remains unimpaired whether in Socialist England or in Communist Russia.[27]

Even though it is true that the government will have the decisive voice in determining the vital sectors of the employer-employee relationship, labor need not fear that without the weapon of the strike it will lose its character as a free labor movement. It merely means that collective bargaining in the main will not be autonomous and private, but will be carried on on the administrative level in a form similar to the NWLB with tripartite representation of management, labor, and the government. In place of the strike, other weapons more suitable to the new economic and political environment will be forged.[28]

There is no way out of the train of events leading to government compulsory arbitration through laws which aim at reversing the trend to official or unofficial industry-wide collective bargaining. In the first place, this trend has to its credit a great many positive democratic values, which we should not destroy. In the needle trades, for instance, it has stabilized a chaotic industry and has prevented cutthroat business competition conducted at the expense of employees working at sweatshop wages and conditions. Since unionism contributes to raising the purchasing power of its members, the trend to industry-wide bargaining has been a trend not alone to democratic equalitarianism by removing interplant inequalities but a fillip to an ever-higher level of economic well-being. Therefore, to the extent that we break up or weaken unions by the application of antitrust laws or some other means we destroy the only force that can be relied on, short of government regulation, to keep purchasing power somewhere near the level where it can absorb the national product. The consequence would not be freedom from government intervention but an acceleration to that eventuality through certain unemployment and economic collapse. There is no analogy between the application of antitrust laws to break up business combinations and to break up unions. While competition among business firms, according to good capitalist theory, should contribute to efficiency of production and the general well-being, competition among millions of workers would tend to reduce the purchasing power of the masses.

Even if it were feasible to break up unions, this would not remain a permanent condition. For the same factors—the quest for power and the need for integration—that have caused business power to grow in concentration and size despite the antitrust laws and have caused unions to expand, would still be operative.

The split-up unions involved in the same industry would somehow manage to arrive at a common understanding in regard to the collective bargaining demands, as businessmen now somehow manage to fix prices. On the other hand, to prevent unions as now constituted from dealing with industry-wide employer associations and from striking a whole industry would weaken the employer side, for then each employer struck would be subject to pressure to settle because of fear of losing his market to his competitors. It is unrealistic, even if it were desirable, to advocate legislation to reverse the trend to official or unofficial industry-wide collective bargaining. Only the government as the integrative agent can deal with the problem in the effectual and democratic manner analyzed.

The Taft-Hartley Act is not the answer to the problem of settlement of labor disputes. The pertinent provisions of the act exhibit the vices and none of the virtues of government intervention. Independent of the personality of the incumbent a single federal mediation and conciliation director is likely to command less prestige and power than would a board.

Since it is not obligatory on the parties to reach an agreement, the requirement that unions must bargain collectively will not prove of any value in reducing the incidence of strikes. The requirement of a 60-day written notice of proposed changes in an existing contract, together with an offer to negotiate and the prohibition of strikes for the sixty days is no more in substance than the present practice of including a no-strike clause in collective contracts which applies for their duration. Indeed, the effect of the Taft-Hartley Act's throwing labor relations questions into the courts will make many unions reluctant to include no-strike clauses in their agreements for fear of being held legally responsible for unauthorized strikes.

The real mischief, however, resides in the procedure created to deal with "national emergencies." This procedure may be invoked by the President when in his opinion an impending or actual strike in an entire industry, or a substantial part of it, threatens to affect the public health and safety. He may then obtain a court injunction to preclude the workers from striking for approximately eighty days. Unlike the Railway Labor Act, this act does not provide for the maintenance of the status quo during the waiting period. While workers are prohibited from striking, employers may meanwhile impose their own terms after their contracts have expired. This provision is open to grave constitutional doubt because it tends to deprive workers of their property without due process of law by making the employer's will supreme and not subject to the decision of an arbitrational tribunal.

The act authorizes the President to appoint a board of inquiry to investigate the dispute, but unlike a board functioning under the Railway Labor Act, the board of inquiry has no power to make recommendations. It merely serves as a sounding device for the contentions of the parties. The employer, given the power to impose his own terms of employment, is further released from any embarrassment which may flow from recommendations by impartial experts, which are likely to be adverse to the employer's position. It is a matter of recent history that the 1946 strikes in General Motors and other industries were continued after the respective fact-finding boards made their reports, because the employers, not the unions, refused to accept the recommendations.

The Taft-Hartley Act is careful to remove this possible onus for continuing a strike from the shoulders of the employer and place it on the workers. These are given the doubtful privilege of voting by a secret NLRB ballot before the waiting period expires whether to accept the last offer of the employer as reported by the board of inquiry. Frustrated for over two months in their demands and angered at the employer's immunity, there is little doubt that the employees will justify the expectation that they would vote to stike. The waiting period under the Taft-Hartley Act will produce a temperature equal to that of the "heating-up" period of the War Labor Disputes Act. The blame for the paralyzing strike will rest squarely on the union and the workers.

The ensuing public anger against labor will not be blocked. It is likely to have expression in antilabor legislation. One of the principal aims of sound labor relations is to remove the settlement of labor disputes from the exigencies of varying political influences and to entrust them to regular agencies. It is regrettable that the President in recent years has become involved in every major strike. The Taft-Hartley Act not only perpetuates this deleterious evolution but adds Congress itself as an ad hoc settlement tribunal for each major strike. While the act precludes the board of inquiry from making recommendations, it makes it mandatory at the end of the heating-up period for the President to dissolve the injunction and to throw the whole dispute into the lap of Congress "together with such recommendations as he may see fit to make for consideration and appropriate action."

In the antilabor hysteria and bedevilment induced by the threat of a paralyzing strike, there's no doubt that Congress would act to stop the strike by further antilabor restrictions, including breaking up of national unions. Any lingering misgiving on the point should be removed by the recollection of what the railroad and coal strikes brought in their wake. The Taft-Hartley Act in effect outlaws major strikes in the basic industries, which affect the health and safety of the public, by preparing the ground for panic legislation to render labor impotent, even though this might cause social strife and economic collapse. This is not calculated to be a well-wrought system for the peaceful and equitable settlement of labor disputes. It should not be confused with the over-all plan advocated in this analysis, which integrates the wage-price-profit relationship and is operative within the framework of our democratic traditions with equity to both labor and management.

CHAPTER XV

Industrial Democracy and Freedom

---

1. INDUSTRIAL DEMOCRACY AND CIVIL LIBERTIES

The realities of labor relations and of the growth of organized labor are not only leading to the emergence of the administrative state, but are equally essential to making the administrative state free and democratic, industrially and politically. This is but a projection of an evolution already well on its way.

The adoption of the National Labor Relations Act was in itself a landmark in recognizing that a legal right—in this case the right to organize—is meaningless unless there is a correlative duty upon others to refrain from interfering with its exercise. In protecting the right of workers to organize against economic retaliation by employers, the act reaffirmed and enforced our civil liberties.[1]

If these liberties are valid and desirable, then they must be protected against aggression from any quarter. It is not enough that these liberties are protected against the government. If they are to be enjoyed they must also be defended against encroachment by private interests. If a worker joins a union, it is small comfort to him not to be arrested for it if in doing so he loses his chance of making a living. That paralyzing fear has been removed by the Wagner Act. Now when American workers foregather in a meeting to determine matters which vitally concern their livelihood and whether to form or to join a union, they really can enjoy their constitutional liberties. They enjoy freedom of assembly, for their meetings are not dispersed by hired thugs, and spies and agents provocateurs may not find entry. When a worker rises to speak his mind or to distribute leaflets urging his fellow workers to join a union, he enjoys to the fullest freedom of speech and of the press, for he knows that he will not be discharged from his job for doing so. And those who listen or read also enjoy the same liberties and for the same reason. It was when labor sought to exercise its "right" to organize or to strike that the most fruitful soil was prepared for the wholesale violation of our civil liberties by government officials. Government does not function in a vacuum. Particularly in a democracy it is subject to stresses and pressures of economic and social interests. Because of the economic dependence of the community, especially the smaller ones, upon the payroll of frequently a single enterprise, the employer was able to dragoon, directly or indirectly, the leading elements of the community against labor. Court injunctions, citizens' committees, arrests for alleged vagrancy or other trumped-up charges, running organizers out of town, mayhem, even murder, were some of the expressions of vigilantism which made a mockery out of the constitutional liberties of the workers. It was by proceeding against the very source of the anti-union miasma that the act and the board were able to liberate whole communities from the feudal control of the dominant economic interest. As a result, the incidence of violations of civil liberties is much less now than it was before the act was adopted. The gain is not only to the workers involved but to whole communities and to the nation at large, for liberty like peace is indivisible. The liberties of no one are secure where the liberties of anyone are lightly considered.

The violence and civil liberties violations customarily associated in America with labor disputes may not loom large in the consciousness of a world numbed by the atrocities of Maedanek and Dachau. Let us not, however, underestimate the importance of what the act and the board have accomplished in eliminating vigilantism from labor relations.

The humanizing and civilizing conditioning of the Wagner Act should not be ignored. That is the direction in which we labor. To those of us who believe that cultural traits of nations are modified with great difficulty and slowly, this is a promising token of the viability of the American democratic way of life.

2. PLANT DEMOCRACY AND SECURITY

Not only has the Wagner Act bolstered our liberties, it has been even more decisive in laying the foundation for the new economic liberties within the framework of industrial democracy. The National Labor Relations Act has contributed immeasurably toward the realization and establishment of the fundamental right to a job along democratic lines. In preparing the legal basis for the organization of

15 million workers, the act to that extent is responsible for the creation of a social and political force which must, because of the logic of its own self-interest, work for the goal of full employment in the field of politics. Even short of that ultimate goal, organized labor is a power operating in the direction of economic security within the framework of democratic techniques. Collective bargaining agreements reduce the individual worker's economic helplessness and feeling of insecurity. For that reason protection of foremen's right to bargain is as necessary as that of ordinary employees.[2] In excluding the unionization of supervisors from the protection of law, the Taft-Hartley Act constitutes a retrogression in America's struggle for economic security.

Wage determinations through collective bargaining, seniority practices in dismissal and promotion, grievance procedure, job classification, merit rating, and other aspects of rationalized personnel practices, which follow in the wake of collective bargaining, serve to introduce a measure of democratic give-and-take in place of industrial absolutism. Of course, they are no panacea against injustice or favoritism in personnel relations. But collective bargaining does convert industrial relations into a government of laws and not of men in the sense that management has to mold its actions so that at least they might have the appearance of logic and justice and be persuasive enough for acceptance by the representatives of the employees. Collective bargaining is neither a hindrance to nor a substitute for scientific management but an impetus to its development. The principles of scientific management must be applied within the framework of union-management relations, to be fruitful. It is futile to rely upon them to evade dealing with the union or to make union organization unnecessary. Establishment of better communication between management and employees should not be used to create neo-company unions to rival legitimate unionism.[3] The Taft-Hartley Act facilitates the return of company unions by permitting them to appear on the ballot in employee elections, although ordered disestablished.

Adequate minimum-wage laws are no substitute for collective bargaining, for the latter supplies necessary psychological values lacking in the former. The sustaining sense of being part of an effective community like a union reduces the atomization of the individual. The act of participating through his chosen representatives in the determination of his own economic destinies should add to the sense of power and therefore security euphoria of the individual worker. Only thus can he become part of a democratic "plant community." In the economic realm too, not only in the political, the worker becomes an individual with rights that others are bound to respect.

The employer too must undergo profound psychological revision of his personality structure under the pressure of collective bargaining. For the latter demands sharing of power—the most explosive phenomenon in individuals as well as cultures. Of such stuff are revolutions made. Strict enforcement of the law will of course result in outward compliance with the law, but it requires an arduous and long educational process to bring about a conversion not only intellectually but on the deep emotional subconscious level. It is one thing to favor collective bargaining in the abstract but it is quite something else to accept it as one's own industrial mode of life. That economic considerations are not paramount in this is indicated by the emotional difficulty many government officials experience in employing the collective bargaining process. It is because the Wagner Act required such a profound and arduous psychological readjustment that it became such a bitterly fought-over statutory enactment. Unionization is as essential in government as it is in private industry.[4]

In order for industrial democracy to make its appearance, the employee interest had first to be recognized. The Wagner Act has often been blamed for substituting a philosophy of conflict for one of co-operation in industrial relations. The complexity of modern industrial operation renders co-operation between management and labor essential. But in making labor independent and strong the act prepared the indispensable condition for co-operation, because co-operation, like freedom of contract, is conceivable only among those who are independent and are approximating equality. Only when an individual worker joins a union can he participate in the co-operative process between management and labor. This is true under public ownership as well as under private operation of industry. The economic and psychological problems of management-labor relations are essentially the same under both systems. Public ownership does not do away with the need for a free and independent labor movement.

Modern democracy has on occasion been attacked as being too distant in its seats of power from the individual voter.[5] Modern political democracy, because of the complexity of government, does not perhaps sufficiently involve the citizen as a participant. Industrial democracy can help to remedy this defect and supply this lack. In voting for a collective bargaining representative, in passing upon the terms of an agreement, in participating in the grievance settlements, in attending the union local's meetings, the workers are called upon to participate in the determination of issues which are of the most vital interest to them. If the democratic premise has any validity, it is here that it should prove itself. The high percentage of voting in NLRB elections as compared with political elections is an indication that the democratic premise is not baseless. Are we to believe that the democratic habits learned in the industrial field will fail to be transplanted to the political realm with consequent benefit to the latter?

Ever since Plato it has been observed that democracy's greatest enemy is pronounced inequality—of the economic type.[6] Our democratic culture too could not endure for long divided against itself: politically democratic and industrially absolutist. By introducing democracy into the industrial field, the fatal breach is being attended to, and political democracy fortified. The economic framework of our civil liberties has been strengthened.

3. INTRA-UNION DEMOCRACY

Every measure in the social field, however it may have the character of a solution, in turn raises problems of its own which demand attention. The National Labor Relations Act is no exception. It aimed at the establishment of industrial democracy through the protection of the employees' right to bargain through their freely chosen representatives. But if the republican form of industrial government is to endure, the representatives themselves, that is, the labor organizations, must be democratically oriented. If power is to continue to flow from those represented up to the representatives, then responsibility must flow from the leadership down to the rank and file. This is the bloodstream of the democratic organism. The right to choose representatives is the right to make mistakes. Although the law can create the conditions favorable to democratic functioning, it cannot guarantee it. That is up to the electorate.

Although the Wagner Act omitted prohibitions against "unfair labor practices" by unions, significantly the problem of "union responsibility"[7] was not shirked by those entrusted with the administration of labor relations. The public may be amazed at the extent and pervasiveness of union regulation already in operation, and all of it springing from the federal protection of the right to bargain collectively, although the statue involved is silent on the point. This highly important evolution of the law was on an empirical case-by-case basis, in response to specific needs, not a priori assumptions. The result would prove disappointing only to the enemies of labor, for it demonstrates that unions can grow in strength and power while (or because) they must comply with democratic controls.

At the nexus of this legal evolution is the principle that if the bargaining union has the power to act for and obligate the workers it also has the duty to exercise fairly the power conferred upon it in behalf of all those for whom it acts, without hostile discriminations against them. This principle found application as the most important minority problem of our society—race—impinged upon labor relations. Although labor organizations have an ideological and functional life peculiar to themselves, they, because they are mass organizations, also reflect the characteristics of their society. It is therefore not surprising that some labor organizations—few, to be sure—should be found to discriminate in regard to membership on the basis of race, particularly in sections of the country where the race issue borders almost on the irreconcilable.

The problem of racial discrimination came before the National Labor Relations Board in several indirect and marginal ways. The expressions of antiunionism have frequently been crisscrossed and exacerbated by racial hostility. In such cases when the board eliminated antiunionism it had to that extent mitigated these expressions of race conflict.[8] But the board has had to confront the problem squarely in the determination of the bargaining unit. Despite repeated requests, the board has refused to define the unit along racial lines.[9] Thus the board has not only protected the economic liberties and interests of the Negroes but those of the whites as well, for it has prevented the building up of a large competing reservoir of cheap labor which would undercut the bargaining position of the white workers. It has also ruled that, although it will not dictate to a union its membership eligibility, it will not certify a union, or it will revoke its certification, if it should discriminate in representing its constituency on the ground of race.[10] Nor will it permit the discharge of a Negro under a closed-shop contract of a union which bars Negroes from membership.[11] These rulings were made although the "Board has no express authority to remedy undemocratic practices within the structure of union organization.[12] The Supreme Court has adopted a similar policy in interpreting the Railway Labor Act. It declared void a contract which disqualified from certain employment Negro workers who were not admitted to membership in the contracting union.[13]

The effect of protecting racial minorities against union discrimination should not be underestimated. To the extent that collective bargaining gains ground, job discrimination on the ground of race will tend to be eliminated. This is not an argument against federal and state antidiscrimination statutes, but it is well to remember the great benefits the American people have derived from the Wagner Act, even from one of its unexpected by-products.

Not only racial but other types of minorities have been protected against discrimination. Because the employer must bargain exclusively with the union, the Supreme Court held, the union must therefore represent without discrimination nonmembers as well as members, those who voted against it as well as those who voted for it, those it welcomes and those it does not.[14] A union could not by means of a closed shop discriminate against dissident groups who were formerly affiliated with a rival union.[15] The NLRB will not permit a craft union to slough off the less skilled from the unit it represents.[16] It has indicated that it will revoke certifications as a penalty for restrictive practices and economic reprisals aimed at each other's members in jurisdictional disputes.[17] The NLRB's evolving technique of "policing" certifications held out great promise for supervision of the collective bargaining arena.[18] One could conclude that political minorities were equally protected against union discrimination. This is of the utmost significance in view of labor's increasing participation in politics.

The administration of the wartime labor policy has witnessed a further development of union regulation. In regard to maintenance of membership, the National War Labor Board's standing practice was to deny it to unions which violated the wartime no-strike policy, refused to hold reasonably frequent elections, refused to make reasonably regular financial reports to their members, or coerced employees into joining; also disputes concerning expulsion from membership had to be decided by an impartial arbitrator.[19] In the case of the newspaper publishing business NWLB adopted the Newspaper Guild constitution's provision against expulsion from membership because of a member's conviction or what he has written.[20]

This legal evolution would appear to be fortified by the Taft-Hartley Act, which makes it an unfair labor practice for a union to cause an employer to "discriminate against an employee with respect to whom membership in such organization has been denied or terminated on some ground other than his failure to tender the periodic dues and the initiation fees uniformly required as a condition of acquiring or retaining membership." It may be ventured that this provision would be interpreted to outlaw the various types of discrimination mentioned when they result in loss of a job or other disadvantage in employment.

Not only job discrimination but denial of admission and expulsion from a union per se for the discriminatory reasons indicated, including views and actions in the realm of intra-union politics, should be outlawed and made reviewable by the NLRB. Union leadership should be deprived of such proscribed conduct as instrumentalities for maintaining themselves in power.

The enumerated and other measures should become the nucleus of a system of techniques calculated to promote intra-union democracy. This will not weaken, but strengthen labor unions; and though union officers are much more accountable to the rank and file than corporation officials are to stockholders, there is no doubt that there is room for democratization of union structure. But no easy solution is available. As a matter of fact there is a great deal of heat but very little light on the crucial problem of union structure and the institutional relationship between union leaders and membership. There is need for disclosure of critical information on this point before a specific program of legislation can be recommended.

Some information along that line should be forthcoming as a result of the Taft-Hartley Act's requirement that as a prerequisite to the processing of NLRB cases a union must file certain data with the secretary of labor, including its constitution and by-laws, its name and address, compensation of officers, manner in which officers were selected, amount of dues, fees, assets, liabilities and disbursements, a detailed statement of union procedure with respect to "(a) qualification for or restriction on membership, (b) election of officers and stewards, (c) calling of regular and special meetings, (d) levying of assessments, (e) imposition of fines, (f) authorization of bargaining demands, (g) ratification of contract terms, (h) authorization for strikes, (i) authorization for disbursement of union funds, (j) audit of union financial transactions, (k) participation in insurance or other benefit plans, and (l) expulsion of members and the grounds therefor," and that all the members were furnished with copies of its financial report.

This should bring together and make easily accessible information which, though at present largely public, is scattered. Objectionable is the conditioning of access to board machinery upon compliance with registration requirements. This may cause some unions, unwilling to furnish the information, to resort to strikes to achieve their ends rather than to use NLRB procedures. This provision may leave out some unions that seldom avail themselves of the NLRB machinery.

To equalize the obligations, the technique of disclosure should be made to apply to business and other associations and firms and to members of Congress.

Whatever democratizing modifications are effected in union constitutions, it should not raise the utopian hope that union leadership will lose its power and its reason for existence. Labor unions, like any other organizations, are necessarily in need of leadership, are pyramidal in power structure, and are subject to the "iron law of oligarchy."[21] At the base of the pyramid are the union members. The leadership is distributed on the middle and upper tiers. This is manifested both in income and in control over the machinery of the union. What democratic controls may aim at is to establish procedures which would make it possible for union leaderships to compete for the consent of the governed—the essence of democracy. This would tend to do away with dictatorial self-perpetuating union administrations which feel a proprietary interest in their office. But this is not an easy task. Union members are preoccupied with their jobs. Only the leaders are free to devote all their time to union matters. While in certain maritime trades union officials may in rare instances return to the ranks of the workers, in industry generally the rule holds with few exceptions that once a labor leader never again a "working stiff." Union leadership in point of standard of living and other indicia of power become assimilated into the middle and upper classes of society, psychologically, economically, and socially. Though labor leaders compete with leaderships in other forms of power, they are psychologically conditioned not to disturb the foundations of the pyramidal structure of society in which they are well established. For that reason, contrary to popular belief, trade-union officials have been predominantly conservative and inimical to radical changes in the economy and structure of society.

Under present dispensation, with few exceptions, changes in union leadership come about in connection with union fissures. This is obviously not conducive to regular changes. What is necessary is to provide an economic and legal base for a broad leadership which would not be monolithic. The analogy of the parliamentary system may be invoked. Leadership on the plant level may be furnished by giving economic means to free men from production tasks for union business. Election systems should be canvassed to provide for greater responsibility to flow from the top to the bottom layer of officials and membership.

The importance of protecting individuals or minorities operating within a group should not be underestimated. The democratic faith in the worth of the individual is grounded on biosocial truth, for man, unlike the insect, is not an automaton indistinguishable from his fellow beings, but an individual with a personality structure all his own.[22] The modern period of democratic capitalistic development since the feudal era has seen the progressive atomization of the individual and the dissolution of his social ties.[23] But once again the economic complexities of our society are projecting the trend to institutional or organizational development. Increasingly, even in the economic realm, the individual can protect his individual rights only through group action. Our democratic problem is not how to limit collective action but how to make it responsive to individual needs and desires. Minorities, too, must suffer if majorities are rendered powerless. In terms of collective bargaining, the task will not be accomplished through making majorities ineffective, but by making their representatives responsible to their constituencies.[24] The Taft-Hartley Act has diminished the security and freedom of the individual union member by weakening the union vis-à-vis the employer.

4. FREEDOM OF ORGANIZED LABOR UNDER PLANNING

It has been objected by some that the evolving governmental controls in union regulation, even before the passage of the Taft-Hartley Act, denoted a tendency to fascism, to the end of free unionism. As a matter of principle, so the argument runs, workers should be able to choose whomever they want as representatives, and the government should not circumscribe the power of those chosen, however praiseworthy is the specific limitation imposed. Why such a unique immunity should obtain in industrial democracy is difficult to see. In political democracy too we place limitations upon the action of the representatives of the electorate and indicate areas, such as our constitutional liberties, which are to be free from their encroachment.[25] If we are convinced that it is bad for society to discriminate against workers because of their race, color, religion, or national origin, it is equally an evil whether the discrimination finds origin with the union or with the employer. Hence the union as well as the employer should be precluded from engaging in such proscribed conduct. It is no reflection on labor that labor organizations must function within the orbit of law. Like all human institutions, they are not immune to functional disorders in their internal and external relationships.

It is no answer to plead that, while the controls imposed by a liberal administration upon labor may be sympathetically administered for socially worthy goals, in the hands of an antilabor administration these controls may be turned to shackles of bondage. This is no argument against the controls but rather for labor and liberals generally to be vigilant in keeping the government out of the hands of democracy's enemies. For when reaction or fascism gets into the seats of power it does not waste its energies on finding precedent for its actions. Possibility for abuse of power is no reason for denial of its legitimate use, unless the abuse inevitably follows. Freedom does not lie in the absence of power, but in its proper use and control. Dangers for misuse of power there are but it is the task of a strong and intelligently functioning labor movement to guard against them. This task will not be discharged by an indiscriminate opposition against all governmental controls but only against those which are socially hurtful. Only then can the labor movement form the nucleus of the anti-Fascist forces. Governmental controls are per se neither conducive nor hostile to freedom. It all depends on the kinds of controls and the methods of their exercise.

The projection of labor's role in the administrative state, both in the industrial and in the political fields, is that of an independent labor movement. Organized labor's history has thus far passed two stages: from legal taboo to independence and freedom. Would a planned economy necessarily bring organized labor to its third and final stage of evolution: absorption by the state as an agency of government in the industrial field and loss of independence? This is precisely what happened to organized labor in Soviet Russia, Fascist Italy, and Nazi Germany.[26] But again it must be pointed out that concerning labor, as well as other aspects of democracy, it was not the planned economies of these countries that were decisive but their dictatorial philosophy. Labor in the United States, Great Britain, Australia, and New Zealand operated with no loss of freedom and independence in governmentally controlled war economies. There is no reason why this should not obtain in a peacetime planned economy. In a democratically oriented administrative state, labor will face expanding opportunities for making its contribution to freedom, security, and democracy.

5. FREEDOM OF EMPLOYMENT UNDER PLANNING

Economic planning is not incompatible with freedom of employment. To workers as well as to employers a planned economy will bring expanded economic freedom because of larger opportunities for making economic choices. The right to a job will become an actuality instead of a shimmering phantom, and man will gain surcease from the haunting, debilitating, and demoralizing fear and pressure of unemployment. In a planned economy all those who can and want to work would be able to find jobs. There will of course be the unemployables and small numbers of those temporarily unemployed because of shifts in production. But over-all, in an economy of full employment, there should be more vacancies than workers seeking jobs—a work seller's market. No one will be entitled to any particular job, but he will have greater oportunities than ever for work commensurate with his capacities.[27] In this kind of economic order liberty to choose one's work would be so much greater than in an unplanned economy. In an economy of chronic, severe unemployment freedom to choose a job is a fraud and a delusion. Only in an economy of full employment is that liberty meaningful.

In that type of economy liberty and security coalesce. Nor is it the security of the barnyard or the slave enclave. It is true that economic planning would involve shifting of manpower from industry to industry or from one location to another. But this will be done not under the urgency of war or of an exhausted economy, as in England, but in response to deliberate planning. There would therefore be no general necessity for compulsion. The dynamics of a planned economy would be fully matched by the mobility of labor. In all likelihood, at least in the beginning, the manpower problem would be not how to uproot people from their jobs but how to keep them in their jobs and maintain stabilized employment. In any case the necessary, directed shifting of manpower could be obtained through inducements rather than compulsion. This would involve a much-needed rationalization of the wage structure of American industry within plant and among industries, which was just begun under impetus of war and would contribute greatly to production efficiency. This, however, involves the whole problem of incentives in the administrative state.[28]

Above all, in the democratic administrative state, the employee would not be a nonentity buffeted by economic exploitation and unemployment but an individual whose rights are advanced and protected through the collective action of his union. In the making of over-all economic decision and in their application to specific situations the interests of labor, management, and the consumer would be represented. Liberty implies choice, and choice involves a voice in the making of decision. This is implicit in the democratic character of the administrative state.

6. UNION RESTRICTIVE PRACTICES

While unions in the administrative state would protect freedom of employment against assaults from other sources, a planned economy would tend to remove the conditions that in the past have induced some unions to impose restrictions on production and job opportunities.

Just as in the case of business monopolies or professional restrictions on admission beyond considerations of merit, labor restrictions on production are expressions of the use of private political power to defend economic interests. From a moral standpoint, labor restrictions on production are on a higher level than those of business or of the powerful professional organizations, for labor is trying to protect a precarious livelihood, not riches. But, whatever the moral question is, there is no doubt that restrictive practices irrespective of source must be removed since they interfere with efficient production, one of the sine qua non conditions to increasing satisfaction of needs.

In our basic industries it is a rare collective contract which does not provide for labor-management co-operation "to reduce waste, improve products and equipment and increase efficiency."

Where are now the prophets of doom who were certain that the private operation of industry and industrial efficiency are incompatible with collective bargaining? We were able to turn the industrial miracle in America which was the determining factor in winning the war the while labor has reached the highest peak in history. Industrial absolutism can work in an absolutist society, for then there is no schizophrenic ideology to create cultural conflict leading to mass neuroses. Even psychologically America could not long remain politically democratic and industrially absolutist. Hence, by tending to remove the psychological conflicts through the introduction of the practices of industrial democracy, the Wagner Act has demonstrated that in our type of society liberty is not only compatible with efficiency but the very condition of its fullest realization. It would be well for business if this principle of management would gain wide acceptance.

The baseless doctrine of "management prerogatives" (reminiscent of the royal prerogative) should not be used to limit the scope of collective bargaining. Employers should welcome, not resist, labor's ever-widening interest in the conduct of industry. With such interest must also come responsibility for industrial efficiency even in the few crafts and industries where make-work practices exist. Reprehensible and shortsighted as "featherbedding" may be, its effect on our economy is minute compared to the monopoly practices and cartel agreements which aimed to restrict production even in wartime.

Make-work practices are caused by fear of unemployment and of destitution due to industrial hazards, and can be removed effectively only by a policy of economic security for the worker. Public opinion may become outraged by the methods of some labor leaders, but in lashing out against them let us deal justly and intelligently with the causes they represent. Technological developments have thus far increased the total reservoir of employment but that is small solace to the workers who are displaced by new machines. Since the individual business, the industry involved, and society as a whole are the gainers from technological changes, it is just and proper that they and not the hapless individual worker should bear the burden of the consequent employment shifts.

The parties immediately involved can best determine the area where the slowdown ends and the speed-up begins. Regularization of employment through the elimination of occasional fluctuations will be one result of a planned economy, but temporary unemployment in consequence of shifts due in part or in whole to technological changes would be covered by unemployment compensation. Labor's restrictions on production should be eliminated, whether these are practiced independently or in combination with employers. Similar to these restrictions are those which are caused by jurisdictional disputes including secondary boycotts. By creating a forum for their peaceful settlement the Taft-Hartley Act is removing the necessity for a trial of strength in the economic realm, as the state has already done in the field of private criminal law.

The Taft-Hartley Act prohibition of featherbedding practices will prove troublesome administratively and of doubtful effectiveness and justice. It declares it to be an unfair labor practice for a union to "force or require an employer to pay any money in the nature of an exaction for services which are not performed or not to be performed." It is similar to the prohibition in the Lea Act aimed at Petrillo, which was declared constitutional on its face by the United States Supreme Court[29] although the court did not rule whether the prohibited force or coercion could constitutionally include strikes and picketing. It is so broad in scope that it could proscribe many legitimate union objectives, such as vacations, rest periods, safety and health measures. Since many a featherbedding practice is the outgrowth of a legitimate safety and health measure, no generalized definition can be made and the determination must be limited to the circumstances of each particular industry and firm. But in this task the board would be hampered by the irrational denial to it by the Taft-Hartley Act of the services of an economic staff.

The chief objection to the provision, however, is that it attempts to eliminate make-work schemes at the expense of the workers by failure to provide for the framework of economic security which planned full employment alone can vouchsafe. This provision in the Taft-Hartley Act is neither just nor holds the promise of effectiveness.

Another type of labor restriction refers to manpower. Since a planned economy is a full-employment economy, the government would have to remove all restrictions on the training, availability, and proper allocation of manpower to fulfill the necessary industrial projects. In the few rare instances of old-line crafts, where restrictions on the admission of workers exist either in the form of high admission dues or by any other method, they would have to be eliminated through government regulation of the amount of dues and entrance requirements. The regulation of union fees under union-shop agreements has been entrusted to the NLRB by the Taft-Hartley Act.

Since a planned economy would offer jobs to those who can and want work, there would no longer be any reason for members of crafts to protect their jobs against the competition of newcomers. To the extent that a union shop and other forms of union security would through union admission and expulsion of members interfere with manpower requirements and union democracy they would have to be modified. It may well be that union restrictions on entrance to a trade might under certain circumstances be subsumed under the provision of the Taft-Hartley Act, which makes it an unfair labor practice for a union to cause an employer to discriminate against an employee whose membership in the union has been denied or terminated for any reason other than nonpayment of dues. It is for the government, not private bodies, to determine the manpower requirements for each occupation. This applies equally to the professions. The federal government ought to establish objective qualifications and entrance requirements for admission. The state system of professional admission is confusing, burdensome, subversive of merit, and incompatible with an economy that is national in scope and cannot be compartmentalized.[30]

Labor itself in its most progressive sectors is already indicating an awareness of the impact of the developments indicated on collective bargaining. While the leaders of craft unionism can afford to concentrate on wages and conditions of employment of their membership, the leaders of mass industrial unions cannot remain indifferent to any aspect of industry, including price structure, efficiency measures, finance, production controls, and the competitive position of the industry. The trend in the evolution of collective bargaining is toward an expanding range of subjects to be included within the proper sphere of the negotiators. In severely competitive industries, such as the needle trades and coal, the unions have been the greatest stabilizing force. It is no accident that by the end of the war the C.I.O. was demanding the establishment of industry councils for each of the basic and mass production industries, to be composed of representatives of management, unions, and government. The function of these councils was to plan for the industries during reconversion. It is also other than fortuitous that the C.I.O., as well as industrial unionism generally, has made greater strides in the direction of political action than have the craft unions. The logic of industrial organization leads to government participation in industry and labor interest in politics.

Collective bargaining has and will accomplish a lot toward increasing workers' security. Regularization of employment through the elimination of seasonal fluctuations is one goal toward which labor and management increasingly direct their attention. Concomitant with that is the guaranteed annual wage. But it is futilitarian to rely on collective bargaining to furnish our people adequate social security and full employment. Collective bargaining is not a substitute for a planned economy. Only the state through a planned economy can provide for full employment. Emphasis remains on politics.

CHAPTER XVI

Labor's Role in Politics

1. RETROSPECT AND PROSPECT

Labor's role in politics is sure to become one of the chief issues of any campaign and one around which swirl the emotions, hopes, and fears, synthetic and otherwise, of fervid partisanship. To some extent the sound and fury aroused by labor's major participation in the 1944 election was a bit surprising. Yet it did not set a precedent. Labor has always been in politics.[1] The Knights of Labor were definitely oriented toward political policy and action. And even the conservative American Federation of Labor, which has always emphasized its preoccupation with purely industrial trade-union policies, has not abjured political action. Samuel Gompers's injunction to labor "to reward your friends and punish your enemies" certainly was not a call to political teetotalism. Of course, he advised against labor's organizing into a separate party or forming a permanent alliance with one of the two major parties; but that injunction addresses itself to the method of political action rather than to a negation in principle of such action. Indeed, the A.F.L. on all levels of organization has never been frugal in handing out endorsements to political candidates of both parties even for the same office in local, state, and federal elections. Nor, on the other hand, can it be noted that candidates for public office ever felt reluctant to seek or accept such endorsement. Labor's Educational and Political League is A.F.L.'s answer to the Taft-Hartley Act.

What was significant about labor's participation in the 1944 election campaign was that at least one great branch of labor's fighting family was implementing its endorsement of political candidates with elaborate organizational work along the lines of political machines from the bottom up. But even in this respect C.I.O.'s Political Action Committee was not a first. Labor's Non-Partisan League, organized in 1936 by the C.I.O. under the presidency of John L. Lewis, had as its immediate paramount aim the re-election of President Roosevelt. But it also had plans for throwing labor's political weight around— plans which it sought to execute along pragmatic lines. In New York the league gave impetus to the organization of the American Labor party, which gave promise of acquiring the balance of power between the Democratic and Republican parties until the Communist fight for control sapped its strength. In other industrial states too the league entered the arena of practical politics, though not with signal success. The league received its coup de grâce after the 1940 presidential election when John L. Lewis backed Mr. Willkie and was jolted into the realization that labor leadership does not necessarily encompass political leadership even among one's own dues-paying miners.

Even in the 1944 campaign C.I.O.'s P.A.C. was not the only one of its kind. Little noticed in the national limelight was Dave Beck's well-established machine alliance between labor and the Democratic local organization.

Included in the happy family of labor for Roosevelt was the Liberal party of New York, which consists of the right-wingers who broke away from the American Labor party when the latter came under the control of the Communists in 1944. Though not based exclusively on labor, its nucleus was the International Ladies' Garment Workers whose president is shrewd, capable David Dubinsky.

Yet in the center of the national limelight was C.I.O.'s PAC. This is true because it has been an organization on a national scale and represented the more aggressive and politically the more ambitious, though numerically the smaller, of the two labor branches.

The person most immediately responsible for the formation of P.A.C. is Representative Howard K. Smith of Virginia. The immediate occasion was the passage by Congress in June of 1943 over the President's veto of the Smith-Connally Act, which placed restrictions on labor's right to strike during the war and forbade contributions by unions in political elections. Galvanized into a realization that labor must become politically articulate to protect itself, the Executive Board of the C.I.O. organized the Political Action Committee at a meeting held in Washington on July 7, 1843. There is a parallel to this in British politics, where impetus to the development of the Labor party was furnished by the Taff-Vale and Osborne decisions of the House of Lords which sought to destroy or limit labor's industrial and political activities, respectively.

It will hardly be contradicted that Roosevelt's hold upon the labor vote did not depend upon the support of labor's leaders. American labor, which is heterogeneous, does not think of itself as a class. For these and other reasons the votes of even disciplined unions cannot be delivered by a labor leader. Miners will follow Lewis in strike action but would burn his effigy when he called upon them to vote against Roosevelt—as they did in 1940. American workers are not yet conditioned to look to their union leadership for political guidance. Those union members who were inclined to vote against Mr. Roosevelt were hardly persuaded to change their minds by Mr. Hillman. With the Roosevelt magic gone, P.A.C. participation in the 1946 campaign did not prevent a Republican landslide.

This is not to imply that P.A.C. and the other political bodies in labor have no function to perform. Their function, as that of any political machine or organization, is not primarily to change the minds of the voters but to get them out to register and vote in accordance with their wishes. And labor did help to mobilize its voting strength.

What of the future? Is labor participation in politics a transient phenomenon? If the premise is correct that the economic and political processes are becoming increasingly interpenetrated—and there is no reason to doubt its validity—then labor's participation in politics, and at a faster tempo, at that, is indicated. Autonomous collective bargaining, even on an industry-wide basis, is insufficient to cope with such problems of our economy as unemployment, social security, the price structure, monopoly, housing, and the like. Even foreign affairs are not strangers to the interests of labor. Exports and imports, for instance, are functions of our economy and complementary to our domestic problems. These are facts which are known to an increasing number of labor leaders, not only in the C.I.O. but also in the A.F.L. The pronouncements of David Dubinsky reveal a political consciousness no less sensitized and articulate than that of Mr. Murray. Were it not for the antagonisms and hostilities born of labor's strife, the A.F.L. leaders might have shown a greater readiness to endorse political action than we have been led to suspect.

The Taft-Hartley Act of 1947 administered a needed shock to labor, particularly the A.F.L., which should awaken it to the realization that organized labor's very survival as an effective collective bargaining instrument is not assured unless it presses forward its political action with greater intensity and persistence than it has ever deemed necessary or even possible.

There are two levels on which labor must be expected to participate in the political process: the administrative and the politico-elective. The two, though interrelated, are nevertheless distinct. The administrative phase encompasses labor representation on various administrative and executive agencies. Thus the National War Labor Board was a tripartite body composed of representatives of labor, employers, and the public. Other war agencies, though not formally organized on an interest-representation basis, nevertheless did provide for such representation. With multiplied government regulations and controls of the industrial process, administrative participation of economic interests, labor's, the farmer's, and management's, is going to increase in scope and power.[2]

Political consciousness, however, should not lead logically to the political strike. This was invoked, according to reports, on one occasion to cause the government to bring back our troops from overseas. This is a strike against government action which has no relation to the employer-employee relationship. As such it would appear not to be protected by the Labor-Management Relations Act[3] and constitutes a subversion of our democratic system. Government policy in foreign and domestic affairs must be determined and executed not in response to economic coercion but in response to persuasion. Neither labor's strike weapon nor the employer's economic action should serve as a veto of our government's military and political decisions.

Political consciousness of government policy must of necessity encompass interest in the nomination and election of members of the legislative and executive branches of the government who would promulgate policies favored by labor and oppose policies deemed detrimental to labor. It is therefore to be expected that labor's participation in politics is neither a transient phenomenon nor will it lapse into the casual, sporadic, innocuous phase of "endorsement" typical of the past. How soon these external conditions will become transmuted into the consciousness and drives of labor leaders it is difficult to gauge.

2. TECHNIQUES AND FORMS OF POLITICAL ACTION

The form labor participation in elections should take involves problems of the utmost importance to labor as well as to the public generally. These problems do not admit of easy solution or of a casual answer. They merit at least some analysis.

Will labor organize into a separate labor party? The question has thus far been answered in the negative by labor, except for the Communist dominated small minority in back of the Wallace candidacy in 1948. Even from long-range perspective it is unlikely that a separate labor party will in the United States be the mold of political action by labor. The presidential form of government and the electoral college render it possible only for parties commanding large voting masses nationally distributed to capture the Presidency and thus control government administration.[4] It should also be noted that state election laws make it rather difficult for new and small political parties to get on and to remain on the ballot.

It is true that the American Labor party and the Liberal party, both of New York, may be cited as refutations of labor's disinclination to organize along third-party lines. But only superficially is this so. Neither of these parties has been a real party offering voters a separate set of candidates, until the purged A.L.P. backed Wallace. Rather, they have been organized and have since operated as coalition bodies supporting the candidates of one or the other of the two major parties in New York. They were organized to appeal to a large block of voters in New York who were conditioned against belonging to either of the two major "bourgeois" parties. The Socialist party has been the chief victim of this strategy.

Labor's rejection of the third-party strategy will save it from the utopian, messianic impotence that is the fate of the Socialist party in America. By working with and through the major parties, labor will give hostages to the principle that politics is the art of the possible. A well-organized and closely-knit labor action in the major parties would afford labor an opportunity for leverage to achieve an influential and powerful role. Party machines subsist on control over a small minority of voters. They are therefore particularly vulnerable to the attack of a well-disciplined bloc of voters. Nothing sinister is implied when the assertion is made that the potentialities of a well-articulated labor vote are incalculable.

But if labor is not to dissipate its strength it must concentrate its activity in one or the other of the two major parties. It might appear attractive to remain on the fence continuously and shift with the greatest of ease to the party offering the most at a particular time. Such a policy might even deliver some immediate returns. But from long-range considerations it is calculated to end in ineffectualness. It is easy to change endorsements. It is slightly harder to change the direction of even a small well-disciplined group. Even the Communist party has lost a few of its riders every time it has made a change in the line of its zigzag course. Men live by symbols. In politics these are called party labels. If labor wants to muster mass support, it cannot keep shifting that mass from one party to the other. The inertia is too great. Labor's voters, no less than others, need conditioning to a specific label. It is better for labor in the long run to be on the losing end of a primary fight and remain in the party than to change parties when a loss is sustained in the primaries. Party floaters rarely gain influence.

Another problem that must be considered in evaluating labor's long-range political activity is the division in labor's ranks, principally the conflict between the A.F.L. and the C.I.O. The problem of lack of unity in American labor is not that all the legitimate unions do not belong to the same federation or that more than one union claims membership in the same industry. Just such a situation obtains in

Great Britain without giving rise to the internecine warfare characteristic of the American scene. The real difficulty is that no modus vivendi has yet been reached by the various branches of the labor movement in the United States. The bitter struggle for sheer survival among the various competing unions still exists. As long as this condition continues, labor's influence and effectiveness in political action will at best be severely limited.

Perhaps even more menacing to the political effectiveness of American labor than the fight between the A.F.L. and the C.I.O. are the everlasting attempts of the Communists to obtain control of the American labor movement. There is no need or space to go into an examination of the trojan-horse, infiltrational techniques developed by the Communists to gain power in any organization. They are too well known through sheer recurrence of their application. If the formula is so frequently successful, it is not because there is any great mystery about it but because men are so prone to sacrifice long-term considerations for the lure of short-term expediency. These "realists" should be well advised that, if the party line at a certain period calls for supporting a particular cause, such help will be forthcoming without a quid pro quo. But even the short-term benefits are illusory, for the taint of communism immediately places every liberal and labor organization and activity on the defensive, and alienates more support than can be derived from Communist participation.

More important, Communist infiltration into any organization is aimed solely at obtaining control of the organization for converting it into an instrument of Communist policy. An organization which manages to escape is weakened at best and frequently fatally injured. The history of popular-frontism is eloquent testimony to the truth of this proposition.

Just as conservative and business organizations have been the happy hunting grounds of fascism, so have labor and liberal organizations been reserved for the special attention of Communists. This practice is in line with the established policy of communism to eliminate all competitive forces and parties from the left of center. Hence the fratricidal conflict with the Socialists. The danger of communism to America is not that it will become strong enough to achieve power, but that it will so weaken and demoralize the liberal and labor forces, in part through the promotion of irreconcilable conflicts, that the path of fascism will be made a highway. It happened in Germany; it can happen here. No army can effectively fight the enemy when it is riddled with a fifth column. In order to fight reaction successfully, liberalism must constantly be on guard against the infiltration of Communists.

Impinging upon all other problems discussed is the relationship of labor organizations to labor's political activities. Whatever form labor's political action takes—whether through a separate party, through one of the major parties, or on a nonpartisan basis—the master question will have to be answered: what should be the connection between the union and labor's political action? So fundamental is this inquiry that it involves a reconsideration of the nature of labor organization, its function in our society, and the character of political parties.

We may best examine the problem against the background of an actual case study of labor participation in politics. In 1936 John L. Lewis's United Mine Workers contributed half a million dollars to the Democratic party for the re-election of President Roosevelt. Also Labor's Non-Partisan League was operated for the same purpose by the C.I.O. By 1940 Lewis had undergone a change of heart in regard to Roosevelt, the reasons for which are irrelevant in this connection. As a result, Lewis backed Republican candidate Willkie. In doing so he called upon and ordered his miners and mine officials to work and vote for Willkie. The command set in motion an intra-union and interunion explosion whose consequences are not yet spent. The rank and file of the miners did not follow Lewis's order but voted overwhelmingly for Roosevelt. Their defiance of Lewis's dictation was demonstrably flaunted at union meetings throughout the mining country. Some mine union leaders, including international officers Philip Murray and John Brophy, as well as certain district officials openly declared their continued support of Roosevelt. These leaders were purged from the Union by Lewis. After the election the C.I.O., which also supported Roosevelt, accepted Lewis's resignation as president. Lewis then withdrew his union from the C.I.O., and there was added another interminable series of bitter jurisdictional disputes. Even the miners' union is not yet free from the effects of the political dispute.

This case exhibits a number of characteristics which are inherent in union participation in politics. First and foremost is the fact that bitter divisive dissensions are bound to arise within and among unions as a result of political action. As long as the interest of labor organizations in politics is limited to promoting a legal atmosphere favorable to their functioning in the industrial sphere, the danger of dissension is minimized though not completely eliminated. But with the broadening of the interest to include every aspect of domestic and foreign policy the chances for dissension are infinitely multiplied, for the issues are highly controversial.[5]

The interunion and intra-union dissensions so detrimental to union strength may be paralleled by the danger to the process of collective bargaining when political action is made part of the process. From the pamphlet *Guide to Political Action* issued by the C.I.O. United Electrical, Radio and Machine Workers of America in 1944, the following excerpt is taken:

> *Labor-Management Committees.* Labor management committees, already in operation or which will be set up in the future, can also be made to serve the cause of political action. These committees seek to increase war production for victory. Enlightened, win-the-war managements will agree that a win-the-war Congress helps production. Such managements will agree that political action on the part of all voters is necessary to elect such a Congress, as well as other public officials.
>
> The Labor-Management committee, in addition to its regular functions, can encourage the registration of new voters, conduct in-plant registration, support the passage of legislation which will liberalize voting laws, and carry on any action which will remove enemies of national unity from production for war. They must also serve the cause of orderly transition to production for peace. The best guarantee of such an orderly and rapid transition is political action of employees and employers alike.[6]

Some employers might be amused if not happy to hear that they have been included in the new popular front of "political action of employees and employers alike." But suppose some employers do not see eye to eye with the union representatives as to who are the "enemies of national unity." Would the U.E.W. consent to the employer's using labor-management committees, grievance procedures, and employee meetings for the purpose of promoting his own favorite set of candidates and policies not approved by the U.E.W.? Were the employer to do so, he might be violating certain state statutes which were adopted to stop the employer from using his economic power to interfere with the freedom of his employees in political elections.

It has been reported that officials of the Amalgamated Clothing Workers did, in 1944, solicit employers with whom the union had collective agreements for contributions to P.A.C. The understanding of a quid pro quo in some form or other may intrude itself coercively here on the part of both the employer and the union. Recognition of this fact is evidenced by a provision in the constitution of Dubinsky's International Ladies' Garment Workers Union prohibiting solicitation of contributions from employers for union causes. Some union officials have been disciplined for violating this provision.

If union political action is to be subsumed as part of the collective bargaining process, the political complexion of the particular union will be impressed upon the workers of the industry over which it claims jurisdiction. The tendency of continued political action will be to proliferate unions along political lines. Would it be a contribution to American unity to have Republican, Democratic, Socialist, Communist, and Catholic unions—a situation which would parallel the European experience?[7] Is it compatible with democratic principles for a worker to be compelled to give his support to a political party favored by the union which he joins when he enters a certain industry? Of course, the individual union member cannot be compelled to vote as the union leader wants him to, as Lewis found out to his dismay. But funds from the union treasury and the work of his union officers to which he contributes may go toward the support of a political program and candidates whom he may wish to oppose. Should a union card involve all these obligations? It is no answer to say that the majoritarian principle of democracy sanctions it, and this for several reasons. For one, membership in a union, our economic citizenship, could justifiably become as widespread as political citizenship. The greater majority of all workers under collective agreements are covered by some form of union security. For them, and even for those not under union security contracts, union membership is part of the industrial environment which they must either accept or to which they must adjust themselves. Should industrial citizenship determine the obligations of political citizenship?

Invoking the majoritarian principle raises the question: a majority of whom? of the union members or of the union officials? Certainly Lewis's support of Willkie in 1940 was not made after obtaining a mandate from the union membership or even from the union leadership. Such conduct can be justified only on the principle that the head of the union knows best at all times what is good for the union politically—obviously an empirically untenable position and politically certain to accelerate the trend toward public regulation of labor unions, as part of the election apparatus of the state.

One of the first proposals that might be suggested would make the political choice of the union dependent upon a majority determination of its membership. Although in accordance with democratic principles of control, such a procedure would be open to other objections. Principally, a decision by the majority of the membership would be sabotaged by a hostile union leadership. If we make union leadership responsible for both industrial and political policy we create explosive situations where a vote of confidence may be obtained in one field but not in the other. The miners who rejected Lewis's political leadership in 1940 and in 1944 have since followed his lead in strikes.

The conclusion is tentatively indicated that perhaps the union is not the most suitable apparatus for political expression by labor. We do not expect a labor union by a majority vote to determine what church the members must support. Even the state, the democratic state, is not looked upon as a reservoir of all societarian activities and functions. And this is true even though we do not accept the pluralistic as opposed to the monistic theory of sovereignty.[8] For the avoidance of indicated inner conflicts, and for consideration of democratic efficiency, it may be best to have a separation of the political and industrial functions. Such institutions as labor unions, farm organizations, chambers of commerce, and employer associations—which exercise economic functions, frequently on an administrative level, and hold considerable power over their constituent membership—are not, it may be suggested, the most appropriate arbiters of the politics of their membership.

This does not ignore the fact that economic interest must of necessity find expression in the political realm. Labor must and should be politically active. But in the election phase as distinguished from the administrative level, the expression must be through an organization independent of the union apparatus in fact as well as in form. Such an organization should have nonlabor elements. It may have its strongest support among the leaders and the rank and file of unions; yet not law but tradition, the ultimate architect even of political mores, must guarantee that the separation will be genuine. Such an organization will, it is true, be handicapped because it will depend financially on small individual contributions. This is a substantial handicap, as was proved in the case of the British Labor party after the general strike of 1926 when a law was passed making it necessary for union members expressly to authorize contributions: to "contract in." But this did not prevent the British Labor party from winning power in 1945. The slush funds in political campaigns always come from the right. But, in compensation, the political organization for labor action will not be geared to the considerations of status quo, always animating such vested interests as labor unions, which must be preoccupied with the day-to-day business of a going concern. The domination of the British Labor party by the trade unions has not contributed to the stature of the party in or out of office. There is nothing in the record of the Bevins, the Attlees, or the Morrisons to lend pride and fire the imagination of mankind looking for guidance to a new statesmanship.

The practicalities of labor leadership will, then, be leavened with the cultivated imagination and expert competence of the liberal intelligence which otherwise could not be tapped within the narrow confines of a labor union. Such an independent organization, not exclusively or even chiefly of a labor character, would make it easier to fuse labor with the liberal middle classes into effective coalitions within the framework of the major mass parties.

What has been said here should not be construed as approving the Taft-Hartley Act prohibition of political contributions and expenditures by labor organizations "in connection with any election . . . or in connection with any primary election or political convention or caucus" for a federal office. The provision is so broad in scope that it might encompass prohibitions against union newspapers' "commenting favorably or unfavorably upon candidates or issues in national elections," as President Truman declared in his veto message. This and other applications may well infringe upon the constitutional guarantees of free speech and press.

The sole restriction on political contributions by unions that is contemplated in the province of the administrative state is contained in the declaration that unions should have the right to make contributions in political campaigns if these are authorized by a majority of the membership and if those voting against authorization are not assessed.

The analysis made and the problems indicated are not the overly fastidious preoccupations with the punctilios of means at the expense of ends. By all means it is desirable to direct our steps to the brave new world, but to do so it is important to make sure that the road leads in that direction.

BOOK FOUR

Law and Government in the Administrative State

CHAPTER XVII

The Role of Law and Government

1. CONCEPTS AND MEANINGS

We have examined the chief forces in society that have influenced the nature and evolution of the state, and of social orders and political systems.[1] We now approach the analysis of the structure and function of the state organization itself—government and law. So intrinsic are goverment and law to the organization of the state that in the popular mind they are virtually inseparable; certain political theory has identified state with government,[2] traditional political science has limited the range of its interest to the study of government, and law has become stamped as the peculiar product and province of the state.[3]

The state, like every other organization, gives rise to two manifestations in its operation as an organization. One is a definition of the state's structure, functions, and instrumentalities, and their interrelationship, as well as that of the interests and elements composing the community as among themselves and in reference to the state, in the context of the state's total environment. This is the law of the state organization. Since a state is a controlled system of power, its law constitutes the analysis of its power system.[4] The other manifestation of the state as an organization is that it necessarily evolves instrumentalities or agencies for discharging its functions. These instrumentalities constitute the government of the state.

Since the functions of a state are ultimately determined by the power relationship within a state, government and law are interrelated. They reflect the sovereignty of the state—the resultant of the crosscurrents of forces influencing government policy—which refers not alone to the formal documents, but to the totality of constitutions, statutes, court decisions, administrative rulings, customs, practices, and government institutions that exist in a state. Their history also mirrors the past evolutions of the state in power structure and function as well as the history of civilization.[5] This is neither fortuitous nor exaggerated. Since man's society is dynamic and the history of man is the tale of his quest for mastery over his physical and social environment, the evolution of the state, man's all-encompassing organization, parallels that fateful struggle and the resultant social forces.

In the study of politics we must ever be concerned that we are dealing both with inanimate forces and with human drives, with our machine civilization and with human habits and traditions. We must ever seek for a synthesis of the rational and the irrational in human affairs.

Emphasis must remain on the individual as the primary unit for observation in political analysis. Society has no being, no existence apart from the individuals who compose it. Conceiving of the state as an organization permits us to discover principles of development of society as a system of power composed of individuals, while it avoids the fantastic efflorescence of the organismic theories of the state represented by Spencer, Bluntschli, and others, which conceive of society and of the state as an integrated biological organism.[6] The ultimate objection to this theory is that society has no mind, no life apart from its component individuals, while in a biological organism the component cells and parts have no life apart from the whole organism. Human society does not even have the automatic cohesiveness of insect society.[7] Nevertheless, the state in its development and functioning does bear more than accidental and metaphoric resemblance to an organism. Both belong to the general category of power organizations, although probably at polarized extremes of stages of development. In all types of organization the laws of canalization of power may be the same or at least similar even though the pattern may differ with the stages of development. The principles of ways and means, of power and responsibility, of ebb and flow, of action and reaction, of centralization and diffusion, of viability, morbidity, and pathology of power may be the same for all organizations in differing contexts of circumstances.

2. THE MECHANISM OF CONTROL: POWER AND RESPONSIBILITY

The state as the over-all organization of the community is the chief focus for the community's efforts to adjust itself to its total environment. The rapid advances in science and technology have greatly accelerated the rate and accumulation of changes in the physical environment and have rendered the social environment both intra- and interstate more fluid in character.

While the state must increasingly keep adjusting itself to a constantly changing complex environment, it must perform its fundamental purpose or function of survival, that is, of maintaining control over its system of power. The mechanism of integration or control cannot be performed without decision. In the dictatorial state, where opposition is outlawed, this is done chiefly through the medium of physical force. In the democratic state through the right of opposition the struggle for power expresses itself in any form of power exclusive of violence. The integrative function of the democratic state is obviously more difficult and more subtle than that of an autocracy. It must constantly maintain a balance of power to prevent the struggle for power from spilling over into violence. Where it does not succeed its existence is placed in danger. In biology, the uncontrolled growth of cancer cells is deadly to the organism. Where the balance of power is successfully maintained, the state is characterized by stability. But to remain stable the state must be constantly dynamic, for its composition and total environment are forever in a state of flux. Not a static but a fluid balance of power is most conducive to the stability of society. In the ideal commonwealth the dynamism of the state would be in exact proportion to the rate of change in the total environment. But this of course is not to be achieved in actual society. Because of men's habits, traditions, vested interests, lack of security, and other factors, change is greatly resisted in society in all fields and there is a constant lag between change and adjustment.[8] Politics is no exception.

In politics, vested interests loom largest perhaps as a cause for resistance to change, if that appears to threaten the power status of those affected. But the lag between change and adjustment in politics is pronounced even without the factor of vested interest.

Cancer spares no class or group. Rich and poor, the high placed and the humble, congressmen and their constituents—none is immune from this scourge of mankind. There is no vested interest in cancer. Yet cancer research must still depend on inadequate private contributions instead of sufficient government appropriations. Why can't we mobilize our talent for cancer research as we have done in atomic energy and for other war purposes? Does humanity lack the imagination to appreciate danger unless it is visible, immediate, certain, and drastic?

The scales of social psychology are heavily weighted in favor of conservatism, and adjustment is expected to fall behind change. Nevertheless, this lag cannot be permitted to widen, for maladjustment then ensues, which in its more pathological expression may result in disabling disease or even in mortality.

The need for adjustment by the state to an ever-changing total environment raises the problem of the establishment and maintenance of control. The relationship or connection between those who command and those who obey, in so far as the execution of the command is concerned, may be characterized as responsiveness or sensitiveness. The degree of control achieved may be deemed to be in direct proportion to the responsiveness of the agent or subordinate to the command of the superior or principal. Responsiveness is significant both in point of time and in exactness of execution of the command.

In management organizations, and particularly in the state, responsiveness is expressed through the power of the principal and the responsibility of the agent. In both autocratic and democratic states there exists the problem of power and responsibility. In dictatorships, power resides in the rulers and flows down in the pyramid toward the ruled, while responsibility or obedience is the duty of the ruled and flows upward to the ruling elite. In representative democracies, power resides among the various pyramids of power of which the people are composed and flows upward to the personnel of the government, while responsibility is the lot of the government and flows down to the people. To the extent that this pattern exists in actuality the government is either autocratic or democratic.[9] Where the government in a democracy through one cause or another loses responsibility for action or lacks the power to act it is paralyzed. If the situation demands prompt and vigorous action, failure to act may result in catastrophe.

There can be no responsiveness unless power flows from the one in command to the one executing it. But that power has two aspects: power to perform the task to which the command relates and power to bind the subordinate to perform the task in accordance with the will of the superior. The latter aspect is expressed in the superior in his power of control and in the subordinate in his duty of responsibility. Every organization, including the state, has to deal constantly with the problems of transmission of power to subordinates to execute commands and enforcement of responsibility for execution. Because in the modern world the problems that we have to deal with demand great concentration of power in the government, the surpassing issue of modern representative government is how to reconcile powerful government with responsible government, authority with freedom. In this connection the dichotomy between power to act and power to control is of greatest significance.

The problem of power and responsibility will be dealt with in its various manifestations.

CHAPTER XVIII

Political Integration of the State

1. THE STAGES AND PROCESS OF INTEGRATION

A dynamically planned economy, which is of the essence of the administrative state, raises the problem of the political integration of the state, for economic integration is geared to the extent to which the state has evolved as a political unit. Planning for a national economy impinges directly on our federal system. In order to gauge this influence we must ascertain the nature and evolution of federalism and its relationship to freedom and democracy, and to the problem of power and responsibility in government.

The problem of power and responsibility is involved in the very process of integration of the state as a unit, which in the form of federalism has loomed so large and portentously in American political and constitutional history and spilled over at least once into military annals. But the phenomenon is not peculiar to American soil, though it has manifested here its most extravagant growth. It is germinal to the growth pattern of states. It is a manifestation of the tendency of organizations to expand in size, in intensity, and particularly in concentration of power.

The stages of integration may be roughly identified as alliances of individual states, leagues, confederations, federations, and unitary states. In alliances, a common interest is found in the need for safety against a common foreign menace. Hence only external security is the prime interest and cohesive force of that stage which keeps the allied powers together. The business of the alliance is discharged through government representatives of the component states. If the alliance proves durable, a league may emerge with a permanent body to deal with the common interest. This body is composed of the representatives of the member state of the league. Perhaps a more integrated form than a league is a confederation, which is brought about when common nationalism, economic interests, and other factors supplement external security as cementing material for the expanding state. But a confederation is still essentially a composition of states which retain their identity, for the government of a confederation is still an assembly of representatives of the member states. If a confederation does not fall apart or is not destroyed by outside military pressure, it passes the critical stage of coalescence and becomes a federation, which has the sine qua non criterion of a real state: in its proper sphere of functions a federation does not act through the government representatives of the component states but has direct jurisdiction over its subjects or citizens. Yet in a federal state the central government does not perform all the functions of the state, but only those which are deemed of common interest, such as external security and commerce, the governments of the component states retaining functions presumably of only local interest. In the course of time the centripetal forces of society lead to an ever greater concentration of power in the central government, resulting in the emergence of a unitary state, whether or not officially recognized as such. In the unitary state, the authority of the state and the functions it performs are concentrated in one government, and not divided between the co-ordinate central and local governments, as is the case in federal states.[1]

This is the endemic, or autonomous, pattern of the political growth and integration of states. Where the endemic evolution is complicated by conquest, then the resulting expanded state may not be federal but unitary, for conquest leads to domination, since the tendency of men is not to relinquish power willingly. Absent the factor of conquest, the pattern of evolution from diffusion to integration of the locus of authority is universal and aboriginal. When the unicellular family state began to break up and expand into sibs, gentes, and tribes, the superior units evolved in accordance with the indicated cycle. Even the city-states of classical antiquity and of the Renaissance were no exception and passed the shadings of federalism before they became unitary. The history of the structure of their government exhibits the traces of their development. The early basis of representation in the Roman senate and in the upper chambers of other classical cities of the Mediterranean was tribal, not individual, reflecting the formation of city-states out of converging tribal states.[2]

2. THE AMERICAN PATTERN

The endemic pattern of political integration has strikingly impressed itself on American history. British colonial rule endowed the American colonies with a common cultural, economic, national, and political background, and furnished a common foreign menace to bring the colonies together in the War of Independence. The Articles of Confederation that followed victory could not remain static. The loose confederation gave way to a genuine federal state, for the centripetal forces already mentioned were stronger than the centrifugal particularism that was operating. The process of integration continued unabated after the Republic was founded to the present day, though not in a straight line. Originally only the House of Representatives of the branches of the federal government was elected by popular vote on a nonstate basis of representation. In the course of time the political changes that have taken place were in the direction of national representation. Although in the United States Senate the principle of equal state representation remains, the Constitutional Amendment providing for popular election of senators served to free that body from control by the state official hierarchies. A similar result has been obtained in regard to the Presidency through the development of the party system, and the consequent actual election of the President by popular vote, although the electoral college election fiction and the state unit rule are still retained.

Even more impressive than in representation has been the integration trend in government function. Despite periods of serious judicial and political obstacles, the over-all historical picture is one of inexorable accretion of power and functions to the federal government and a progressive atrophy of state government.[3]

What is responsible for this compulsive tendency to integration? Fundamentally, our technical advances in communication and industry, resulting in division of labor on a continental scale, made the United States one nation and indivisible. The quest for power operated to provide political integration to parallel the economic sphere. From the beginning of our national life until the turn of the century it was the commercial interests whose quests for power, spearheaded by the genius of Hamilton, promoted national integration through the formation and expansion of the Union.[4] When the growth of national corporate power succeeded in freeing itself from effective state regulation, it was the people, as farm groups, labor, and small business, that became the apostles of national integration.

The revivification of the cry for states' rights should not be mistaken for a renaissance of state government. It has served in the past and will be used in the future as a political rationalization of vested economic and social interests at the expense of the national and popular welfare. Our economy is national and demands uniform treatment, and therefore only the federal government can effectively and salubriously regulate it. Our industrial concerns and labor unions are national in scope. What a horrible mess the states would create in the bargaining process if they proceeded to set up forty-eight different types of union regulations and other requirements in employer-employee relations. Only when state regulations are in harmony with the corresponding federal prototypes can they be of benefit.[5] The Taft-Hartley Act abandons the principle of the uniform application of the federal law in at least one respect. It would waive the application of its union security provisions in states where greater restrictions exist. This invitation to chaos and industrial strife constitutes a regressive step in the evolution of our form of government. What justification is there for the confusion that now exists in the conflicting state divorce laws, tax laws, admission to professional practice, and state social security systems?

The inadequacy of our public school system, particularly because of the scandalously low pay for teachers, will not be remedied until the federal government assumes financial responsibility for education. Federal intervention is not incompatible with sectarian education. A good case may be made out for integrating religious education with the public school system or making it supplementary to it. Segregation of children on the basis of sectarianism is no more in the public good than segregation on the basis of race or color, and the result is detrimental even though the segregation is not compulsory. It is not a denial of the value of cultural diversification or of religious freedom to affirm that it might lessen racial and religious prejudice, if during their most impressionable years children of various cultural environments were to share common contacts, institutions, and cultural influences.[6]

Uniform state laws are inadequate, for forty-eight political subdivisions cannot regulate an integrated economic unit. Nor is it intelligent to set up an interstate system of law and government to rival the federal. This is not to deny the value of localism and regionalism. Municipalities are viable political units, for they perform useful cultural and governmental functions on a local scale. It is also true that economic planning would duly recognize the necessity for regional economic development. But states do not correspond to either local or regional boundaries or interests.

3. FUNCTIONAL FEDERALISM UNDER PLANNING

Economic planning in the administrative state would further increase the functions and importance of the central government. In the framework of democratic controls this should enhance and not weaken the enjoyment of our freedoms. There is no necessary connection between democracy and federalism or between a unitary state and dictatorship. The English, French, and Scandinavian countries have enjoyed both democracy and highly centralized and unitary systems, while imperial Germany and the dictator-ridden South American republics have been federal. The history of the United States does not lend support to the contention that local government is democratic and centralized government is dictatorial. Boss rule and maladministration have been more characteristic of the state and city governments than of the federal government. The reason for this is that, contrary to general assumption, the federal government is closer to the voter than are the state and local governments. The Platonic and Aristotelian[7] assumption that democracy could flourish only in direct form and locally within narrow geographical limits, such as the Greek city-state, has been exploded by modern technology. The press, radio, and other means of communication, as well as the fact that the important issues of government which vitally affect our lives gravitate increasingly from the local to the national and international fields, have completely invalidated that view. We may not know the name of our councilman or of our state legislator, but we have managed to keep up with the Roosevelts. We know much more about what is going on in Washington than in our state capitals. For that reason alone it should be easier to keep the central government more responsive to democratic control than state officials, for attention leads to information, the basis of supervision and control.

There is great need for evolving projects to obtain greater participation by citizens on all levels of the complex government of today. But the functions of the federal government offer greater opportunities for that than do those of the states. Our war experience ought to be studied for clues to a methodology for combining centralized direction with local participation.

As the trend of events concentrates more and more controls and functions in the federal government, the problem of decentralization assumes focal interest. Administrative considerations alone demand progress toward decentralization. But that problem can be solved best within the framework of the central government, not in the federal system. The proper rationalization of administration in terms of centralized planning, direction, and supervision, with a certain measure of decentralized autonomy in execution, can be accomplished only when the central authority has control over the circumference of power. In our constitutional federal system, where the states and the national government are co-ordinate, no such reliable and endurable co-operative integration can be achieved. Rivalry between state and federal officials offer interminable sources of dispute. The difficulties between TVA and the local political machines are not accidental.

Because the states are no longer suited as agencies of control over a national economy, they can no longer serve as laboratories for social experiments as fully as some states like Wisconsin and New York did serve during the first quarter of our century. The federal government in co-operation with the municipalities can best undertake needed experimental programs.

The states have tended to become not reservoirs of progressive thought and action but strongholds of local prejudice and reaction. The preservation of our very civil and political liberties has come to depend on the intervention of the federal government even in the state administration of justice and conduct of elections. It is to the federal government that racial minorities have come to look for the protection of their elementary economic and social rights, and even life itself. The reason why the government representing the nation is less likely to be subservient to a particular discriminatory influence is that local prejudice becomes diluted in a more generalized confluence. This is of salutary effect in a democracy, for in that type of state the government is more likely to reflect the prevailing sentiments of the community than in a dictatorship. The Soviet government was able to outlaw anti-Semitism and other forms of racial discrimination. Without detracting from this laudable measure one may inquire to what extent this policy has taken hold in the population. According to available information, the Ukrainian population actively collaborated with the Germans in exterminating the Jews. It may well be that the rate of change in emotional attitudes of populations is no faster in a dictatorship than in a representative state.[8] This is no argument against using government measures to eliminate racial discrimination, but it underscores the value of using federal action which is not so rooted to local prejudice as is local government.

When the Supreme Court declared the Wagner Act a constitutional exercise of national power over interstate commerce, it ended politically induced paralysis of government which endangered our democracy by depriving the national government of capacity to deal with the economic crisis. This paralysis was the cumulative result of judicial decisions over several decades. The result was a crisis. Now we are in a judicially sanctioned era of functional federalism in which the central government has the power and the responsibility to act in matters of national concern.[9]

Centralization of power is not per se dictatorial. It all depends on the character of the controls over the government. We will not render safe but will endanger our freedoms by denying our central government the power to act. We can defend them only by retaining control over the central government to make certain that the delegated power is executed in accordance with the popular mandate.

Because of the national character of our economic and social life, federalism has served its purpose in the United States. In its role as a synthesizer of local particularism and the general interest, it has a great future on a world stage to coalesce racial, national, economic, and political entities into ever greater units culminating in the world state.

CHAPTER XIX

Differentiation of Government and Law

1. DIFFERENTIATION OF FUNCTIONS AND FORMS

The problem of power and responsibility is not limited to the political integration of the state. It exists in the interrelationship of organs of government and of types of law. Understanding the pattern of these interrelationships is crucial to the task of effectuating a dynamically planned economy within the framework of freedom and democracy. However, before the interrelationships can be analyzed, it is essential to trace the differentiation and crystallization of the various types of law, and forms and organs of government from the simple family state to the present complex government mechanism. This evolution should throw a revealing light on the functions and limitations of the tools we are to use in fashioning a democratic administrative state.

Speculation about the nature of law has had as extravagantly luxurious a growth as has theorizing about the nature of the state.[1] In these related fields the varying concepts were inevitably conditioned by man's ideas about what the state and law should be and do. They have been rationalizations of man's quest for power in the framework of the total environment that prevailed when the philosophers' systems were constructed. Justice is what each man thinks he is entitled to; law is what he gets. Justice is what each man wants from society; law is what society accords him. Obviously, justice is subjective; law is objective. Since law is what exists and justice is man's idea of what law should be, man in his struggle for justice has attempted to conceive of law in the special image of his own drives and in the cultural symbolism of his age. Just as in the case of the nature of the state, speculation about the nature of law has tended to equate certain sanctions, agencies, sources, and types of law with the whole phenomenon of law.[2] But law throughout history and at any particular period is a highly variegated tapestry of forms.

Law, like the state, transcends any of its forms, sanctions, or any other manifestations connected with it. It can be understood only as a continuous process undergoing change in response to its interrelationship with its conditioning environment.

Law as an analysis of the power system composing the state shares the history and destiny of the state. The evolution of law is inseparable from the evolution of the state. As soon as a community becomes independently organized as a state, law thereby comes into existence, and the presence of law indicates the existence of a state. One without the other is inconceivable. Since the state is as old as society itself, law by definition should also be as old as society. The history of civilization and of primitive cultures discloses no evidence of the existence of a society without a system of laws.[3]

The form of the state is reflected in the character of its legal system. The first state, being a patriarchal and family state, was grounded in the same type of legal system. The undifferentiated family state was an absolutist, unlimited, hereditary monarchy. The source of its law was custom and its sanctions were a thick stew of magic, religion, and force.[4]

In the assemblage of family patriarchs when the family state began to evolve into the expanded state was the germ of representative government and of the legislature. It may or may not be true that the idea for the specific form of representation for the British Parliament came from Rome through Spain. But that does not negate the fact that wherever the familial state began to expand into the larger states the representative form of government was an evolutionary stage.[5]

The evolution of the representative system has been along two main lines. In regard to the representation principle proper the trend has been away from the representation of states as the process of federalism gave way to unitary states. Likewise, the process of democratization has led to the establishment of a nexus of control in the electorate and responsibility in the representative.

In regard to function the evolution has been equally decisive but more complex. Since only gradually did the functions of the assemblage of patriarchs displace those of the family states, their role in the field of internal security involved adjudication of disputes among the constituent families. The judicial function is thus the principal one of the postfamilial state in the realm of domestic policy. The only other one in that inchoate state which began to be differentiated was external security. Even when tort law was merged into the "King's Peace" and a wrong became a crime against the expanded state, adjudication was still the most important function of the government. One of the names of the English Parliament is the "High Court of Parliament." The judicial functions of the House of Lords are well known.[6]

Indeed, out of the adjudicatory power of the government developed the executive and legislative functions in the postfamilial state. As the expanded state became solidified and a criminal law emerged, the state became impressed with the function of enforcing and administering the laws. As the integrative power of the state, operating in an ever more complicated environment, added more and more services to the category of state functions, the executive organs of the government become crystallized and in turn diversified.

While the executive function emerged from the enforcement need of the adjudicatory power, the legislative function evolved from the process of promulgation of laws. The earliest source of law was custom, society's equivalent of habit, and the result of trial and error in man's adjustment to his environment.[7] When the elders became judges, custom was law. Since custom was anonymous, impersonal, and diffused, the idea gained currency that judges do not make law but merely apply it as they find it. There is no longer any need to argue the point that the judicial act involves lawmaking, whether the decision involves common law or interpretation of a statute or of a constitution. Nevertheless, the concept of the judiciary as simply an innocent vehicle for a superior will, be that deity, reason, the people, or the constitution, depending on the ideological sanctions of the times, has proved one of the most pertinacious legal fictions in history.[8] Although not the result of excogitation, it is extremely useful to the legal priesthood, for it leaves them full power in the premises without any responsibility for their action. It possesses also great attractiveness as a social doctrine. By giving law the ultimate sanction of society and making it immutable in appearance, it satisfies the human drive for security and makes the law acceptable to the community.

As the elders proceeded to adjudicate disputes, the lawmaking process began to emerge from the amorphous and unconscious stage into the more precise and conscious stage. But the abrupt mutative changes that have been the lot of states throughout their life histories could not be contained within the mold of gradualist legal evolution. They gave rise to legal codes, which by their very selectivity of subject matter, unlike the all-inclusive modern codes, proclaimed a reshuffling in the power relationship of the state. Most of them constituted innovations but in some the attempt to turn the clock back has left its imprint.[9] In time even code making proved inadequate as an instrument of adjustment to the needs of a changing environment. Both in ancient Rome and in England the rise of equity jurisdiction was to meet the needs of a changing environment which could not be fitted within the procrustean world of established legal procedures.[10] But in time equity too fell victim to the pathology of arteriosclerosis, which affects all human organizations. The haphazard, fitful, and occasional code making was transmuted into the regular and orderly procedure of statutory enactment. The emergence of the legislative process inaugurated a signal advance in the evolution of the state. It meant that the state had reached such a developed stage of integrative power that it could substitute for the slow, amorphous, planless, diffuse, and irresponsible judicial lawmaking, the planned, concentrated, quicker, and more responsible policymaking through promulgation of statutes. In place of the vague authority of custom and of the heaven-sent lawgiver the dominant will of the state was enthroned and thus authority and responsibility became tangible and localized in the governors. In the course of democratization of the power of the state the legislative process became responsive to the popular will. One of its chief manifestations is constitution making, in which the framework of the state and its government are determined.

The triumph of the legislative process has not, however, meant the supplanting and elimination of the judicial process. Every statute, constitution, and code becomes overlaid in time with a body of judge-made law in applying and interpreting them in the adjudicating process. Lawmaking oscillates in the cycle of diffusion leading to centralization and purposefulness, and then again to devolution.[11]

Dovetailing with and accentuating this cycle is the administrative process, whose universality in all types of highly developed states should be conclusive proof that it owes its existence not to a theory but to a condition.[12] That condition is the multiplicity of functions that the highly integrated state has to perform and the complex business that it has to manage or administer. The modern state is a creative state, a welfare state, an industrial state, and above all an administrative state, for in the performance of any of its functions administration is involved.[13] Government has come to be so much involved in business that government must be conducted as a business. For the conduct of the government's business the traditional techniques proved inadequate. The legislature could not possibly draft laws in the realm of economic and social activities which would be self-executing and undemanding of day-to-day application, adaptation, and rule making. This could not be performed by the courts, for many reasons. The diffuse, planless, nonexpert, litigious, adversary character of the judicial process having general jurisdiction, particularly when encased in the rigidity of encrusted rules of procedure, was ill adapted for purposes of planned management and flexible administration demanding expert specialization and uniformity of policy making and administration. Only the administrative bureau or tribunal combining the relevant features and techniques of the executive, legislative, and judicial processes could perform the tasks entrusted to modern government. In the development of the administrative agency, government reaches the climax in the evolvement of organization from the simple to the complex in structure and function and from the unconscious to the intentional and planned in objective. To the extent that our economy becomes a planned economy will administration gain in importance and lend its character to the whole state.

The development of administrative law has demonstrated that Sir Henry Maine's generalization that law has evolved "from Status to Contract"[14] needs qualification and is incomplete as a description of the growth pattern of law. The idea of contract is ingrained in man's cause and effect, stimulus and response psychology. It is operative in man's adjustment to his environment. In return for certain labor, the world affords him the wherewithal to satisfy his wants. Child behavior is conditioned on contract. Rachel will get a balloon if she keeps her promise to be a good girl. Contract was the nexus of primitive man's relationship to the strange and hostile world about him. It was the pattern of his religion and magic.[15] It is the essence of his propitiation of the deity. If the gods would fructify his lands, his cattle, and his mate, and would drive his enemies before him, he would offer them sacrifices and worship no others, a clear contractual quid pro quo. The Old Testament is replete with mutual promises between God and man. Man has ever tended to cover a coercive or organic situation with the fiction of contract. In return for "protection" by the racketeer the storekeeper promises to pay tribute. The formation of organized society or the state has been "explained" by the fiction of the "social contract."[16]

Nevertheless, it is true that in the highly concentrated and evolved familial state the individual's activities, rights and obligations were determined wholly by the state's "definition" of his status or position in society. As the familial state began to break up and merge into the expanded forms, the law tended to emancipate the individual from the obligations of the familial state and endow him with rights and duties as an individual citizen of the larger state. In consequence, the individual acquired rights of contract in matters which were formerly not left to his discretion. Thus far the development was from status to contract. But as the expanded state developed to ever greater integration of its environment, more and more of the individual's activities were regulated, and when the feudal state reached an advanced stage of evolution, society was again ruled by status, not by contract. It is interesting to observe that though status was the essence of the feudal relationship the ritualistic formula of the contract between the lord and the serf was retained. In return for the lord's promise of protection, the serf owed him certain services. This harks back to a period when contract did play a greater role in society although the fiction of freedom of contract tended to camouflage a relationship based on coercion. At the height of feudalism, the pattern of evolution was from status to contract to status.[17]

With the rise of capitalism and the enthronement of the laissez-faire state there occurred a return to contract, which became the legal basis of capitalism.[18] As the developing economic inequalities rendered freedom of contract a fiction, the state's integrative function has been called in more and more to redress the balance and to protect the weak against the depredations of the strong by hedging in the rights of contract with limitations and by defining the rights and obligations of individuals by law instead of leaving them to be determined by contract. The individual agreement between employer and employee must give way to the collective bargaining agreement.[19] The law is becoming socialized, and the evolution of administrative law is in a sense a response to and manifestation of this political phenomenon. We are reaching again the status stage in the legal cycle. Maine's thesis of a two-stage direct evolution is wrong. There is no universal straight-line evolution. There is a cycle of development depending on the integration by the state of the environment. With reference to a specific environment, the development is not from status to contract but the reverse, from contract to status. Historically, the cycle in broad outline has led from familial status to early contract, to feudal status, to capitalist contract, and now to administrative status. In the framework of our civilization man's freedom will find expression in collective and political organization, not in a fictitious freedom of contract. There is no freedom of contract or any other kind of freedom among unequals, without state intervention.[20]

Tracing the differentiation of governmental functions and legal systems would not be complete without some attention to the evolution of governmental forms. When the familial state began to expand, the absolutist hereditary monarchy of the patriarch gave way in the course of time to the gerontocratic representative government of the assembled patriarchs. Their power of adjudication may have been only mediatory at first, and then became compulsory as their control over the component states increased.[21] The process of state integration could not of course leave unaffected the diffused government of the elders. Where experience is the only school, age affords a presumption of wisdom and knowledge. But soon other characteristics of personality, position, and forms of power began to assert themselves in the competition for leadership.[22]

In the course of countless generations the loosely organized gerontocracy, producing temporary leadership for each emergency and activity, gave way to a monarchy. At first the monarch or chieftain may have been elective, particularly where conquest was not involved. But in time leadership became associated with certain families and became inheritable, as any other form of property. Once again, as in the familial state, authority is concentrated in a monarch who is absolute, at least in theory, and whose power is inherited. Whether the king is derived from the priesthood, warrior, or propertied classes, he soon becomes the "father" of his people, and at least nominally the religious head and the possessor of divine rights.[23]

The business of government of the expanded state cannot, however, be carried on by one person. The process of devolution begins before the trend to centralization is completed. The elders and other emerging leaders become the nucleus of a nobility or hierarchy which performs the judicial and executive functions of the king. They also serve as a conciliar body advising the king on matters of state. With the emergence of representative government the conciliar body acquires legislative powers and the modern legislature begins its evolution. The tripartite division of government into executive, judicial, and legislative and the corresponding differentiation of law into judicial, legislative, and administrative have become crystallized. Likewise, the monarcho-aristocratic, or dictatorial, and representative forms of government.[24]

2. THE ROLE OF THE FATHERHOOD SYMBOLISM

There remains to be differentiated one other aspect or division of government, which, though less tangible than the other parts and therefore less recognized, is no less essential to the viability of the state. This is the fatherhood symbolism with which every government is informed. When its hold on the people is weakened, it is a sign that the unity of the state is in danger of dissolution. Democracies possess it no less than monarchies and dictatorships though in different forms. The implications are significant.

When on the fateful April 12, 1945, the news reached the world that the chief architect of victory was denied entry into the promised land of peace, the first blush of incredulity gave way to long, deep, and sincere mourning. The behavior pattern of the American people was that of children who had lost their parent. This was true not only of those who voted for him or of the young who in their political awareness knew no other president, but also of the older generation and of those who voted for his opponents. The feeling of a void and of a rudderless ship of state that needed a captain was rendered more poignant by the crisis of war. Who was going to take care of us now, and of the larger human family? The welling up of sympathy and goodwill that first greeted President Truman was a reflection of the deep need that the people felt for someone to fill the terrifying void at the head of the table.

This was an unusual demonstration of the operation of fatherhood symbolism in the body politic, but not fortuitous. It has its origin in the familial history of the individual and of the race, already analyzed.[25] When the family state began to evolve into the expanded forms, the family imagery became attached to the new units. The fatherhood of the patriarch was displaced toward the tribal chief and then toward the king. The subjects were the king's children. The brotherhood of the king's subjects was proclaimed under the fatherhood of the king. Kingship is derived from kinship. Man's anthropomorphic familiocentric imagination was operating not only in heaven but on earth. The divine right of royalty was an inevitable consequence of the all-pervasive influence of religion in primitive society. So strong was the sense of family kinship in the developing states that the factor of territoriality was not easily assimilated in the early state. Since the expanding state included peoples of diverse stocks, territoriality was not at first acknowledged as a basis of citizenship even in the Greek city-states. Rome solved the problem through the fiction of adoption and through the myth of a common ancestor as the founder of the state.[26]

The monarchial form was of course ideal as a symbolic representation of the family. The royal family completed the anthropomorphic illusion and figment of the family character of the state. In the course of centuries the territorial element in the state played havoc with the kinship principle. The hold of monarchy was correspondingly weakened. When a division among the elites took the form of revolution, two lines of development occurred. In one of them representative government developed in the form of a republic, and to a limited extent direct democracy evolved in the city-states of antiquity.[27] In the other pattern of evolution, representative government developed under a constitutional monarchy. The British system is the classic example of this form.

In the republic or democracy the fatherhood symbol becomes an abstract principle like monotheism in the Hebraic religion, the least anthropomorphic of the Western forms. The people or the constitution is deified. But the mass mind strives to incarnate the symbol in personalized form. For a period the Supreme Court of the United States became the sacrosanct repository, but the sacerdotal varnish was definitely rubbed off by that august tribunal's resistance to popular demands for liberal social measures. The continuing public divisions among its members, though desirable in clarifying public policy, do not contribute to perpetuating the illusion of oracular communion with divine authority as the essence of the judicial process. Presidential leadership offers a more promising target for people in search of father authority, for it is more personalized and concentrated. The Roman imperator was deified. Modern dictators are nearly so.[28] Great presidents from Washington to Franklin Roosevelt have been noted as great father figures.

That during their lifetime they were viciously attacked is not a denial but an affirmation of their father role. The ambivalence of love and hate of the offspring toward the father as the incarnation of protection and authority engenders a complex of guilt, Oedipus-like in intensity and explosiveness. Great presidents have been men of great personality and positive action. They at once attracted attachment and aroused opposition, frequently in the same circles. The consequent guilt feeling has taken expression in billingsgate, which has always been characteristic of American politics. Washington and Lincoln were as maligned as Wilson and Roosevelt. Only after death can veneration of them be unalloyed.

In the British system, by a splendid fiction, the monarchy retains the appearance of power, without its essence. It can therefore receive veneration as the bearer of the father symbol without an admixture of animosity. Power resides in Parliament and the Cabinet, and opposition can be directed against them without engendering a feeling of guilt. British politics are therefore lively but without the unrestrained aggressions prevalent in the United States. In dictatorships the same catharsis is obtained by deflecting the hate to internal or foreign scapegoats, and the leader can be apotheosized as the father image.[29]

There is no denying the excesses of American politics, but withal they are more redolent of the democratic spirit than is the deferential brand in more stratified societies. It is a positive democratic value that Americans need not bend the knee before any human being, even as a symbolic gesture. It is well that our education should be directed toward focusing our veneration on the impersonal symbolism of headship and unity. And if the price for the dynamism of American democracy is that those who may temporarily bear the responsibility of headship and fatherhood must be the targets for sound and fury, they themselves, by their eagerness to serve, give eloquent testimony that the price is not too high.

CHAPTER XX

Integration of Representative Government

1. THE HISTORICAL PATTERN OF GOVERNMENT INTEGRATION

Democratic dynamism must not be equated with centrifugal explosiveness if the state is to exist. The differentiation of the functions, agencies, and forms of government and of law is a manifestation of the phenomenon of the division of labor operating in the governmental sphere. But division of labor demands co-ordination of the component parts in relative order if it is to lead to a common objective, and for that reason government differentiation makes integration or unified control imperative.

This becomes evident from an examination of the historical pattern of government integration. In the tracing of the evolution of government, two fundamental forms were crystallized: the monarcho-aristocratic, or dictatorial, and the representative, or democratic. While kingship gave way to the representative form when the kinship element in society weakened, this form does not remain a permanent fixture. In Rome, for instance, the republic in time is supplanted by the imperium of the Caesars. In the new monarchy, the kinship hereditary principle is of course less influential than in the kingship era, and as a result the imperial succession, elective in theory, becomes the prize of military power.[1] Nevertheless, this constitutes a return to the dictatorial system. The Roman example is not unique. In Germany, Kaiserdom was dissolved in the Weimar Republic, which was in turn succeeded by Hitler's dictatorship. In Italy, the representative form under the constitutional monarchy was snuffed out by the sawdust Caesar. In France, the Bourbon dynasty was supplanted by the republic, which in turn was overthrown by Napoleon. His defeat led to the restoration of the monarchy, which after the revolution of 1848 led to the establishment of the Second Republic which again evolved into Bonapartism. The Third Republic, which succeeded it, proved more viable but the fortunes of France are again under the shadow of dictatorship, this time Communist or DeGaullist.

The pattern of historical sequence is, then, (1) familial-monarchical; (2) tribal-gerontocratic-representative; (3) kingship; (4) democratic-representative, of either republican or constitutional monarchical form; (5) dictatorial, etc. This constitutes a cycle in which representative government alternates with dictatorship, each succeeding appearance being influenced by its historical period. The classical cycle of Aristotle, anticipated by Plato, consisted of monarchy, aristocracy, oligarchy, tyranny, democracy, and then back again to monarchy, and the repetition of the cycle.[2] Allowing for differences due to political development peculiar to the Greek city-states, Aristotle's cycle fundamentally resembles the indicated pattern of the representative system alternating with the dictatorial.

What causes representative government to be supplanted by dictatorship? Let us discriminate between conditions which are unavoidable and those which may become responsive to our collective will. If man is not yet master of his destiny, he has come a long way from being its helpless prisoner.[3] Economic cycles have been eliminated under economic planning.[4] Are there not also factors in the mechanism of government which strongly influence the stream of political systems? If there are, then knowledge of them may assist us in breaking the vicious circle and gaining insight into principles which throw light on the fateful transition from representative government to dictatorship.

The Greeks, in their characteristic worshipful attitude toward moderation as a guiding ethical precept,[5] emphasized that excessive development of any dominant trait of a political system leads to a reaction toward the system containing the opposite characteristic.[6] When monarchy deteriorates into tyranny, the ground is prepared for democratic revolution.[7] According to Plato, "excess of liberty" is characterized by impatience with authority and leads to slavery and tyranny.[8] Stated in more modern terms, the weakening of political authority and the dissolution of social bonds lead to disorder, anarchy, and political paralysis. The control of the power system known as the state starts tottering and, if the state is not then destroyed by conquest, it is reintegrated by strong government in the form of a dictatorship. Extreme weakness is compensated by excessive strength. The man on horseback is acclaimed as the savior of the state and the protector of the people, who are glad to escape the state of paralysis and to surrender the responsibility of adult independence to the great leader, in whose power they find surcease from interminable and wasteful conflict. Just as tyranny leads to democracy, anarchy precedes dictatorship.[9] The cycle is concentration to devolution to looseness and back to concentration.

In a dictatorial system, the inevitable conflict of the component pyramids of power is suppressed and held in check until in time it explodes into revolution. When this is ultimately succeeded by a representative system the competing pyramids of power have greater freedom for expression of their conflict. Where the conflict is fundamental it may in time become irreconcilable. This is particularly true in times of transition from one economic system to another.[10] In consequence, the representative government becomes weak and impotent to perform its necessary tasks in adjusting the state to its changing environment. The result of impotent government is anarchy and paralysis. Since each of the competing pyramids of power becomes consolidated in time, the situation at that stage is one of oppression of the many at the bottom of the pyramid of power by the powerful few near the top. This anarchic oligarchy which threatens the unity of the state is resolved by the emergence of a strong apex that finds support in the lower levels of the pyramid against the oppressive power of the few in the middle.[11]

In terms of agencies of government, the cycle described represents a conflict between the executive and the legislative. When representative government gains power against a tyrannous dictatorial executive, the interests of the people find protection in the legislature. As the representative system becomes encrusted with the consolidated pyramids of power, the legislature is transmuted into a vehicle for vested interests which seek to maintain the status quo against the interests of the people. It is then that the integrating, unifying, positive power of a strong executive is transmuted into a shield for the popular cause. It is no accident that historically dictatorships and strong executives in democracies have had popular support. Caesar was sincerely acclaimed as a popular hero. They have done, or gave the appearance of doing, those things which needed to be done in order to adjust the policies of the state to the new demands of a changing environment, and which the divided, impotent legislature was unable to perform. The executive offers positive, dynamic government, while the impotent legislature is negative and static. The executive that has the power to act wins over a weak and paralyzed legislature. The danger to democracy does not arise from a strong responsible government but from a weak and negative government. Impotence of government is the graveyard of democracy.

With the establishment of dictatorship, the state acquires a positive executive government that can act in the crisis, for it has the power, but since that government lacks responsibility to the people, freedom is lost. The pathology of the representative system is the tendency of the legislature to lose the power to act and thus become negative. By losing power it also loses responsibility. Thus, the nature of the vicious cycle.

2. THE BRITISH CABINET SYSTEM

Is there no escape from the fateful dilemma in modern representative government? Great Britain and the United States, the two greatest democracies in the world, where representative government has shown highest vitality, represent contrasting approaches to the problem of power and responsibility in government and of the relationship of the various divisions of the government.

In the cabinet form of government, as it has been crystallized through centuries of evolution in Great Britain, all powers of government are concentrated in Parliament, the crown retaining the father symbolism for the unity of the state. All power to Parliament.[12] To this repository of all power the judiciary is subordinate, for it has no power of constitutional veto. In this virtually unicameral container of all governmental power the legislature and executive are differentiated but at the same time integrated and operating as a whole in the process of government. The legislature selects the executive and delegates to it all necessary powers of government. In granting adequate power to the executive, it retains control over it through its power to dismiss. The executive has full power to act but coupled with responsibility to the legislature. The legislature itself, however, is not without responsibility to the executive. In case of disagreement between executive and legislature, the executive can call for new elections, and both must go to the people for a new mandate. The check that the legislature and executive have on each other's tenure of office becomes a check by the electorate on both and enforces responsibility of the government to the people. It also removes the possibility of a deadlock between executive and legislature in regard to policy. Positive government is unthinkable unless the legislature and executive are in agreement on affairs of state. The power of calling elections for a popular mandate is a highly significant adaptation by representative government of the referendum technique of direct democracy to ascertain the will of the people.

What, it may be inquired, is there in the British system to prevent Parliament and the Cabinet from voting themselves perpetual tenure and becoming a dictatorship? Nothing but the tradition of democracy of the British people and leadership. This is true in America as it is in England. There is no mechanistic formula which could guarantee against government usurpation of dictatorial power. Denial of power to govern is no answer; it is an invitation to chaos followed by dictatorship. The British system, however, provides reasonable safeguards against usurpation. It is unlikely that a coup d'état could be accomplished by an improvised conspiracy in Parliament. Even in the same parties there are always tendencies for division and antagonisms, particularly between those in the center of power and those on the circumference. Only a party subject to dictatorial control, such as the Communist or Fascist, can establish a dictatorship in a democracy. In the framework of a democratic tradition, the check that Parliament and the Cabinet have on each other's tenure results in the control of the government by the people. The power of the Cabinet at any time to go to the people for a new mandate is likewise the greatest safeguard against the tendency of legislatures to become paralyzed through lingering divisions among vested interests blocking action. Renewal of the people's mandate gives power to the government to act while at the same time it exacts responsibility. Great Britain has the advantage of a strong government of integrated executive and legislative branches acting in unison and of democratic control and responsibility. Thus has Britain in the flexible structure of its government escaped the vicious cycle of democracy and dictatorship.

The British formula for government integration does contain, contrary to textbook maxim, a check and balance system. But, unlike the American equivalent, the British checks are not on the powers of government or through their separation but on the tenure of office vested in Parliament and in the Cabinet. Through this technique Britain has admirably solved the problem of power and responsibility and of legislative executive conflict.

3. THE AMERICAN PRESIDENTIAL SYSTEM

The American approach to the problem, having a different historical conditioning, diverged materially from the British model, and its experience is a less happy one than that of the British. Indeed, in this matter we are at the crossroads of decision. Unless we undertake drastic measures to resolve what has proved a chronic inadequacy of our governmental system, our democracy and our very survival might be endangered.[13]

Since at the time of the American Revolution, the supremacy of Parliament had not yet sufficiently crystallized to be appreciated, the Founding Fathers were of the impression, shared by Montesquieu, that the British system was one of separation of powers into independent executive, legislative, and judicial branches with mutual checks and balances.[14] Since the Revolution was directed against the policies of the crown, and since fear of government was exceeded only by distrust of the people, the framers of the Constitution entrusted their security to a system of checks and balances directed at the powers of government. Even in those of decided mercantilist convictions, like Hamilton, the fear of the popular will stilled any predilections for powerful government.[15]

Delilah's scissors did a thorough preventive job. It cannot be gainsaid that the written Constitution, when combined with the doctrine of judicial review usurped by an independent judiciary, served to impose restrains on the will of the people and on the ability of the American commonwealth to adjust itself to the needs of a changing environment.[16] Judicial supremacy has been a negative influence on the powers of government, for its expression is censorial. Nevertheless, the Supreme Court has a great role to play in our system in defending civil liberties against local encroachment, and in assimilating the administrative process within our general legal framework. Let us hope that the future composition of that tribunal will be such as not to handicap our government in dealing with the social and economic inperatives of our age.

Though the American government, at least for the time being, freed itself from judicial bondage, it is still afflicted with the creeping paralysis that is inherent in our presidential form by reason of the checks and balances and separation of powers between the executive and the legislature. We have been precipitated into one of the recurrent critical deadlocks between the Congress and the President by reason of each branch being controlled by a different party as the result of the midterm election of 1946. It is the twenty-eighth time this has occurred in our history. It delayed reconstruction after the Civil War for a generation. It destroyed the peace after World War I by preventing the United States from taking its part in its preservation. It prevented effective action for economic reconstruction between 1930 and 1932. It has laid the groundwork for a catastrophe after World War II, by creating a grave stalemate.

The reason for this is that, if government is to have the power to govern, the legislature and the executive must be in agreement on the policies of government. When these are controlled by different parties, the mechanism of agreement is wanting and stalemate ensues. However, the absence of organization for harmony between executive and legislature is a permanent feature of our system, and in consequence conflict and deadlock between the two are the usual state of affairs, even when both are controlled by the same party, except during war and briefly in times of domestic crisis.

Congress as a representative assembly constitutes a hodgepodge of views and sentiments about public affairs. It is an unorganized system of power, and in order for it to function positively it must be organized or controlled. For that, leadership is necessary. But leadership to be effective must have means of enforcing compliance even with majority decisions. But no such controls are available. The fixed terms of office in the House and Senate prevents any effective control by a would-be leadership from Congressional ranks. Decisions of party caucuses in Congress in matters of policy are not effective instruments of organization and are being ignored with impunity.

Neither was the Presidency intended to provide such leadership. The President was given the power to make legislative recommendations through his annual message but no power to organize support behind them. He was given the power of veto over Congressional action, which meant that he could block any positive Congressional initiative, but that is of no assistance to him in promulgating his own program. Congress and the President were given checks on each other's powers, which meant that each could negate the action of the other. Had they been given checks on each other's tenure of office, as Parliament and the Cabinet have in the British system, the basis would have been prepared for the emergence of a common state policy, the essential of the power of government. The fixed term of office of Congress and the President eliminated any procedural make-weights for co-operation and made conflict and recurrent paralysis the usual condition. No sooner was the Republic established than the grave defects became apparent. Washington's experience with the Senate in the matter of treaties did not add measurably to his reputation for control of his temper. Ironically, that which the framers feared most of all, the spirit of party, and which they hoped to avoid, soon asserted itself to make government workable.[17] Since political parties are the mechanism through which the general quest for power seeks to control the government and its policies, they are inevitable. In democracies they are useful vehicles through which various leaderships may mobilize and crystallize public opinion in behalf of specific political programs, in addition to being instruments for the attainment of political power.[18]

The ballot for the individual voter in a modern democracy constitutes the climax of a complex evolution of political sanctions and techniques. In primitive society, balloting was originally in the form of a lot, leaving the choice to the intervention of the supernatural, as in the case of trial by ordeal. It also constituted a recognition of the political equality of the tribal chieftains and was associated with rotation in office. The transition from the lot to voting constituted a secularization of state power and its materialization within the coalescing tribal state. It was a transmutation from the unconscious to the conscious.[19] With the democratization of the state power suffrage expands and the phenomenon of power devolution sets in. It is through this medium of the party system that the necessary integration of the devolved power takes place for the conduct of government.

With the rise of popular parties, the electoral college became a ceremonial seal for the popular election of the President. This extra-constitutional turn in the evolution of presidential leadership as the chief characteristic of American politics emerged with Jefferson. It is in the person of the President that party leadership is focused and it is to him that the country looks for leadership in carrying out the policies of government.[20] On entering office, however, he finds that he has no regularized machinery for promulgating his legislative program. The honeymoon induced by novelty and patronage spoils is short-lived and the marriage of convenience soon settles down to a tug of war of mutual conflict and frustration. Even the presidencies of strong leaders in the midst of crises have been productive only for the first half of their first terms in office. By 1936 the New Deal was virtually over as an aggressive program. After then all it could do was to fight defensively to consolidate its power. The President has no means of control even over the members of his own party. The primary system for the selection of candidates deprived the party of its unifying power, since leaders have no control over determining who the party candidates should be. In the context of our system of checks and balances, the primary system aggravated government irresponsibility and has exercised antidemocratic influence.

It is, to be sure, fallacious to infer that our major parties offer no real choice to the American voter because each of them constitutes a federation of parties. What is important is the point of emphasis and direction of the component social forces and of the leaderships. In retrospect there appears to be no doubt that on the two over-riding issues of our time—internationalism and domestic control over the economic environment—the Democrats produced Wilson's New Freedom and Roosevelt's New Deal, while the Republicans have been the standard bearers of isolationism and resistance to government regulation of our economy. Nevertheless the operation of our party system leaves much to be desired in point of integration.

The usefulness of major parties lies in eliminating extremism from the main stream of American politics. The welding of divergent elements into a functioning unit necessitates compromise, and compromise abhors extremism. If our governmental system placed a premium on party solidarity and control, paralyzing divisions and bitter conflict would tend to mellow into mutual accommodation. But since parties have no means or impelling need to act as a unit, compromise does not prevail in party councils. What we get is a false front of pre-election unity, which disappears once the votes are counted. In consequence, American party divisions become particularly meaningful when great leaders emerge.

Throughout our history national destiny and the popular cause have rested on the powerful shoulders of strong executives. The history of our nation has been propelled forward by the leadership of Jefferson, Jackson, Lincoln, Wilson, and Roosevelt. The periods of Congressional ascendancy have been times of reaction, stagnation, deadlock and inaction. The vested interests, the numerous lobbies, the solidified pyramids of power have become entrenched in the structure and procedure of Congress. Numerous committees with overlapping jurisdiction, undue power of committees to block legislation, senatorial filibuster and other excrescences of the legislative process have combined to put a premium on minority power to block action when action is needed. Is it any wonder that Congress has fallen into public disrepute and that the people look to the unifying power of the strong executive for political leadership? Here too the mass of the people at the bottom of the pyramid unite with the strong executive at the apex against the anarchy and oppression of the few representing economic feudalities.

The destiny of our country cannot be permitted to be at the mercy of the chance that greatness should tenant the White House. We have been extremely fortunate in having great war leaders, but in the no less critical reconstruction eras fortune frowned on us. No system of government is adequate, if it is workable only during periods of great stress under the brief spell of the blessed of the Lord. The machinery of government must provide techniques for resolution of conflict and for orderly crystallization of national policy. Failure to do so has converted our system into a crisis government, able to function effectively only in times of great domestic and war emergencies. This has made for spasmodic operation consisting of long periods of stagnation alternating with brief spurts of hectic attempts to make up for lost time. Only the great genius of the American people for democratic self-government has lessened the danger to our liberties flowing from a negative government. And even that would not have sufficed had it not been for our great economic strength and our geographic isolation. The proximity of France to Germany made the impotence of its government, induced by its deep social cleavages and aggravated by its anarchic party system, fatal to its national survival.

The sands of destiny's tolerance for our dawdling political system are running out. The tempo of change in the total environment is ever accelerating and the need for rapid adjustment through positive government is correspondingly greater. Airpower and atomic energy must endow our foreign policy with triggerlike sensitiveness. Our highly interdependent economy can no more be operated without government integration and planning than a great plant or business can be run without management control and direction. The answer is positive government, government that can act. That is what we do not have now. Because our constitutional system does not provide for orderly exercise of necessary powers by the government, it has created constant temptation for executive usurpation. Just as the Roman consul was endowed with unlimited powers for a temporary period of an emergency, when he acted as a "dictator," the President is constantly tempted to strain his executive powers and his powers as commander in chief in peace, and particularly in war, to the utmost to compensate for his helplessness vis-à-vis Congress. The irony is that the President has the power as commander in chief to make himself a dictator were he so minded, but has no power to function as the democratic head of government.

4. A PROGRAM OF GOVERNMENT REORGANIZATION

What should be done? The Legislative Reorganization Act of 1946 is a step in the right direction, in reducing the number of Congressional committees, regularizing their jurisdiction, providing the nucleus of an expert staff for Congress, and in other attempts to modernize Congressional procedure.[21] But that does not go to the core of the problem.

It is regrettable that the House eliminated from the original bill the provision for the establishment of a Joint Legislative-Executive Council, which should have contributed in some measures to advancing co-operation between Congress and the President. But even at best it would have been inadequate to crystallize a harmonious relationship. The reason is that it would have left the executive and the leadership in Congress helpless to enforce responsibility on the members of their party. Only if the executive has the power to call elections to obtain a popular mandate can such responsibility be enforced. At present, by the time the fixed election comes around, important issues get buried in the hopper of local issues and slip from the surface of public consciousness. The public has no means of knowing on whom to place responsibility for government policy, whether on the President, on Congress, or on any specific members. If the executive could call a special election, attention would be focused on the controversial national problem and candidates would be forced to commit themselves and could not escape responsibility.

The public mind would also be clarified, for the people would be able to distribute rewards and punishments in accordance with the success or failure of specific policies. This would not result in frequent elections or changes in administration. On the contrary, it would stabilize the system, for members of Congress reluctant to face defeat would follow the guidance of the executive, unless they believed their views were in accord with public opinion. The chaotic condition of French politics has been due to the French premier's powerlessness in practice to dissolve Parliament.

If the American representative system of separation of powers and checks and balances, is to perish from the earth, its epitaph, as that of all other similar systems in history, would read: "Here lies a government that had no power to govern."

If it is to endure, our government will have to cease being divided against itself. In government as in individuals, internal conflict which cannot be resolved is pathological and must end in breakdown.[22] A strong dictatorship is one way to compensate for a weak government. But that should not be our way.

We should follow the British example. One way is to adopt the British parliamentary system with mutual checks and balances on the tenure, not on the power, of Parliament and the Cabinet. Another proposal would retain the popular election of the President and would make his term and that of Congress coextensive, giving the President the right to dissolve Congress and call for a special election for Congress and the President at any time in case of disagreement between him and Congress. The Cabinet could be composed of the President, his own appointees, and those appointed from Congress.[23]

It is doubtful whether this could be accomplished in the foreseeable future by extraconstitutional evolution. A constitutional amendment would be necessary to accomplish this imperative objective. But whether this could be done short of another domestic crisis is equally open to doubt. Humanity has apparently irrevocably matriculated in the school of hard knocks.

The projected reorganization of our presidential system might in time eliminate the bicameral structure of Congress. Representation of states in the Senate, it might be argued, is no longer compatible with the unity of our nation or democratic equalitarianism before the law. The share of an American in his government should not vary in reverse ratio to the population of the state wherein he happens to reside. Nor is there any evidence that the virtual elimination of the

House of Lords has made the process of government in England hasty or its politics unstable.

It would be at variance with the genius of representative government to have an upper chamber based on direct representation of economic or other interests, despite the fact that the administrative state is engaged to the hilt in dealing with such interests. It is the genius of democracy that individuals, not interests, should be represented by the legislature-executive. Conflicting economic and other interests constantly strive to influence and control government, but it is best that this influence on the highest level of policy making should be sifted through the integrating power of the personality of the individual voter. It is best that in choosing his government to integrate all his interests the ultimate voice should be that of the voter, not of those who represent a particular interest. This affords the individual voter a final check over those who claim to speak in his behalf as a member of a union, employer association, or other type of grouping. It is in the administration of government that the influence and representation of interests should find their direct and useful expression.

CHAPTER XXI

Administrative Integration

---

1. DEMOCRATIC CONTROLS OF THE ADMINISTRATIVE PROCESS

"The 1940 presidential election—which may well have been the last regular presidential election in the history of this country, or, at most, the next to last—was a symbolic landmark, a guarantee of the course of the future."[1] So wrote James Burnham in 1941 in predicting the triumph of administrative dictatorship in America. Yet though the war multiplied the administrative controls and powers, as well as the administrative personnel, to unprecedented degree, the Republican party in 1946 managed not only to remain on the ticket, but to gain control of both branches of Congress. Even before that, government controls were rapidly dismantled and administrative personnel drastically reduced by a Democratic Congress and Administration. Strangulation by reduced appropriations and curtailment of functions threaten to reduce the remaining agencies to impotency. Does that conform to the lurid propaganda bogey of an omnipotent bureaucracy, a "new despotism," an administrative leviathan, a Frankenstein which is about to do away with representative government and the liberties of the people?[2]

Of course the new dispensation will be a short-lived, costly, and perhaps even catastrophic interlude of madness. Government controls and the administrative bureaus will return in greater numbers and functions than ever before, for they are called for by the inevitability of an administered economy. But the very fact that the administrative agencies proved to be so amenable to the control of the legislature, executive, and judiciary, and that the party identified most closely with government administration suffered defeat, is irrefutable proof that the administrative process can be, and has been, assimilated as an integral part of the democratic representative system. Administrators are the servants, not the masters, of the people.

This should not be surprising to those who have had access to the facts. The administrative process in a democracy demands that sufficient power be granted to the agencies to perform their tasks, while effective controls are retained over the agencies, so that their operation is in accordance with their mandate. Such controls were retained. The President and Senate, through the respective powers of appointment and confirmation, retain fundamental control over policy-determining administrative personnel. Control over budget and appropriations afford the President and Congress a strangle hold over administrative function and discretion. Continuous supervision over administrative operation can be exercised by Congress through its standing committees and special investigating committees. The special type has proved undesirable, dominated as they have been in many cases by representatives of interests with a special ax to grind in embarrassing the operation of a particular agency. The standing committees under the Legislative Reorganization Act, paralleling as they do administrative agencies in function, should serve as valuable channels of constant supervision of administration and vehicles of consultation. The danger, however, is that these committees might assume covert minority control over administration, where a frontal attack is politically inadvisable. Congress must realize that the administrative agencies stand in the same relation to Congress as the latter stands to the electorate. It is humanly impossible and administratively inadvisable for Congress to do more than lay down general lines and directives of policy. The rest must be filled out by day-to-day administration. Congestion of authority and paralysis of operation would result if Congress attempted to do more.

In this day-to-day operation, administrative tribunals are subject to judicial review of their action This review exacts the requirement that administrative action be within the purview of the legislative mandate and that it comply with the fundamental concepts of procedural and substantive due process of law The "rule of law," which originally referred to the judicial process under the supremacy of Parliament, has been distorted out of context to assert that the administrative process is not consonant with it.[3] Administrative acts, even as are judicial decisions, have to conform to basic concepts of fair play and equality before the law. The tendency indeed has been for courts to usurp the function of administrators and decide for themselves the administrative problems involved.[4] The peculiar usefulness of the administrative agency in affording specialized expert treatment of economic and social problems is to that extent impaired. The danger is not that administrative law and procedure will evaporate into arbitrary whim, but that they will lose their necessary flexibility and congeal into rigid formulas as equity and common law did before them. Administrators, no less than judges and legislators, are devoted to the ideals and aspirations of American democracy. In requiring that "so far as practicable" U.S. District Court rules of evidence shall apply to NLRB proceedings, the Taft-Hartley Act would encumber the administrative process with unnecessary legalisms. It disregards the Administrative Procedure Act of 1946.

2. STRUCTURE AND FUNCTION

The power necessary for the performance of their tasks would be dangerously impaired if the proposal were adopted to decompose administrative quasi-judicial tribunals into independent sections for the performance of the administrative, policy-making, and judicial functions.[5] It is the integrating unitary control of the administrative process that is its peculiar genius, for it focuses attention and responsibility on one locus of authority for carrying out a specific national policy. Should we apply to the administrative process the doctrine of separation of powers and checks and balances which our historical experience in the relationship between the legislature and executive has proved so detrimental to the national welfare? Within each agency the functions are of course divided among the staff, but in order for the tribunal to operate effectively these have to be coordinated under unitary control. It is just as subversive of good government and management to break up the quasi-judicial administrative tribunals as to decompose the other government and private agencies into independent, unco-ordinated units for planning, organizing, staffing, directing, co-ordinating, reporting, and budgeting just because these are separate functions.[6] Without control there is no organization. It is the purpose of the infant science of administration not only to analyze the functions of management, but to synthesize them most effectively. In breaking up the Review Section of the NLRB, the Taft-Hartley Act will render necessary cumbersome duplication of work. Most mischievous, however, is this act's provision for an independently appointed general counsel who would have sole power over the enforcement policies of the act. This will diminish the effectiveness of administration and runs counter to the Administrative Procedure Act of 1946.

Too great a preoccupation with administrative analysis has tended to overrefine structural or functional blueprinting. The imperatives of organic growth and of subject matter are too readily sacrificed to considerations of symmetry. The genuis of the British system would argue against such overemphasis. No administrative planning can be generalized outside the context of the particular subject matter and function involved and of the surrounding traditions. For instance, representation of economic and other interests affected is desirable in administrative agencies but no over-all generalization can be made. In agencies such as the National Labor Relations Board, involving enforcement of duties which do not permit of compromise, representation of the interests involved would be subversive of good administration. In agencies, such as the National War Labor Board, whose functions involve accommodation of interests and where compromise is feasible, representation of the interests affected at least in an advisory capacity is desirable. An eclectic empiric approach is indicated.

It is interesting that the same sources which advocate breaking up the unitary character of administrative agencies recommend, in the name of government responsibility, placing the independent administrative tribunals in dissected forms within the executive department.[7] Here, again, no universal generalization is possible. Functions of a quasi-judicial character, as that of the National Labor Relations Board, which admit of continuity and independence from the policies of the administration in power, had best be administered by independent agencies. Matters relating to economic planning and administration should be placed under the direct control of the administration in power.

3. A PROPOSAL FOR ADMINISTRATIVE REORGANIZATION

There is no question that the multiplicity of functions makes necessary government reorganization. But a certain quality of ad hoc improvisation and accommodation may have been actually useful in circumventing vested bureaucratic interests and introducing new blood into the administrative cadre. So interdependent and fluid has the subject matter of administration become that no rigid demarcation along traditional classifications is feasible. The variety and ramifications of labor problems are so extensive that there is virtually no field of foreign or domestic government activity which does not impinge on labor and does not necessitate the establishment of a bureau to perform the function. Duplication of functions should be avoided, but it is completely unrealistic to conclude that all functions dealing with labor should be incorporated into the Department of Labor. Nor is it possible to formulate immutable tests for permanent exclusion or inclusion.

Modern democratic government bears resemblance to the following managerial setup: The legislature, composed of leadership with peculiar aptitude for personal contact and popular appeal, has the function of an intermediary between government and the people and the task of ultimate ratification and supervision of policy making. The executive, composed of the President and his Cabinet, should function as a more cohesive board of directors. Their leadership, equally of a popular character, must include over-all government management. For that reason members of the Cabinet should not be burdened with administrative duties and should not be responsible for the operation of any department. They should serve without portfolio under the President in determining and executing the overall policy of the Administration.

The administrative branch proper should be staffed with a leadership of experts whose chief attribute is expertness in the manipulation of specialized techniques in addition to the requisite skills in human relations. They should perform the tasks of actual administration. The administrative agencies should specialize in the performance of the analyzed functions for which they were created. They should be grouped according to administrative needs in general departments whose heads are not members of the Cabinet. The organizational synthesis should not be rigid and permanent. Agencies and sections should be shifted around within and among departments to conform with the changing tides of administrative integration.

Our tasks of government have become so overwhelming and intricate that government and public administration itself has crystallized as a distinct and worthy subject for research and administration. There is imperative need for the creation of a Department of Government, whose functions would include, in addition to those of the Civil Service Commission, co-ordination and sponsorship of government research and personnel training in the universities of the country. It would also be the task of the Department of Government to keep constant supervision over the process of administration and advise the President and his Cabinet on reorganizational projects and administrative techniques. In order that this department should not become a conflicting source of authority, its power should be only advisory, with the exception of those of the Civil Service Commission.

4. A MICROCOSM OF DEMOCRATIC ADMINISTRATION

A microcosm of administrative integration in a democracy is afforded by the administration of the controversial Wagner Act.[8] What accounts for the encompassing ramifications of the act? The fact that it dealt superbly with fundamental social forces is not to be gainsaid. But in order for the act to have become a living dynamic reality instead of an innocuous symbol, the character of its administration has to be considered. Its administrators took the Congressional mandate seriously. If it is the law of the land that workers should have the freedom to self-organization, then that law must be enforced. And enforce it they did.

What enabled the board and its staff to follow the mandate of Congress with which it was entrusted was the sustaining faith that the act they were called upon to administer represented the healing truth and would ultimately come to prevail. This was done by a staff which never exceeded a few hundred and whose yearly budget has averaged not much above $3 million. Never in the peaceful tasks of protecting civil liberties and industrial democracy has so much been accomplished by so few at so little cost.

The moral equivalent of war was found in being the servants of the people. The American people do possess the intelligence, the education, the talents, and the spirit of dedication necessary to administer the laws of a complex democracy. This was abundantly proved by the successful prosecuton of the war. What is imperative for an enduring democracy is to keep the communications open so that these qualities may ascend to the seats of power.

Social reform is not necessarily grounded in personal or class considerations and self-interest.[9] Labor's Magna Charta was not labor's handiwork. Labor was too weak even to furnish effective political impetus to its passage. The architects of the Wagner Act and its administrators did not come from labor's ranks. They have come from that growing reservoir of public-spirited, informed intelligence which possesses to a high degree the equipment and above all the social and national approach to see the problems of our complex society as a whole without distortion by the special interests of pressure groups.

The administrators have not, however, been starry-eyed crusaders. The remarkable judicial record of the board is persuasive that the substantive and procedural rights of the parties coming before it have been scrupulously observed.

This retrospective glance at the administration of the Wagner Act is particularly appropos now at the dawn of the new era ushered in by the regressive Taft-Hartley Act. It should not be forgotten that it was under the Wagner Act that American industry enjoyed unprecedented expansion and productivity, to become in fact the arsenal of democracy in peace as well as in war.

More than ever our generation will have to be preoccupied with one of the master problems of politics—means and ends. From the standpoint of authority in a democracy, it is one of administrative techniques: how to establish a favorable legislative climate for public administration; how to establish democratic controls and traditions and make the administrators responsive to their trust; and how to educate, attract, and keep the necessary talent.

CHAPTER XXII

Freedom Through Government

---

1. FREEDOM AND ORGANIZATION

In the development of the thesis of this study—that a planned economy is inevitable in the light of the historical evolution of social forces, but that we do possess a collective choice whether to make the administrative state dictatorial or free and democratic—there was a constant alternation in point of view between consideration of the desirable and of the possible, between ends and means. No study of social relations has ever been free of a choice of objectives, of an indication of preferred progress, however camouflaged that was under the claim of being "scientific."

Progress implies direction and that means some conscious purpose. No science of social techniques is conceivable without a hierarchy of social values.[1] Though every science must ever maintain the distinction between its specific techniques and its ethical or cultural purposes, the study of means presupposes a determination of ends. One has to know where he is going before he can go about finding out how he can get there. Politics as the study and application of power reaches its fruition in the actual world through the realm of ethics. The "mature man" of modern psychiatry, no less than the "good man" of traditional morality, is ultimately an ethical concept conditioned by the specific culture.[2] Ethical ideas are in turn conditioned by man's concept of his relation to the universe, which is an expression of his quest for power and mastery over his total environment.[3] But man's quest for power is socialized by his society. Thus, even conceptually, man's problems are neither wholly individual nor wholly social. They must be treated from both approaches.

At the end as at the beginning of our study we are confronted with the duality of man's nature: his individuality as well as his membership in society. This duality is sharpened in view of the densification of social relations brought about by mechanization and organizational growth of our civilization. It may well be that judged in proportion to the social activities covered, the number of laws and regulations, both public and private, have not increased. But the number and intensity of social activities and relations have immensely multiplied. And so have the social organizations with the state as the encompassing agency.

Athwart our path to a free and democratic administrative state is the question whether freedom is compatible with organization. Throughout this study certain techniques and conditions of freedom and democracy have been suggested. But no pretense is made that all the springs of human action, particularly in his social relations, have been laid bare. There is greater need than ever for the evolvement of a science of human relations, of authority and sanctions.

Emphasis on a scientific approach to the problems of administration, particularly the psychological expression of authority, is imperative in view of the strongly knit organizational pattern of our social living. With few exceptions we make our living not as independent entrepreneurs but as members of ever-growing organizations, in private industry and in government. This is the inevitable consequence of our technology and mass production. More and more, therefore, we are drawn into the vortex of immediate personalized hierarchy with its increased opportunities for tyranny and sadism in all the unlovely expressions of man's inhumanity to man.[4]

Coercion must remain for the foreseeable future the ultimate sanction of the state and its monopoly. But the very complexity of our industrial process makes blind obedience and sullen submissiveness inimical to effective public and private management. We are at the threshold of greater awareness, if not new discoveries, about human motivations, on which to build a science of techniques of control, sanctions, and incentives. It is well that modern administration seeks to depersonalize authority and to reduce domination by rationalizing power in terms of function, aptitude, and techniques for evaluation of effort and co-operation. We may expect much-wanted illumination on personality adjustment, abilities, and aptitudes.[5] But, whatever scientific truth may be gleaned, there is a constant danger that in actual application these might deteriorate from aids to administration into rationalization of the dominance of the bureaucratic elite. "Science" and "psychology" may follow birth, race, and breeding as sanctions for the perpetuation of the power of the elite. An elite of science, not subject to democratic controls, may yet prove the most tyrannical because it will wield more power than any elite in history. Efficiency ratings and decisions on promotion are largely subjective despite the impressive legerdemain of so-called objective analysis of performance. Particularly in work on the professional level, denial of promotion may mean not lack of merit in the victim but abundance of merit, sufficient in fact to inspire uneasiness in the hierarchical superior, or that the inferior does not "belong" to one or another of the ruling factions within the hierarchy. It is a fallacy for management to feel that it must support the decisions of its supervisors in matters of personnel irrespective of their merits. Superior and articulate ability, when combined with a lack of sycophancy and an absence of ruthlessness in the drive for power, is not conducive to the advancement of an administrative career. The Republic of Florence could ill afford not to avail itself of the genius of Machiavelli, yet death came to vegetative "Old Nick" without the proffer of his service having been accepted.[6]

If "scientific" management is to fulfill its ambition to be scientific, it will need the impetus of strong unionism in government as well as in private employment. This would serve to some extent as a check on arbitrariness in management.[7]

Maintenance of competition and check of social forces is particularly important in view of the growth of large organizations both in industry and in government. Being in a hierarchy exercises some limitation on one's freedom of action in the political arena. For instance, in the case of two independent legal practitioners a difference in income does not involve control of the opinions and activities of the less by the more affluent. However, though the supervisor in government or in private industry may receive only slightly more than those under his supervision, the conscious and unconscious control he exercises over their wills is immeasurably greater, for on his opinion about them their careers depend. In the case of the inarticulate masses, labor organization and the secrecy of the political ballot protect them. But what of the articulate leaders on the lower rungs of the hierarchy? Will our society continue to have room for the emergence of the Darrows, the dissidents, the rebels, the maladjusted? Our democratic traditions and the competition of many pyramids of power should make us optimistic on this score, for they will furnish the economic support for many independent conflicting leaderships. A democratic society should cherish its nonconformists, for out of their mouths, come the ideas that challenge the prevailing modes and enable society to shake off the paralysis of vested interests. Man can learn only by contrast, and progress implies freedom of dissent.

Every culture has its inarticulate premises, its myth, Plato's "royal lie," through which its members look upon the world. Their effectiveness is lessened as soon as they reach the conscious level, for then they become targets of critical examination. Since the tendency of social systems is to overlay their foundations with a crust of tradition, social criticism can perform no greater service to freedom than to uncover and challenge society's basic assumptions.

2. SANCTIONS, REMEDIES, AND INCENTIVES

One of the basic assumptions that will be challenged in the democratic administrative state is that mankind is impaled on the dilemma of choice between the yogi and the commissar,[8] between powerless government and a dictatorship. Man's inner growth finds greatest promise for expression in the framework of a democratic society organized in the administrative state.

In the planned state democratically controlled man reaches the climax of his social progress from unconscious purpose to conscious design. In it the conflict between power and responsibility is theoretically resolved. What man is helpless to achieve individually he does through his democratically controlled state.[9] Man's economic inequality makes a mockery of his legal freedom of contract. Through law and government man gains a social status in which he finds the greatest possibility for the satisfaction of his wants—freedom. Law in a democratic society is a collective contract. The golden age of the "social contract" may be in the future, not in the dim past, in the highly evolved state, not in the primitive society of the fictitious "state of nature." That man's rights depend more and more on law rather than on individual contract is an impetus to freedom in a democratic state. With the increase of man's power, his ability to plan keeps pace and he becomes more independent of his natural environment. The restraint on man's freedom to fulfill his needs becomes visible and personal rather than hidden and impersonal. This is a gigantic, revolutionary advance in the direction of freedom. Before a slave can be free, he must first become aware of his slavery and that he need not remain a slave. In a laissez-faire society the individual worker accepted the general mores that he had only himself to blame if he was unemployed and did not get more pay than he did, and that "natural" laws determined the relationship between his wages and his work as well as the state of his employment. It was a great emancipating step for workers to realize that their economic betterment is dependent not on laws outside their control but on their collective action through a union. It was still more significant for people to realize that they themselves through their government were the captains of their economic destinies. Since man is impelled by his quest for power to strive to remove the restraints that he is aware of, the effect of dynamic economic planning in a democratic state is to focus responsibility and to increase mass pressure for economic betterment. It is of course true that even in democratically planned societies there will emerge the ideological premises that will justify the pyramidal structure of society, but nevertheless the tendency of democracy is to remove pronounced inequalities. This mass pressure for economic betterment operates to increase efficiency, since that is the ultimate limit to society's capacity to satisfy its needs. Since in a dictatorship this mass pressure has no free expression, dictatorially planned societies are likely to be less efficient than democracies.

Another of the basic assumptions that will be challenged in the democratic administrative state is that man's energies in the economic field are most sensitive to fear of want and of privation. Man's unending quest for power should dispel any such motion. The rich go on striving, accumulating, and functioning long after their fortunes have exceeded their capacity to consume. Man's quest for power is very plastic and has been socialized along many lines within the same and among many cultures. Even in terms of economic rewards the desire for more should prove more effective in liberating the energies of men than the mounting fear of privation, which is degrading and paralyzing of spontaneous effort.

But the need for maintaining stability will compel the administrative state not to comply with the ever-growing demands of competing interests. In that situation the administrative state would have to resort to its arsenal of authoritative sanctions. What should be the policy of the government in order to avoid strikes against government determination of the wage-price relationship? In terms of priority of remedies the government will have at its disposal sanctions, first against union officials, then against unions, and last against employees. It will not be necessary or desirable to resort to imprisonment of union leaders or workers or to draft strikers into the armed services. Nor should NLRB union certifications be denied or revoked except as a last resort, and even then it should not be done at the expense of interrupting the bargaining process or the right to resort to the peaceful processes of the law.[10] Chief reliance against strikes, however, must be placed not on sanctions but upon the conviction gaining ground that a strike would not cause the government to alter its decision. This may require a transitional period during which a rash of strikes would occur to test the firmness of the government. But once that firmness is demonstrated there would be no need to apply sanctions and strikes would cease to be a problem. In time, resort to the strike weapon would become as antiquated and rare as violence is now to redress a private wrong.

The history of the frequent use of injunctions in labor disputes, climaxed by the decision of the Supreme Court upholding the right of the government to enjoin the coal strike when in possession of the mines, would preclude any serious contention that the strike as a technique cannot be constitutionally eliminated under certain provisions. One such provision would be not to prohibit employees from quitting work, although if they did they could be deprived of certain economic and legal benefits connected with their employment. It is highly doubtful whether the strike technique could be immunized under the constitutional injunction against involuntary servitude.

Nevertheless, a persuasive argument could be advanced for the proposition that the strike is a collective weapon for the protection of the workers' fundamental property rights. Legislation, therefore, which would prohibit strikes but not quitting work, would still be of doubtful constitutional validity, for it would leave the employer all-powerful to determine the employment contract, thus depriving the employees of due process of law. Open to this objection is the provision in the Taft-Hartley Act that prohibits strikes for a period of approximately eighty days where stoppage would affect the health or safety of the public but does not provide for the maintenance of the status quo, thus leaving the employer free to impose his terms.

No such objection can be made against compulsory arbitration, since neither the employee nor the employer is left supreme. The property rights of both are preserved. Because of the imperative of maintaining the fundamental duty to preserve communal life, the government finds it necessary to deprive the employer and employees of their customary economic sanctions of the lockout and strike, respectively. But in compulsory arbitration it affords them a forum for the protection of their respective rights through new remedies and sanctions. Democracy and freedom will find impetus in a doctrine which does not bestow sanctity upon specific techniques for the protection of fundamental rights, but allows the substitution of new techniques, remedies, and sanctions more suitable to the changing needs of the social environment. The same old wine in new and better bottles.

In order for the government's role as umpire to be accepted, its reputation for firmness against labor will have to be combined with a similar attitude toward business interests. It did not measurably add to acceptance of government as supreme economic arbiter for it to have lifted meat ceilings in response to a strike by meat interests against the health of the people, and soon after to have cracked down against a strike by miners. Morally a miners' strike for higher wages is on a higher level than cattlemen's strikes for higher profits. The government's policy against labor strikes would have to be implemented with equally stringent measures against attacks on the price structure. These should include requisitions, fines, and promotion of competitive enterprises. Where the government has to resort to plant seizure by reason of the refusal of the employer to accept a decision on wages or on another arbitrated issue, the profits for the duration of the seizure should not accrue to the employer.

Again, the critical period of the administrative state will be the transitional period, when it will have to resort to its powers of sanctions in the economic realm. In the course of time the conflict of economic interests will be canalized in more orderly channels. Then the era of sanctions will be transmuted to one of incentives. Our specific administrative techniques in the economic realm will improve and with them public sentiment. No drastic change in public attitudes will be required; only a continuation of the evolution of administration in the framework of democracy already well on its way.

3. LIBERTY AND AUTHORITY

Generalized attitudes are less amenable to change than specific techniques. The British genius has been to leave untouched the old symbols and landmarks of authority and install the most drastic changes in the course of generations.[11]

The American people will do well not to make a fetish out of the means used to achieve liberty and the fullness of life. There is nothing sacred or devilish about governmental or nongovernmental means. It is all a matter of what means are best calculated to achieve certain desired social purposes at any particular time. Social intelligence is the better part of vigilance. Authority is the enemy of liberty, shout those who also claim that security is inimical to freedom. The former is as fallacious as we have seen the latter to be.[12] Far from being necessarily its enemy, authority is the condition that makes liberty possible, for law is the foundation of freedom.[13] Without law there is freedom only for the most powerful and chaos prevails, philosophical anarchism to the contrary notwithstanding. Even revolutionaries against a particular legal order appeal to what appears to them a higher law—traditionally the law of nature, of God, or of the proletariat.[14] The absence of government is not the condition of liberty; it is rather the basis of bondage. In the democratic administrative state freedom is to be achieved through government.

If we are to preserve our liberties we must reject easy generalities and replace them with an eclectic approach. If we do not like some laws we should work to change them. But we should not be hoodwinked into thinking that our freedom lies in the absence of law. Laws always restrain somebody's freedom, regiment him, if you please. But it is imperative to inquire whose freedom and what liberty and to weigh the social values. Of course, the Wagner Act in granting freedom of self-organization to millions of employees has abridged the freedom of employers to discharge workers for belonging to a union. The question to consider is whether it is, from the interest of our society, more desirable to protect the freedom of employees to organize than that of the employer to punish them for exercising that right.

As America and the world are entering into a period of greater governmental controls, let us not be befuddled into the defeatist attitude that governmental authority necessarily leads to bureaucracy, authoritarianism, and loss of freedom. Here, again, it is not a problem of black and white but one of discriminating wisdom. Authority and freedom, power and responsibility—these and other everlasting problems of politics are, if not resolved, at least in dynamic equilibrium in the democratic administrative state. Its politics is not the desiccated abomination that Samuel warned against, but the process of creative controls.[15] The administrative state incorporates the principle that to be good it is not enough for government to be strong, but without being strong it cannot be good.

The democratically controlled administrative state is no panacea, no automatic device designed to inaugurate and maintain a static and utopian order.[16] Not a Leviathan,[17] nor a Moloch, nor some mystic essence superior to man,[18] but man's greatest organization and implement for social living. It is through the democratic administrative state that man's quest for power to master his environment can be dynamically socialized. As man's society expands into a global community and a world order is established, it is through the democratic administrative state that his pursuit of freedom and security can best be advanced.

Footnotes to Chapters

CHAPTER I

1. "The satisfaction of our wish may end it, but for every one that is satisfied there remain at least ten which are denied; further, desire lasts long, while its demands are infinite; the satisfaction is short and scantily meted out."—Arthur Schopenhauer, *The Wisdom of Life*; ". . . the cause of all these things was the pursuit of power animated by covetousness and ambition."—Thucydides, History, Bk. III.

2. Thomas Hobbes, *The Leviathan*, XI. See Niccolò Machiavelli, *The Prince, The Discourses*.

3. Francis Grant, *Oriental Philosophy*, 44.

4. Elbert D. Thomas, *Chinese Political Thought*, 55 (Hsun Tzu); 24 (Lao Tzu).

5. See Hobbes, *op cit.*; Reinhold Niebuhr, *The Nature and Destiny of Man*; see footnote 14, infra.

6. See Ralph Linton, *The Cultural Background of Personality*, 13; W. M. Wheeler, *Social Life Among the Insects*; W. C. Allee, *The Social Life of Animals*; Robert Redfield, "Levels of Integration in Biological and Social Systems" in *Biological Symposia*, Vol. VIII; Abraham Myerson, *Social Psychology*; L. Bernard, *Instinct*.

7. See Roderick Peattie, *Geography in Human History*; Montesquieu, *The Spirit of the Laws*; E. Huntington, *Civilization and Climate*; H. J. Mackinder, *Democratic Ideals and Reality*.

8. See Nikolai Lenin, *The State and Revolution*; Marx and Engels, *The Communist Manifesto*; N. Bukharin, *Historical Materialism*; Sidney Hook, *Towards the Understanding of Karl Marx*. On economic determinism see also Aristotle, *Politics*; J. Harrington, *The Commonwealth of Oceana*; James Madison in *The Federalist*; Charles Beard, *The Economic Basis of Politics*.

9. On technological influence see Thorstein Veblen, *The Theory of the Leisure Class*, and J. Dorfman, *Thorstein Veblen and His America*. On other theories of social causation see William F. Ogburn, *Social Change*; Robert M. MacIver, *Society*, 391-528; J. H. Randall, *Our Changing Civilization*; A. G. Keller, *Societal Evolution*; Pitrim Sorokin, *Social Mobility*. On the philosophical problem of causation see C. E. M. Joad, *Guide to Philosophy*, 170-250, and Bertrand Russell, *A History of Western Philosophy*.

10. Compare footnote 9, supra; Jerome Frank, *Fate and Freedom*; R. N. Anshen (ed.), *Freedom: Its Meaning*.

11. See Linton, *op. cit.*; Myerson, *op. cit.*; G. Murphy, *General Psychology*.

12. "The object of man's desire is . . . to assure for ever the way of his future desire . . ."—Hobbes, *op. cit.*, XI; Linton, *op. cit.*; G. Murphy, *op. cit.*; K. Young, *Social Psychology*; Bertrand Russell, *Power*; Alfred Adler, *Understanding Human Nature*.

13. "If I do not associate with mankind, with whom shall I associate?"—Confucius; Linton, *op. cit.*; Edmund Sapir, *Language*; Aristotle, *Politics*, I; Lucien Lévy-Bruhl, *The Soul of the Primitive*. See George Catlin, *The Story of the Philosophers*; Elbert D. Thomas, *op. cit.*; Hobbes, *op. cit.*; John Locke, *Two Treatises on Civil Government*; Jean Jacques Rousseau, *The Social Contract*; J. W. Gough, *The Social Contract*; Sir Henry Maine, *Ancient Law*, 312; Ernest Barker, *The Study of Political Science, and Its Relation to the Cognate Sciences*, 19; Sumner and Keller, *The Science of Society*, I, 461, 464; Edward McChesney Sait, *Political Institutions*, 101-106; also Chap. IV for origin of the state.

14. See Sigmund Freud, *The Basic Writings of—*, Modern Library ed.; Erich Fromm, *Escape from Freedom*; Karen Horney, *New Ways in Psycho-analysis*; Gregory Zilboorg, *Mind, Medicine and Man*; Harry Stack Sullivan, *Conceptions of Modern Psychiatry*; Franz Alexander, *Our Age of Unreason*.

15. See Hobbes, *op. cit.*; Bertrand Russell, *Power*; Adler, *op. cit.*; Niccolò

Machiavelli, *op. cit.*; Gaetano Mosca, *The Ruling Class*; Pareto, *The Mind and Society*; Robert O. Michels, *Political Parties*; George Catlin, *A Study of the Principles of Politics*; E. S. Bogardus, *Leaders and Leadership*; Friedrich Nietzsche, *Thus Spake Zarathustra* and *Beyond Good and Evil*; Chaps. III and XI.

CHAPTER II

1. See footnote 14, Chap. I.

2. See George Berkeley, *The Principles of Human Knowledge;* Joad, *Guide to Philosophy*, 56, 70-73.

3. A gratifying introduction to the heavenly cities is to be found in James Hastings' (ed.) *Encyclopedia of Religion and Ethics*, 817 et seq.

4. In *Mishkat al-Masabih*, XXIII, 13; "Musselmen will be given strength and vigour in paradise to have connection with many women. It was said, 'O Messenger of God,' will a man be able to connect himself with many women? His Majesty said, 'The powers of one hundred men will be given to one man.'"

5. Being preoccupied with social justice, classical Hebrew religion is virtually without a hereafter. "In the world to come," said Rabbi Rab, "there is neither eating, drinking, nor sexual pleasure, nor strife, but the righteous with their crowns sit around the table of God, feeding on the splendour of His Majesty."—Ber. 17a, Hastings, *op. cit.*, 835. See C. F. Burney. *Israel's Hope of Immortality*.

6. "They have no rest day and night. saying, Holy, holy, holy, is the Lord God, the Almighty which was and is and which is to come."—Rev. 4; "Of all the emotional states experienced on earth the profoundest and the most uplifting is the sense of boundless adoration, joined with abject self-abasement, which thrills through the devout soul as it contemplates the infinite perfections of God. In heaven this rapture of adoration will never cease."—Hastings, *op. cit.*, 835. See Dante, *The Divine Comedy*.

7. The most vivid and stirring parts of Dante's *Divine Comedy* are the descriptions of hell.

8. Marx and Engels, *The Communist Manifesto*; Freud, *The Future of An Illusion*.

9. See Harold Lasswell, *World Politics and Personal Insecurity*; Erich Fromm, *Escape from Freedom;* also Chaps. XI and XIX.

10. See footnote 9, supra.

11. See Chap. V; R. H. Tawney, *Religion and the Rise of Capitalism*; Sidney and Beatrice Webb, *History of Trade Unionism;* Richard R. Morris, *Government and Labor in Early America*.

12. See Chap. XIII; Manya Gordon, *Workers Before and After Lenin*.

13. See Frederick J. Turner. *The Influence of the Frontier on American History;* Vernon L. Parrington, *Main Currents in American Thought*.

14. See Veblen, *The Instinct of Workmanship;* Dorfman, *Thorstein Veblen and His America*.

15. See footnote 14, Chap. I.

16. See E. Bevan, *Stoics and Sceptics;* Marcus Aurelius, *Meditations*; Gilbert Murray, *The Stoic Philosophy*.

17. See Aristotle, *Ethics;* Bertrand Russell, *A History of Western Philosophy*.

18. See G. B. Chisholm, *The Psychiatry of Enduring Peace and Social Progress*.

19. See Nietzsche, *Thus Spake Zarathustra, Beyond Good and Evil;* Richard M. Brickner, *Is Germany Incurable?;* Paul Winkler, *The Thousand Year Conspiracy;* Rohan D'O. Butler, *The Roots of National Socialism;* Franz Neumann, *Behemoth*.

20. Joseph Rosenfarb, *The National Labor Policy and How It Works*, 75-76.

21. See footnote 9, supra.

22. For a discussion of the function of the father-image symbolism in the state see Chap. XIX.

23. "The Lord is my shepherd; I shall not want."—Psalm 23; see footnote 6, supra.

24. Compare Robert Hunter, *Revolution;* William Henry Chamberlin, *The Russian Revolution;* Leon Trotsky, *My Life;* Frederick L. Schuman, *Soviet Politics at Home and Abroad*.

25. See footnote 14, Chap. I; Lasswell, *Psychopathology and Politics;* also Chap. XIX.

26. See Chap. XV.

27. John Dewey, *Human Nature and Conduct.*

28. See Sir John Frazer, *The Golden Bough;* Alexander Goldenweiser, "Totemism" in V. F. Calverton (ed.) *The Making of Man;* Freud, *Totem and Taboo.*

29. See Freud, *Basic Writings;* Horney, *New Ways of Psychoanalysis.* In striking out against the contents of traditional morality, psychoanalysis would also eliminate the emotional content of guilt feelings. (Chisholm, *op. cit.*) It remains to be proved, however, whether guilt feeling, quite apart from the occasion for its evocation, is not a fundamental psychological response.

30. See footnote 14, Chap. I.

31. See Bertrand Russell, *A History of Western Philosophy.*

32. See Lasswell and Blumenstock, *World Revolutionary Propaganda;* Edmund Taylor, *The Strategy of Terror;* F. C. Bartlett, *Political Propaganda;* Plato's "royal lie," *The Republic,* Bk. III.

33. See Chap. XI.

34. See Bertrand Russell, *Power;* Charles E. Merriam, *Systematic Politics,* 74-117.

35. See Chaps. XI and XIX.

36. See Hunter, *op. cit.*

37. See Machiavelli, *The Prince;* Vilfredo Pareto, *The Mind and Society;* Leon Trotsky, *A History of the Russian Revolution;* Thomas Carlyle, *The French Revolution.*

38. See Franz Alexander, *Our Age of Unreason;* Lasswell, *World Politics and Personal Insecurity.*

39. See Aristotle, *Politics;* Chap. XI.

40. "Men are very rarely either entirely good or entirely bad."—Machiavelli, *The Discourses,* Chap. 27.

CHAPTER III

1. Chaps. I and II.

2. See George Catlin, *A Study of the Principles of Politics,* particularly 57-99 for a further analysis of this principle.

3. See Chap. II; Bertrand Russell, *Power.*

4. Harold Lasswell, *Politics: Who Gets What, When, How.*

5. See W. R. Agard, *What Democracy Meant to the Greeks.*

6. R. M. MacIver, *Society,* 143-323.

7. See Book Three.

8. See George Soule, *The Strength of Nations,* 99-129.

9. See Chap. VI.

10. See Chap. X.

11. See Book Four.

12. On the central position of division of labor as a welding force in society see Emile Durkheim, *Division of Social Work.*

13. See Chap. XVIII. See also Catlin, *op. cit.;* Herbert Spencer, Principles of Sociology.

14. Roberto Michels, *Political Parties.*

15. See Chap. XI.

16. See A. J. Toynbee, *A Study of History;* L. Urwick, *The Elements of Administration;* Gaus, White, Dimock, *Frontiers of Public Administration;* Henry Dennison, *Organization Engineering;* Gulick and Urwick (eds.) *Papers on the Science of Administration.* See Chap. XXI.

17. Vilfredo Pareto, *The Mind and Society.*

CHAPTER IV

1. R. M. MacIver, *Society,* 145-165.

2. Compare William C. MacLeod, *The Origin and History of Politics,* 3.

3. See Chap. XVIII for an analysis of federalism.

4. See Chap. XVII.

5. In support of this position see Woodrow Wilson, *The State,* 1-16. For a contrasting view see MacLeod, *op. cit.,* 23-40. As evidence he analyzes some unconvincing observation about the "Anarchy of the Yurok." Yet he states that "These peoples possessed a common or customary law. But there were no authorities to enforce compliance," p. 25. I sub-

mit that wherever law exists, there also is the state organization, and society has never been without law. (See Chap. XIX.) The fact that no governmental organ had become crystallized merely shows that the state organization of the Yurok was of a rudimentary (or perhaps a degenerated) character, and not that there was no state. There is even less justification for his failure to consider the "gerontocracy" of East Africa a state. A human being can be identified as such through infancy, childhood, adolescence, youth, middle age, and old age. So can the institution of the state through the various stages of its development. See Sumner and Keller, *The Science of Society*, Vol. I, 461, 464.

6. See Peter Kropotkin, *Fields, Factories and Workshops;* Michael Bakunin, *God and the State*.

7. Sorel, *Reflections on Violence*.

8. See Karl Marx, *Capital* and *The Communist Manifesto*.

9. As Herman Finer does in *The Theory and Practice of Modern Government* (2 vols., 1932), 8-9.

10. Franz Oppenheimer, *The State;* L. Gumplowicz, *Race and State*.

11. For a criticism of the conquest theory of the origin of the state see MacLeod, *op. cit.*, 144-147; MacIver, *The State*, 222; John Seeley, *Introduction to Political Science*, 73-75; Edward McChesney Sait, *Political Institutions*, 81-136; R. H. Lowie, *The Origin of the State*.

12. Wilson, *op. cit*. See footnote 11, supra.

13. For a pluralistic concept of sovereignty see Harold J. Laski, *The Grammar of Politics;* G. D. H. Cole, *Self Government in Industry*.

14. See Books Two and Four.

15. See footnote 13, supra: on sovereignty compare Sait, *op. cit.*, 137-157.

16. See Chap. XI.

17. See Nikolai Lenin, *The State and Revolution*.

18. See John Locke, *Two Treatises on Civil Government;* Catlin, *Anglo-Saxony and Its Tradition*.

19. See Books Two and Four.

20. See Sigmund Freud, *A General Introduction to Psychoanalysis;* Gregory Zilboorg, *Mind, Medicine and Man*.

21. See Chaps. II and XIX; Lasswell, *Psychopathology and Politics;* Franz Alexander, *Our Age of Unreason;* Richard M. Brickner, *Is Germany Incurable?;* Erich Fromm, *Escape from Freedom*. See footnote 22, infra.

22. Sir Henry Maine, *Ancient Law;* Edward Westermarck, *The History of Human Marriage;* A. A. Goldenweiser, *Early Civilization;* R. M. MacIver, *Society*, 116; Malinowski, "Kinship," *Encyclopaedia Britannica;* Sait, *op. cit.*, 81-136.

23. See footnote 22, supra.

24. For advocacy of the matriarchal theory, see Robert Briffault, *The Mothers*. For refutation see footnote 22, supra.

25. See footnote 22, supra.

26. Compare Wilson, *op. cit.*, 17. For an opposite view see MacLeod, *op. cit.*, 23-40, and see footnote 5, supra, for comment. "The commencement is in the family and State; the consummation is in the Empire," in *Shu King of Confucius*. See Elbert D. Thomas, *Chinese Political Thought*, 39-66. See Chap. I for argument against "social contract" origin of society and the state.

27. See Chap. XIX.

28. MacIver, *The Modern State*, 31.

29. MacIver, *op. cit.*, 43; Wilson, *op. cit.*, 17-29; Maine, *op. cit.;* Sir James G. Frazer, *The Golden Bough;* W. J. Perry, *The Origin of Magic and Religion*.

30. See footnote 29, supra.

31. Maine, *op. cit.;* W. E. Heitland, *The Roman Republic*.

32. See C. J. Hayes, *Essays on Nationalism, The Historical Evolution of Modern Nationalism;* Ernest Barker, *National Character;* Frank H. Hankins, *The Racial Basis of Civilization*.

33. During the war Alexander Nevsky, Suvorov, Kutuzov, and Mazeppa found a niche beside Lenin, Marx, and Engels in Soviet official hagiolatry. See Eugene Tarle, *Napoleon's Invasion of Russia, 1812*.

34. See MacLeod, *op. cit.*, 160-283; Senator Elbert D. Thomas, *op. cit.*

35. See Sait. *op. cit.*, 81-136; MacLeod,

op. cit., 75-97; Maine, *op. cit.*; Sumner and Keller, *The Science of Society;* Wilson, *op cit.*, 17-127.

36. See William Seagle, *The Quest for Law*, 36-101. For a further analysis of legal evolution see Chap. XIX.

37. See Chaps. XVIII and XIX.

38. See footnote 36, supra.

39. See Silas Bent McKinley, *Democracy and Military Power;* Lynn Montross, *War Through the Ages.*

40. See footnote 36, supra.

41. See Chaps. XI and XIX.

42. For emphasis on the assertive or enterprising individual see MacLeod, *op. cit.*, 98-102; on property see Sait, *op. cit.*, 124-129; on force or conquest see Oppenheimer, *op. cit.*; on magic and religion see Frazer, *op. cit.*, and Perry, *op. cit.*

43. See Chaps. V and XIX.

44. As that of Perry, *op. cit.*, in ascribing to Egypt only the origin of kingship, MacLeod's work too belongs in the diffusionist school.

45. See Oswald Spengler, *The Decline of the West;* see Book Four.

46. See Book Two.

CHAPTER V

1. See Chap. IV.

2. See Chaps. III and XI. For a contrasting view see Franz Oppenheimer, *The State;* Nikolai Lenin, *State and Revolution;* Friedrich Engels, *The Origin of the Family.*

3. See Chaps. IV, XI, and XIII.

4. See Robert M. MacIver, *The Modern State*, 31; M. J. Herkovitz, *The Economic Life of Primitive Peoples.*

5. But see Plato, *The Symposium.*

6. See Chaps. II and IV; MacIver, *op. cit.*, 32.

7. Compare Edward M. Sait, *Political Institutions*, 124-136; Oppenheimer, *op. cit.*, 22-81.

8. Compare Oppenheimer, *op. cit.*, 82-120, 174-228; William C. MacLeod, *The Origin and History of Politics*, 160-205; Woodrow Wilson, *The State*, 221-267.

9. Compare Oppenheimer, *op. cit.*, 121-173; MacIver, *op. cit.*, 69-114, 291-316.

10. See footnote 9, supra.

11. See Oppenheimer, *op. cit.*, 174-228.

12. See Lynn Montross, *War Through the Ages;* Silas Bent McKinley, *Democracy and Military Power.*

13. For other manifestations of the same principle see Chaps. VI, XI, and XX.

14. See G. L. Beer, *Origins of the British Colonial System;* Richard B. Morris, *Government and Labor in Early America.*

15. See Osborne Taylor, *The Medieval Mind;* St. Thomas Aquinas, *Summae Theologiae; Commentaries on the Politics of Aristotle;* C. H. McIlwain, *Growth of Political Thought in the West;* George Catlin, *Story of the Political Philosophers*, 146-186; Michael W. Shallo, *Scholastic Philosophy;* Bertrand Russell, *A History of Western Philosophy*, 308-487.

16. See Bertrand Russell, *op. cit.*, 525-540; Ionides, *Stars and Men;* A. Wolf, *A History of Science, Technology, and Philosophy in the Sixteenth and Seventeenth Centuries.*

17. See St. Augustine, *The City of God.*

18. See R. J. Tawney, *Religion and the Rise of Capitalism;* Weber, *The Protestant Ethic and the Spirit of Capitalism.*

19. See Erich Fromm, *Escape from Freedom*, 40-102. On the further atomizing process of democracy see Chaps. IX and XV and: "Thus not only does democracy make every man forget his ancestors, but it hides his descendants, and separates his contemporaries from him; it throws him back forever upon himself alone, and threatens in the end to confine him entirely within the solitude of his own heart."—Alexis de Tocqueville, *Democracy in America*, Vol. II, p. 106, in the World's Great Classics.

20. "Men can do all things if they will," cried Alberti. See Ralph Roeder, *The Man of the Renaissance;* Pietro Aretino, *Dialogues;* J. Burckhardt, *The Civilization of the Renaissance in Italy;* J. A. Symonds, *The Renaissance.*

21. See Niccolò Machiavelli, *The Prince, The Discourses.* Said "Old Nick" in a letter to a friend: "I come now to

the last branch of my charge: that I teach princes villainy and how to enslave ... if any man will read over my book ... with impartiality and ordinary charity, he will easily perceive that it is not my intention to recommend that government or those men there described to the world, much less to teach men how to trample upon good men, and all that is sacred and venerable upon earth, laws, religion, honesty, and what not. If I have been a little too punctual in describing these monsters in all their lineaments and colours, I hope mankind will know them, the better to avoid them, my treatise being both a satire against them, and a true character of them ..."

22. See Martin Luther, *On Civil Government*; Valeriu Morcu, *Accent on Power, The Life and Times of Machiavelli*; Giuseppe Prezzolini, *Niccolò Machiavelli*; George Catlin, *op. cit.*, 187-220; Bertrand Russell, *op. cit.*, 491-674; footnotes 18-20, supra.

23. See Morris, *op. cit.*; Arthur Schlessinger, Jr., *The Age of Jackson*; De Tocqueville, *op. cit.*; Charles and Mary Beard, *The Rise of American Civilization*; Vernon L. Parrington, *Main Currents in American Thought*, Bk. I.

24. Compare Emil Ludwig, *The Germans, Double History of a Nation*; Rohan D'O. Butler, *The Roots of National Socialism*; Herbert Heaton, *Economic History of Europe*; C. W. Hasek, *Introduction of Adam Smith's Ideas into Germany*.

25. Compare Eduard Bernstein, *Evolutionary Socialism*; Karl Kautsky, *Dictatorship of the Proletariat*; Nikolai Lenin, *Kautsky the Renegade and the Proletarian Revolution*.

CHAPTER VI

1. See Adam Smith, *The Wealth of Nations*, 1776; Bertrand Russell, *A History of Western Philosophy*, 491-674. Compare R. H. Tawney, *The Acquisitive Society*, 10.
2. Jeremy Bentham, *An Introduction to the Principles of Morals and Legislation*; James Mill, *An Essay on Government*; J. S. Mill, *Representative Government* and *Principles of Political Economy*; Harold J. Laski, *The Rise of Liberalism*; Alfred Marshall, *Principles of Economics*; Karl Polanyi, *The Great Transformation*.
3. See Thomas Hobbes, *The Leviathan*.
4. See Sir Arthur Salter, *Recovery: The Second Effort*; O. F. Boucke, *Laissez-Faire and After*; J. M. Keynes, *The End of Laissez-Faire*; Eli Ginzberg, *The House of Adam Smith*.
5. For instance, W. Stanley Jevons, *Theory of Political Economy and Money and the Mechanism of Exchange* (correlation with sunspots); H. L. Moore, *Economic Cyles: Their Law and Cause* (correlation with planet Venus).
6. See Sir William Beveridge, *Full Employment in a Free Society*, 40-90; Chap. V.
7. See Chaps. III and IV, and Book Four; Herbert Spencer, *Principles of Sociology*.
8. See *Economic Concentration and World War ll*, Report of the Smaller War Plants Corporation to the Special Committee to Study Problems of American Small Business, United States Senate, 79th Congress, 2nd Sess., Doc. No. 206.
9. See Reports of the Temporary National Economic Committee.
10. See A. A. Berle and G. C. Means, *The Modern Corporation and Private Property*.
11. Berle and Means, *op. cit.*, 9.
12. John Maynard Keynes, *The General Theory of Employment, Interest and Money*, 273.
13. See Chap. I.
14. See Thurman W. Arnold, *The Bottlenecks of Business, The Folklore of Capitalism*; Max Radin, *Manners and Morals of Business*.
15. Louis D. Brandeis, *The Curse of Bigness*; Morris Ernst, *Too Big*.
16. See Chap. XV.
17. See Chap. XV; Millis and Montgomery, *Organized Labor*, 1-242; Joseph Rosenfarb, *The National Labor Policy and How It Works*, 1-20.
18. See Chap. XIV for a fundamental analysis of this problem.
19. Adam Smith, *op. cit.*; Friedrich Hayek, *The Road to Serfdom*; Henry Hazlitt, *Economics in One Lesson*.
20. See *The Communist Manifesto*;

Lenin, *The State and Revolution;* Laski, *The State in Theory and Practice.*

21. See Brady, *Business as a System of Power;* Franz Neumann, *Behemoth.*

22. Compare George Catlin, *A Study of the Principles of Politics;* Herbert Spencer, *op. cit.;* Emile Durkheim, *Method of Sociology.*

CHAPTER VII

1. Public Law 304—79th Congress, Chapter 33—2nd Sess.

2. The first members of the council are Edwin G. Nourse, chairman; Leon H. Keyserling, vice-chairman, and John D. Clark.

3. In Section 2, the declaration of policy of the act is set forth as "The Congress hereby declares that it is the continuing policy and responsibility of the Federal Government to use all practicable means consistent with its needs and obligations and other essential considerations of national policy, with the assistance and cooperation of industry, agriculture, labor, and State and local governments, to coordinate and utilize all its plans, functions, and resources for the purpose of creating and maintaining, in a manner calculated to foster and promote free competitive enterprise and the general welfare, conditions under which there will be afforded useful employment opportunities, including self-employment, for those able, willing, and seeking to work, and to promote maximum employment, production, and purchasing power." Although the term "full employment" was stricken from the bill in its path through Congress and "maximum employment" substituted, it is gratifying that the council in its First Annual Report to the President in December, 1946, p. 3, declares: "It is hard to see how a measure can be regarded as 'watered down' which so clearly states the" purposes of the act. Let us hope that this interpretation will prevail, that the distinction between "maximum employment" and "full employment" is one of semantics only. However "alarming" the objective of "full employment" may be to some, no less should or will be accepted by the people over a period of years as the responsibility of government. See Chap. VI. Compare Sir William H. Beveridge, *Full Employment in a Free Society,* on the meaning of full employment, 18-20: "The proposition that there should be more vacant jobs than unemployed men means that the labor market should always be a seller's market rather than a buyer's market. A person who has difficulty in buying the labor that he wants suffers inconvenience or reduction of profits. A person who cannot sell his labor is in effect told that he is of no use. The first difficulty causes annoyance or loss. The other is a personal catastrophe. This difference remains even if an adequate income is provided by insurance or otherwise during unemployment. . . ."

4. Although the council's First Report emphasizes that it has the power to recommend any plan or combination of plans, it remains to be seen what measures will be recommended by the council. It was rather disquieting to have a government agency set up to plan for "maximum employment" foreclose itself for the future by raising the bugaboo of "bureaucracy" by declaring that the act does not "involve that regulation of actual business operation which would constitute bureaucratic 'regimentation' " (p. 16). It was also less than reassuring that the council would leave the working out of the price-wage relationship and recovery from a possible "brief dip" to laissez faire "without benefit of direct Government intervention" (p. 19; see also p. 18). It is to the credit of the Council that under the impact of inflation, it discarded government by exhortation and embraced positive government regulation of the wage-price-profit relationship and the allocation of scarce materials. *The Economic Report of the President,* January 1948.

5. See Henry Hazlitt, *Economics in One Lesson;* Friedrich Hayek, *The Road to Serfdom;* Ludwig von Mises, *Bureaucracy; Omnipotent Government;* Gustav Stolper, *The Age of Fable.*

6. See Chaps. I and II.

7. See Book Two. Compare Council of Economic Advisers Report, *cit.* 16; Sir William H. Beveridge, *op. cit.;* Barbara Wooton, *Freedom under Planning.*

8. See John Maynard Keynes, *The General Theory of Employment, Interest*

and Money and *A Treatise on Money;* Alvin Hansen, *Fiscal Policy and Business Cycles.* For a discussion of the Keynesian analysis see Beveridge, *op. cit.,* 90-105.

9. See footnote 8, supra.

10. The Council of Economic Advisers rejects government "fiscal policy as a panacea" (p. 13). Nevertheless, it declares that the government must "vigorously use ... control of the public purse" as a strategic economic weapon (p. 18).

11. See Chap. XIV.

12. See Chap. VI.

13. See Chap. XIII for an analysis of the relevant aspects of the Russian system.

CHAPTER VIII

1. The proposed plan in its essentials was formulated by the author in 1944.

2. See Sir William H. Beveridge, *Full Employment in a Free Society,* 110-122; War Production Board First Report, Jan. 1, 1945, Second Report, April 1, 1945, and J. A. Krug Report to WPB on *Production: Wartime Achievements and the Reconversion Outlook.*

3. "The outstanding factor in the present situation is that we are working under a strong domestic urge and foreign demand to catch up on durable (producer and consumer) goods, whose production had to be postponed during the war at the same time that, because of high income and war savings, the majority of the population are eager and able to maintain a higher than prewar level of consumption also of nondurables. Added to these two more-than-ordinary supports of employment and productive enterprise is a third—the need to reconvert plant, reequip it for these particular types of production, and expand these industries to meet the accelerated rate demanded by this race to catch up after the war's interruptions. Everybody without a house or a car wants one this year. The success of '47 and '48 is gauged by our ability to make and sell 6,000,000 cars, 1,500,000 housing units, and similar numbers of electric refrigerators, washing machines, and other accessories in each of these years. But the closer we come to this standard of performance in the immediate future, the more pressing becomes the problem of sustaining employment, production, and purchasing power in the years that follow. Automobiles, as we have learned under war conditions, have a normal life expectancy of 8 to 10 years and houses last anywhere from 25 years to generations or even centuries. Hence, the very industries which feature the prosperity of the moment could, if nothing is done, be expected to drop to a replacement basis after a few years.

"This might spell deep depression for some later time—but only if we fail to make the gradual shift in expenditures and resource use that wise foreseeing and astute planning for this inevitable trend of development suggests to sagacious people." Council of Economic Advisers, First Report, cit. 20.

4. Compare Beveridge, *op. cit.;* J. M. Keynes, *The General Theory of Employment, Interest and Money; The Economic Report of the President,* January 1948.

5. "The unfulfilled consumptive desires of the American people are large enough to absorb a productive output many times that achieved in the peak year 1929 ... The trouble is clearly not lack of desire but lack of purchasing power"—Brookings Institution, *America's Capacity to Consume,* 127. For it would be absurd to say that there are not things to do with these resources after the present making up of war deprivations has been completed. We must recognize the real magnitude of our productive power and keep it going to produce for all the things that only the more favored have enjoyed in the past. As progress is made in catching up on the wartime postponables, we must feed into our 'product mix' more of those semiluxuries, those welfare and culture goods, which are put within the reach of our people as a whole by reason of our unparallelled productive capacity. This, as we have said before, will combat depression and even up the years of traditional recession by allowing those able, willing and seeking to work to go on supplying themselves rather than being every few years forced to loaf and want." —Council of Economic Advisers Report, *op. cit.,* 21. See also *The Economic Report of the President,* January 1948.

6. See Chap. XXII for an analysis of the problem of sanctions and incentives.
7. See Book Three.
8. See WPB Reports in footnote 15, supra.
9. See Borkin and Welsh, *Germany's Master Plan;* Franz Neumann, *Behemoth;* Frank Munk, *The Legacy of Nazism.*
10. See footnote 9, supra; R. Liefmann, *Cartels, Concerns and Trusts.*
11. See footnotes 9 and 10, supra.
12. See Chap. XXII.
13. See Chap. III.
14. See Chap. XIV.
15. See Thurman W. Arnold, *The Bottlenecks of Business.*
16. See A. A. Berle and G. C. Means, *The Modern Corporation and Private Property;* Chap. VI.
17. See Chap. XXI; Joseph Rosenfarb, *The National Labor Policy and How It Works,* 450-635.
18. See Chap. IX.
19. See Book Three for an analysis of labor problems in the administrative state.
20. See Chaps. XX and XXI for an analysis of government structure and administration.
21. See Chaps. III and VI.
22. Other aspects of private enterprise in a planned economy will be analyzed in Books Two–Four.

CHAPTER IX

1. See Chap. VI.
2. See Friedrich A. Hayek, *The Road to Serfdom;* Ludwig von Mises, *Bureaucracy; Omnipotent Government;* James Burnham, *The Managerial Revolution;* Hilaire Belloc, *The Servile State,* Hayek equates democracy and liberty with economic laissez faire but not, however, to the extent that his American claque would have us believe.
3. See Chaps VI, XIII, and Book Four.
4. See William F. Ogburn, *Social Change;* R. M. MacIver, *Society,* 391-528; Alexis de Tocqueville, *Democracy in America,* particularly Vol. II; Ralph Linton, *The Cultural Background of Personality;* Oswald Spengler, *The Decline of the West.*
5. See Chap. I; also Bertrand Russell's essay, *Freedom and Government* in *Freedom, Its Meaning,* R. N. Anshen (ed.).
6. "Man is born free and everywhere he is in chains." Thus begins Rousseau in his *Social Contract.*
7. See Chap. I.
8. Compare Hegel, *The Philosophy of History.* "The History of the world is none other than the progress of the consciousness of freedom."—19 in Bohn's Philosophical Library.
9. See Chap. II, Linton, *op. cit.*
10. See Anshen, *op. cit.;* John Dewey, *Freedom and Culture;* Elbert D. Thomas, *Chinese Political Thought;* John Stuart Mill, *Essay on Liberty;* C. E. M. Joad, *Liberty Today;* Erich Fromm, *Escape from Freedom;* George Catlin, *The Story of Political Philosophers;* Everett Dean Martin, *Liberty;* Benedetto Croce, *History as the Story of Liberty;* Charles E. Merriam, *American Political Theories;* Ross J. S. Hoffman, *The Will to Freedom.* On the relationship of liberty to the problem of causation see Jerome S. Frank, *Fate and Freedom;* C. E. M. Joad, *Guide to Philosophy,* 207-252; Jonathan Edwards, *Freedom of Will;* and John Milton, *Areopagitica* in Everyman's Library, 13, for the relationship of the problem of free will to freedom of the press.
11. The first ten amendments to the U.S. Constitution limit the federal government while the Fourteenth Amendment has been held to apply virtually the same restrictions to the states. These limitations do not apply to actions of non-governmental bodies: Civil Rights Cases, 109 U.S. 3.
12. See Charles and Mary Beard, *The Rise of American Civilization.*
13. "The Fourteenth Amendment does not enact Mr. Herbert Spencer's Social Statics . . . a constitution is not intended to embody a particular economic theory, whether of paternalism and the organic relation of the citizen to the State or of laissez faire."—Mr. Justice Holmes in his dissent in *Lochner* v. *New York,* 198 U.S. 45, 74; see also Mr. Justice Stone's dissent in *United States* v. *Butler,* 297 U.S. 1.
14. See Harold Lasswell, *World Politics and Personal Insecurity;* Franz Alexander, *Our Age of Unreason.*

15. Erich Fromm, *op. cit.;* Richard M. Brickner, *Is Germany Incurable?;* Paul Winkler, *The Thousand Year Conspiracy;* Franz L. Neumaun, *Behemoth;* Rohan D'O. Butler, *The Roots of National Socialism;* Martin Luther, *On Civil Government.*

16. See Harold Lasswell, *op. cit.;* Frederick L. Schuman, *Soviet Politics at Home and Abroad;* William Henry Chamberlin, *The Russian Revolution;* Markoosha Fischer, *My Lives in Russia;* Freda Utley, *The Dream We Lost.*

17. "Full employment" would add far more to happiness than to wealth, and would add most of all to national unity, by removing the misery that generates hate."—Sir William H. Beveridge, *Full Employment in a Free Society,* 129.

18. See Barbara Wooton, *Freedom under Planning,* 55-78. The book presents an enlightening analysis in some detail of the various economic freedoms under planning.

19. See Chap. VIII.

20. See Chap. XV.

CHAPTER X

1. See R. M. MacIver, *Society,* 314-388.

2. See Chap. V; C. J. Hayes, *Essays on Nationalism and the Historical Evolution of Modern Nationalism.*

3. See Brooks Atkinson's articles on art in Russia in the New York *Times,* July 7, 8, 9, 1946.

4. See Martin Luther, *On Civil Government;* Erich Fromm, *Escape from Freedom,* 40-102; Charles and Mary Beard, *The Rise of American Civilization.*

5. See Chap. XIII.

6. See Chaps. XI and XV.

7. Mr. Justice Holmes's dissent in *Abrams* v. *U.S.,* 250 U.S. 616, 624; In *Areopagitica,* John Milton said, "The ultimate good desired is better reached by free trade in ideas."

8. See Harold L. Ickes, *America's House of Lords, Freedom of the Press Today* (symposium); Morris Ernst, *The First Freedom;* James Lawrence Fly, "Freedom of Speech and the Press" (as applied to radio) in *Safeguarding Civil Liberties Today,* Cornell University Press, 1945; *A Free and Responsible Press,* by the Commission on Freedom of the Press; W. E. Hocking, *Freedom of the Press.*

9. See Joseph Rosenfarb, *The National Labor Policy and How It Works,* 635-645.

10. See Book Four.

11. See Fly, *op. cit.*

12. Charles G. Fenwick, *International Law,* 359.

13. The problem of democracy will be analyzed in Chaps. XI-XIII. The economic and political liberties of labor will be treated in Book Three. The relationship of freedom to authority and law will be discussed in Chap. XXII.

CHAPTER XI

1. See George Catlin, *The Story of the Political Philosophers.*

2. See W. R. Agard, *What Democracy Meant to the Greeks;* Edward McChesney Sait, *Political Institutions,* 424-433.

3. See Sait, *op. cit.,* 424-433 for references to variations on the democratic theme.

4. Plato, *Republic,* Bk. III.

5. See footnote 2, supra; James Bryce, *Modern Democracies.*

6. See Chap. IV.

7. See John Locke, *Two Treatises on Civil Government;* Jean Jacques Rousseau, *The Social Contract;* Charles E. Merriam, *American Political Theories;* T. V. Smith, *The American Philosophy of Equality; The Democratic Tradition in America.*

8. John B. Watson, *Behaviorism.*

9. See William C. MacLeod, *The Origin and History of Politics,* 100-101; Robert Redfield (ed.), *Levels of Integration in Biologic and Social Systems* (Biological Symposia. Vol. VIII, 1942); W. M. Wheeler, *Social Life Among the Insects;* Vilfredo Pareto, *The Mind and Society;* Gaetano Mosca, *The Ruling Class;* Roberto Michels, *Political Parties;* Plato, *op. cit.;* Niccolò Machiavelli, *The Prince* and *The Discourses;* Paul Pigors,

Leadership or Domination; Ordway Tead, *The Art of Leadership;* E. S. Bogardus, *Leaders and Leadership.*

10. See Chap. III.

11. See Michels, *op. cit.*

12. See Michels, *op. cit.;* Walter Lippmann, *Public Opinion;* James Bryce, *Modern Democracies,* Vol. II, 549; Mosca, *op. cit.;* Pareto. *op. cit.;* Machiavelli, *Discourses,* Bk. I, Chaps. 44, 53, 54; Pigors, *op. cit.* 195-287.

13. See Joseph Rosenfarb, *The National Labor Policy and How It Works,* 152-153.

14. Compare Thomas Carlyle. *The French Revolution; Latter Day Pamphlets;* Toynbee, *A Study of History.*

15. See Chap. IV; MacLeod. *op. cit.,* 100-101; Franz Oppenheimer, *The State;* Sir James G. Frazer, *The Golden Bough.*

16. Oppenheimer, *The State,* 22-81.

17. Compare M. M. Bober, *Karl Marx's Interpretation of History;* Harold J. Laski, *The State in Theory and Practice;* MacLeod, *op. cit.,* 139-159.

18. See Bertrand Russell, *Power.*

19. See Bienstock, Schwartz, and Yugow, *Management in Russian Industry and Agriculture;* Leonard E. Hubbard, *Soviet Labor and Industry, Soviet Trade and Distribution,* and *Soviet Money and Finance;* Manya Gordon. *Workers Before and After Lenin;* John Scott, *Beyond the Urals.*

20. Plato, *op. cit.,* Bk. I.

21. Compare Mosca, *op. cit.;* Pareto, *op. cit.*

22. See footnote 21, supra.

23. Edward M. East. *Heredity and Human Affairs,* 208-212; N. J. Lennes. *Whither Democracy?*

24. See Bienstock et al., *op. cit.*

25. See Chap. XIX.

26. Plato, *Republic,* Bk. III.

27. See Chaps. I and IV.

28. See Plato, *op. cit.:* "Wealth I said, and poverty; the one is the parent of luxury and indolence and the other of meanness and viciousness, and both of discontent."—Bk. IV.; Pareto, *op. cit.,* and Mosca, *op. cit.*

29. Compare Pareto. *op. cit.;* Carlyle, *op. cit;* Robert Hunter, *Revolution: Why, How, When;* Raymond Postgate, *How to Make a Revolution;* Curzio Malaparte, *Coup d'Etat, the Technique of Revolution;* Crane Brinton, *The Anatomy of Revolution;* L. P. Edwards, *The Natural History of Revolution;* see Chap. IX.

30. Compare Leon Trotsky, *The History of the Russian Revolution;* Sir John Maynard, *Russia in Flux.*

31. See Marx and Engels, *The Communist Manifesto;* Karl Kautsky, *The Dictatorship of the Proletariat;* Nikolai Lenin, *The State and Revolution.*

32. See Mosca, *op. cit.;* Pareto, *op. cit.;* Michels, *op. cit.;* footnote 19, supra; George Orwell, *Animal Farm;* Max Nomad, "Rebels and Renegades" and "Masters—Old and New" in *The Making of Society,* 882, edited by V. F. Calverton.

33. Compare Mosca, *op. cit.,* 394; Sait, *op. cit.,* 406-433; see Chaps. XIX and XX for classification of political forms on basis of government apparatus.

34. See Chaps. IV and XIX.

35. See Chaps. IV and XIX.

36. Aristotle, *Politics,* Bk. III.

37. See Chap. XX; Charles E. Merriam, *American Political Theories.*

38. Machiavelli, *The Discourses,* Bk. II, Chap. 29.

39. Compare Mosca, *op. cit.,* 394; Aristotle, *op. cit.,* Bk. III; Plato, *op. cit.,* Bk. VIII; Cicero, *De Republica,* II, 23; see Chaps. XIX and XX.

40. See Book Four.

41. See Chap. X.

42. It is unlikely that public men today in Britain or in America would dare articulate the views of Edmund Burke in *Appeal from the New to the Old Whigs* or of John C. Calhoun in *Disquisition on Government.*

43. See Lippmann, *op. cit.*

44. See Chap. X.

45. "Virtu" in Machiavelli's terminology, *The Prince,* Chap. 18; also Mosca, *op. cit.;* Pareto, *op. cit.;* James Burnham, *The Machiavellians;* Thomas Hobbes, *The Leviathan.* See Chap. I.

46. For an analysis of the problem of sanctions and incentives as it affects administration see Chap. XXII.

47. See Chap. XV.

48. "A prudent prince must therefore take a third course, by choosing for his council wise men, and giving these alone full liberty to speak the truth to him . . ." Machiavelli, *The Prince*, Chap. 23.

CHAPTER XII

1. On the place of the expert in government see Chap. XXI.

2. On the various expressions of man's quest for power see Chaps. I and II.

3. See Franklin C. Palm, *The Middle Classes Then and Now;* A. N. Holcombe, *The Middle Classes in American Politics;* Max Nomad, *Rebels and Renegades;* Lewis Corey, *The Crisis of the Middle Class.*

4. See Joseph Rosenfarb, "Foremen on the March," *Federal Bar Journal*, Winter, 1946.

5. See Sidney Hook, *Towards the Understanding of Karl Marx;* Charles and Mary Beard, *The Rise of American Civilization.*

6. See Rosenfarb, *The National Labor Policy.*

7. Plato, *op. cit.*, Bk. I.

8. For an analysis of the mechanism of governmental checks and balances see Chap. XX.

9. See Chap. XXI.

10. See James Burnham, *The Managerial Revolution.*

11. See Chap. XXI for an analysis of administration.

12. See Max Nomad, *op. cit.;* Waclaw Machajski, *The Intellectual Worker;* Harold Lasswell, *World Politics and Personal Insecurity.*

13. See Chap. XV.

14. Compare Sir William H. Beveridge, *Full Employment in a Free Society.*

15. See John Strachey, *The Coming Struggle for Power;* Harold J. Laski, *Reflections on the Revolution of Our Time.*

16. Originally attributed to Lord Balfour. See Sait, *op. cit.*, 464-466.

17. See Chaps. XVIII and XX for an analysis of government paralysis as a danger to democracy.

18. See footnote 19, Chap. XI; Robert M. MacIver, *Society*, 391-509; William F. Ogburn, *Social Change;* Ralph Linton, *The Cultural Background of Personality.*

CHAPTER XIII

1. See Arthur Rosenberg, *Democracy and Socialism;* Marx and Engels, *The Communist Manifesto;* Nikolai Lenin, *Imperialism;* Peter Kropotkin, *The Conquest of Bread;* George Catlin, *The Story of the Political Philosophers*, 543-648.

2. An operation similar to that performed for the term democracy—Chap. XI.

3. To be found particularly in the popular literature of socialism.

4. See footnote 19, Chap. XI; Max Nomad, *Rebels and Renegades;* Eugene Lyons, *Assignment to Utopia;* F. L. Schuman, *Soviet Politics at Home and Abroad*, 587-599; Sidney and Beatrice Webb, *Soviet Communism: A New Civilization.*

5. Bienstock, Schwartz, and Yugow, *Management in Russian Industry and Agriculture;* also footnote 19 in Chap. XI.

6. See Book Three.

7. Bienstock, et al., *op. cit.*

8. See James Burnham, *The Managerial Revolution.*

9. See Richard B. Morris, *Government and Labor in Early America.*

10. See *The Wealth of Nations;* Weber, *The Protestant Ethic and the Rise of Capitalism;* R. H. Tawney, *Religion and the Rise of Capitalism.*

11. See Chaps. VI and VIII; Sir William Beveridge, *Full Enployment in a Free Society.*

12. See Book Four for an analysis of the political or governmental aspects of democracy, and Book Three for a study of industrial democracy.

CHAPTER XIV

1. See Sidney and Beatrice Webb, *History of Trade Unionism;* Commons and Associates, *History of Labor in the United States;* S. Perlman, *A Theory of the Labor Movement* and *A History of Trade Unionism in the United States;* Millis and Montgomery, *Organized Labor,* 1-242.

2. Some of the observations in this section on the economic compulsives appeared originally in "The Administrative State: Compulsives in Labor Relations," in *North Carolina Law Review,* February, 1945, and in "Trend of Labor Laws," *Barron's,* July 15, 1946.

3. See Report of the President's National Labor-Management Conference, 1945.

4. See Chaps. VI and VIII.

5. Leo Wolman, *Ebb and Flow in Trade Unionism,* 16; 3,442,600 in 1929, and 2,973,000 in 1933.

6. Membership of Labor Unions in the United States—Release L. S. 47-3948, 1947.

7. See Joseph Rosenfarb, "Foremen on the March," *Federal Bar Journal,* Winter, 1946.

8. Man-days lost because of strikes during the war hovered on the average around one-tenth of one per cent of available working time: *Strikes in 1943,* BLS Bulletin No. 782, 2; also 59 *Monthly Labor Review,* 1017.

9. The greatest incidence of strikes in the history of the country occurred in that year: *Strikes in 1943,* BLS Bulletin No. 782, p. 2.

10. 44 Stat., pt. 2, 577 (1926) as amended in 1934, 48 Stat. 1185 (1934), 45 U.S.C.A. §§ 151-164 (1943). See Joseph Rosenfarb, *The National Labor Policy and How It Works;* and Millis and Montgomery, *op. cit.,* for a description of its operation.

11. 57 Stat. 163, 50 U.S.C.A. §1501 (Supp. 1943). There was an increase in the incidence of strikes after the adoption of the act.

12. See footnote 10, supra; also annual reports of the National Mediation Board.

13. See New York *Times,* Dec. 5, 1946, p. 4. The right of the government to obtain the injunction was sustained by the Supreme Court.

14. The experience in this country has been paralleled by that in Great Britain.

15. See Chaps. VI and VIII.

16. See Chap. XXII.

17. For instance, insurance, hospitalization, health: Continental Can Co., WLB Case No. 2860-D (732), June, 1943; sick leave benefits, Van Norman Machine Tool Co., WLB Case No. 111-3956-D, Feb. 18, 1944; severance pay, Carnegie-Illinois Steel Corp. et al., WLB Case No. 111-6230-D, Nov. 25, 1944.

18. See Mills and Montgomery, *op. cit.,* 353-388; Paul H. Douglas, *The Theory of Wages;* Sir William H. Beveridge, *Full Employment in a Free Society.*

19. Carnegie-Illinois Steel Corp. et al, WLB Case No. 111-6230-D, Nov. 25, 1944.

20. For an analysis of the craft-industrial controversy as it is reflected in the determination of the appropriate unit under the National Labor Relations Act see Rosenfarb, *op. cit.,* 316-385.

21. See footnote 18, supra.

22. See Chap. XI for an extensive analysis of the nature of social conflict.

23. See Carnegie-Illinois Steel Corp. et al., WLB Case No. 111-6230-D, Nov. 25, 1944.

24. See the TNEC Investigation Reports.

25. See Chaps. VI and VIII for the main analysis of the economy.

26. The Council of Economic Advisers in their First Annual Report to the President, December, 1946, declare that the American "business men whether in overalls or white collars" still have to demonstrate that "they display an adequate understanding of fundamental economic forces and of how to work out such mutual wage, price and profit relationships as will correlate an efficient system of production with a fluid and vigorous market" (15). Given the greatest of understanding and the best of good will

on the part of labor and management, they cannot accomplish what the Council expects of them without an agency to perform the integration. No autonomous collective bargaining for each business unit or even for each industry can perform that correlation. Nor will the Council perform that function by merely consulting with labor and business leaders (See report, 16). Consultations are desirable, but they are ancillary to, not a substitute for, government regulation of the wage-price relationship. Such regulation was advocated by President Truman to Congress in November, 1947. Compare Sir William H. Beveridge, *op. cit.*, 198-201.

27. See Chaps. XIII and XV; Bienstock, Schwartz, and Yugow, *Management in Russian Industry and Agriculture.*

28. See Chap. XVI for analysis of labor's role in politics, and Chap. XXI for discussion of administrative participation of interests.

CHAPTER XV

1. Some of the observations in this section appeared originally in "Protection of Basic Rights" in symposium entitled *The Wagner Act: After Ten Years*, edited by Louis G. Silverberg.

2. See Rosenfarb, "Foremen on the March," *Federal Bar Journal*, Winter, 1946.

3. Neo-company-unionism would appear to be among the implications of Peter Drucker's articles on labor management in *Harper's* magazine for November and December, 1946, and January, 1947.

4. See Chap. XXII; Rosenfarb, *The National Labor Policy*, 58-60.

5. See Chap. IX; Erich Fromm, *Escape from Freedom*, 129 et seq.

6. "For indeed any city, however small, is in fact divided into two, one the city of the poor, the other of the rich; these are at war with one another." Plato, Republic, Bk. IV. Also Aristotle, *Politics*, Bk. V.

7. For an analysis of the various proposals dealing with that problem see Rosenfarb, *The National Labor Policy*, 646-675.

8. *Rapid Roller Co.* v. *NLRB*, 126 F (2d) 452 (CCA 7), cert. denied 317 U.S. 650; *NLRB* v. *Planters Mfg. Co.*, 105 F (2d) 750 (CCA 4); *Harlan Fuel Co.*, 8 NLRB 25.

9. *Aetna Iron and Steel Co.*, 35 NLRB 136; *U.S. Bedding Co.*, 52 NLRB 382.

10. *Larus and Bros. Co.*, 62 NLRB 154.

11. *Henri Wines*, 44 NLRB 1310.

12. *Larus and Bros. Co.*, supra.

13. *Steele* v. *L. & N. R. Co.*, 323 U.S. 192; *Tunstall* v. *Brotherhood of Locomotive Firemen*, 323 U.S. 210.

14. *Steele* v. *L. & N. R. Co.*, supra.

15. *Wallace Corp.* v. *NLRB*, 323 U.S. 248.

16. *Bethlehem Steel Shipbuilding Div.*, 61 NLRB No 228.

17. *R. K. O. Radio Pictures, Inc.*, 61 NLRB No. 12.

18. Compare *Corn Products Refining Co.*, 58 NLRB No. 263.

19. *Humble Oil and Refining Co.*, NWLB Case No. 11-1819-D, April 1, 1944.

20. *The Patriot Co.*, NWLB Case No. 111-927-D, March 3, 1944.

21. See Roberto Michels, *Political Parties*; also Chap. XI.

22. See Chap. I.

23. See Chap. V.

24. For an analysis of the problem as it affects the government apparatus see Book Four.

25. See Chap. X; *Safeguarding Civil Liberties Today* (symposium), Cornell University Press, 1945.

26. See Chap. XIII for an analysis of union status in Soviet Russia; Franz L. Neumann, *Behemoth*, 400-436, on the labor front under nazism.

27. Compare, "There is in it not the slightest hint that anyone is to be coerced or constrained to labor more than he wants to, with inferior equipment or at anything other than the calling of his choice. The act stresses maximum production and the purchasing power that makes for high consumption; it does not stress mere number of jobs. The freedom

of the worker is fully protected by the expression 'willing and seeking to work.' The danger of resort to leaf raking or digging holes and filling them up is guarded against by the expression 'useful employment opportunities.' "—P. 4 of First Annual Report to the President, Council of Economic Advisers, December, 1946.

28. See Chap. XXII for an analysis of incentives and personnel problems in the administrative state.

29. June 23, 1947. See Sumner H. Slichter, *Union Policies and Industrial Management*. Millis and Montgomery, *op. cit.*, 389-485; Millis (Ed.), *How Collective Bargaining Works*.

30. See Chap. XVIII for an analysis of the problem of federalism.

CHAPTER XVI

1. See footnote 1, Chap. XIV. Some of the observations on labor's political role originally appeared as "Labor's Role in the Election," *Public Opinion Quarterly*, Fall, 1944.

2. See Chap. XXI for an analysis of the administrative process.

3. Compare Rosenfarb, *The National Labor Policy*, 192-193.

4. See Chap. XX.

5. See Chaps. XII and XIII for an analysis of the concept of class interest.

6. Page 45.

7. See David J. Saposs, *The Labor Movement in Post War France*.

8. See Chap. IV.

CHAPTER XVII

1. See particularly Book Two.

2. G. D. H. Cole, *Self Government in Industry*, 119-121: "What is a State? A State is nothing more or less than the political machinery of government in a community."

3. See Woodrow Wilson, *The State*, 587.

4. See Chap. IV; W. Friedmann, *Legal Theory*; William Seagle, *The Quest for Law*; Huntington Cairns, *The Theory of Legal Science*; Edward McChesney Sait, *Political Institutions*, 158-308; Robson, *Civilization and the Growth of Law*; Sir Henry Maine, *Ancient Law*.

5. Robson, *op. cit.*

6. F. W. Coker, *Organismic Theories of the State*; H. E. Barnes, "Representative Biological Theories of Society," *Sociological Review*, Vol. XVII, 1925.

7. See Chap. I.

8. William F. Ogburn, *Social Change*; Clark Wissler, *Man and Culture*; J. F. Brown, *Psychology and the Social Order*; R. M. MacIver, *Society*, 391-528.

9. See Chap. XI.

CHAPTER XVIII

1. *The Federalist*; Charles A. Beard, *The Republic*; Wilson, *The State*, 484 and 566; Theodore Woolsey, *Political Science*, Vol. II, 169; McBain and Rogers, *The New Constitutions of Europe*; A. V. Dicey, *Law of the Constitution*, 142.

2. See William C. MacLeod, *The Origin and History of Politics*, 316-328.

3. Edward McChesney Sait, *Political Institutions*, 374-405.

4. See Louis M. Hacker, *The Triumph of American Capitalism*; Charles A. Beard, *An Economic Interpretation of the Constitution*; *The Rise of American Civilization*.

5. See Rosenfarb, *The National Labor Policy and How It Works*, 409-449.

6. Compare dissent of Holmes, J., in Meyer v. Nebraska, 262 U.S. 390, Bartels v. Iowa, 262 U.S. 404, 412.

7. Aristotle, *Politics* IV, 7; Plato, *Republic*.

8. See William F. Ogburn, *Social Change*; Ralph Linton, *The Cultural Background of Personality*.

9. See Rosenfarb, *op. cit.*, 448.

CHAPTER XIX

1. See footnote 4, Chap. XVII.
2. See Chap. IV for a critique of this tendency as manifested in political theory.
3. Robson, *Civilization and the Growth of Law*, 10; Sir Henry Maine, *Ancient Law*.
4. See Chap. IV, and footnote 4, Chap. XVII.
5. See Edward McChesney Sait. *Political Institutions*, 467-499, for a résumé of the diffusionist positions tracing the evolution of the specific forms of representation. Whatever influence diffusion exercised over the specific forms, it is still true that every political culture passed through the stage of the representative system of family patriarchs and tribal chiefs, in which the representative principle had its origin.
6. C. H. McIlwain. *The High Court of Parliament and Its Supremacy*; Roscoe Pound, *The Spirit of the Common Law*; Maitland and Montague, *A Sketch of English History*; Oliver Wendell Holmes, *The Common Law*; Sait, *op. cit.*, 158-308; A. V. Dicey, *The Law of the Constitution*.
7. See footnote 4, Chap. XVII.
8. For its manifestation in American legal history see Beard, *The Rise of American Civilization*; Robert H. Jackson, *The Struggle for Judicial Supremacy*; Louis B. Boudin, *Government by Judiciary*; Gustavus Myers, *A History of the Supreme Court*; Benjamin N. Cardozo, *The Nature of the Judicial Process*; Jerome Frank, *Law and the Modern Mind*; Dean Alfange, *The Supreme Court and the National Will*.
9. See William Seagle, *The Quest for Law*, 102-117.
10. Maine, *op. cit.*; Seagle, *op. cit.*; footnote 6, supra.
11. See Chap. III.
12. See J. Rolland Pennock, *Administration and the Rule of Law*; J. M. Landis, *The Administrative Process*; John Dickinson. *Administrative Justice and the Supremacy of Law in the United States*; Blachly and Oatman, *Federal Regulatory Action and Control*; Ernst Freund, *Administrative Powers over Persons and Property*; C. T. Carr, *Delegated Legislation*; Zoltan Magyary, *The Industrial State*; C. J. Friedrich, *Constitutional Government and Politics*; Seagle, *op. cit.*, 326-328.
13. See Chap. VIII; Magyary, *op. cit.*; Charles E. Merriam, *Systematic Politics*.
14. Maine, *op. cit.*, 100.
15. See Sir James G. Frazer, *The Golden Bough*; W. J. Perry, *The Origin of Magic and Religion*; Theodor Reik, *The Psychological Problems of Religion*; Sigmund Freud, *The Basic Writings of Sigmund Freud* (Modern Library) *Totem and Taboo*, 807-930.
16. See Chap. IV; Rousseau, *Social Contract*.
17. See Franz Oppenheimer, *The State*, 174-228; Sait, *op. cit.*, 158-308.
18. See footnote 6, supra; Seagle, *op. cit.*, 252-277.
19. See Chap. XV; Rosenfarb, *The National Labor Policy*, Chap. VIII.
20. See Chap. IX; ". . . equality of position between the parties in which liberty of contract begins." Holmes, J., dissenting in *Coppage* v. *Kansas*, 236 U.S. 1, 28.
21. Compare Seagle, *op. cit.*, 61.
22. See Chaps. I and IV; Sait, *op. cit.*, 81-136.
23. *Ibid.*; compare Frazer, *op. cit.*; William C. MacLeod, *The Origin and History of Politics*, 90-97; Oppenheimer, *op. cit.*; Sumner and Keller, *The Origin of the State and the Origin and History of Politics*; Wilson, *The State*.
24. See Chap. XI for further analysis of political systems.
25. See Chaps. II and IV.
26. See footnotes 22 and 23, supra.
27. Sait. *op. cit.*, 406-413; R. M. MacIver, *The State*, 74-91.
28. In George Catlin's, *The Story of the Political Philosophers*, p. 645, is reprinted the following poem from *Pravda*, Aug. 28, 1936:
   "O great Stalin, O leader of the peoples,
   Thou who broughtest man to birth.

Thou who purifiest the earth,
Thou who restorest the centuries,
Thou who makest bloom the spring,
Thou who makest vibrate the musical chords . . .
Thou, splendor of my spring, O Thou,
Sun reflected of millions of hearts."
The solar theme is preeminent in a letter from Russian youth to Stalin on the thirtieth anniversary of the Bolshevik Revolution. Stalin is called "a leader of genius and a teacher, wise father and friend of Soviet youth . . . We are obliged to you for our life, our education, our happy youth, our today and our tomorrow . . . Youth vows loyalty to you, Comrade Stalin—sun of the entire earth."—The New York Herald Tribune, Nov. 4, 1947, p. 1. See also "*I Want To Be Like Stalin*" by Yesipov and Goncharov, trans. by George S. Counts.

29. See Chap. II; Erich Fromm, *Escape from Freedom*.

CHAPTER XX

1. Edward Gibbon, *The Decline and Fall of the Roman Empire*.

2. Aristotle, *Politics*, Bk. III, Chap. 7; Plato, *Republic*, Bk. VIII.

3. Contrast Oswald Spengler, *The Decline of the West*.

4. See Chap. VIII.

5. Aristotle, *Ethics*.

6. Plato, *op. cit.*, Bk. VIII.

7. Aristotle, *Politics*, Bk. III.

8. Plato, *op. cit.*, Bk. VIII; W. R. Agard, *What Democracy Meant to the Greeks*.

9. See Hugh Taylor, *Origin of Government*, 91 et seq., 214, 215; John Seeley, *Introduction to Political Science*, 169-171; Albert Carr, *Juggernaut*; Alfred Cobban, *Dictatorship*.

10. See Chap. XI and XIII.

11. See Chap. V.

12. See Walter Bagehot, *The English Constitution*; A. V. Dicey, *The Law of the Constitution*; Herman Finer, *The Theory and Practice of Modern Government*; A. F. Pollard, *The Evolution of Parliament*.

13. See Woodrow Wilson, *Congressional Government*; Thomas K. Finletter, *Can Representative Government Do the Job?*

14. On the doctrine of separation of powers see Polybius, *Universal History*, Bk. VI; Cicero, *De Republica*; John Locke, *Second Treatise on Government*; Montesquieu, *The Spirit of the Laws*.

15. *The Federalist*; Lynton K. Caldwell, *The Administrative Theories of Hamilton and Jefferson*; Charles E. Merriam, *American Political Theories*.

16. See footnote 8, Chap. XIX; Beard, *The Republic*, 223-241.

17. See *The Federalist*; Washington's *Farewell Address*; Merriam, *American Political Theories*; Charles and Mary Beard, *The Rise of American Civilization*.

18. See M. Ostrogorski, *Democracy and the Party System in the United States*; James Bryce, *The American Commonwealth*; Beard, *The Republic*, 261-276; Merriam and Goswell, *The American Party System*; Robert C. Brooks, *Political Parties and Electoral Problems*.

19. On the origin of the ballot compare William C. MacLeod, *The Origin and History of Politics*, 482-495.

20. See Pendleton Herring, *Presidential Leadership*; Harold J. Laski, *The American Presidency*; Bryce, *op. cit.*

21. See "Congress Wins a Victory over Congress," New York *Times Magazine*, Aug. 4, 1946, p. 11, by Senator Robert M. La Follette Jr., the chief architect of the act; also Floyd M. Riddick, *Congressional Procedure*.

22. Erich Fromm, *Escape from Freedom*; Karen Horney, *New Ways in Psychoanalysis*; Sigmund Freud, *The The Basic Writings of*—(Modern Library).

23. See Finletter, *op. cit.* for a detailed analysis of the problem and proposal here discussed; Hazlitt, *A New Constitution Now*.

CHAPTER XXI

1. James Burnham, *The Managerial Revolution* (1941), 261.

2. Chief among these frightened souls and their Pandora boxes are Lord Hewart, *The New Despotism*; Friedrich A. Hayek, *The Road to Serfdom*; Ludwig von Mises, *Omnipotent Government; Bureaucracy*.

3. Hayek, *op. cit.*, 72-87; On the origin of the "rule of law" see footnote 6, Chapter XIX, also Finer, *Road to Reaction*, 45-67.

4. See footnote 8, Chap. XIX; also Rosenfarb, *The National Labor Policy*, 601-609.

5. Proposed by the so-called Brownlow Report of The President's Committee on Administrative Management, 1937. For an analysis of this proposal see Rosenfarb, *The National Labor Policy*, 461-475.

6. Gulick and Urwick (eds.) *Papers on the Science of Administration*. See F. W. Taylor, *The Principles of Scientific Management*; and Henri Fayol's principles of management as set forth in Magyary, *The Industrial State*, 19 et. seq.

7. See footnote 5, supra.

8. See Rosenfarb, *The National Labor Policy*; Silverberg (ed.) *The Wagner Act: After Ten Years*.

9. Compare ". . . no matter how injurious an existing institution may be to a society in the face of changing conditions, the stimulus to change or abandon it never comes from the individual upon whom it entails no hardship. New social inventions are made by those who suffer from the current conditions not by those who profit from them."—Ralph Linton, *The Cultural Background of Personality*, 23.

CHAPTER XXII

1. See Felix S. Cohen, *Ethical Systems and Legal Ideals*; George Soule, *The Strength of Nations*; John Dewey's *Philosophy* (Modern Library) particularly 925-954.

2. Compare G. B. Chisholm, *The Psychiatry of Enduring Peace* and *Social Progress*. What Dr. Chisholm succeeds in doing, if he does, is to make out a case against the content of traditional morality, not against morality as a phenomenon. "There is . . . an implicit kind of metaphysics, that often goes by the name of No Metaphysics . . ."—Burke, *A Grammar of Motives*. XXII.

3. See Chaps. I and II.

4. "It is better that a man should tyrannize over his bank balance than over his fellow citizens; and whilst the former is sometimes denounced as being but a means to the latter, sometimes at least it is an alternative."—J. M. Keynes in *General Theory of Employment, Interest and Money*, 374.

5. See T. N. Whitehead, *Leadership in a Free Society*; Ordway Tead, *Human Nature and Management*; Elton Mayo, *The Human Problems of an Industrial Civilization*; Mary Follett, *Dynamic Administration*.

6. Valeriu Marcu, *Accent on Power—The Life and Times of Machiavelli*; Giuseppe Prezzolini, *Niccolò Machiavelli*.

7. See Chap. XV; Rosenfarb, *The National Labor Policy*, 58-60.

8. Arthur Koestler, *The Yogi and the Commissar*.

9. "The task of transmuting human nature must not be confused with the task of managing it."—Keynes, *op. cit.*, 374.

10. See Chap. XV. Wartime strike prohibitions included criminal sanctions and plant seizure under the War Labor Disputes Act, 57 Stat. 163, 50 U.S.C.A. §1501 (Supp. 1943); sanctions against strikers and union officials by the director of economic stabilization under authority of Executive Order No. 9370. Paragraphs B and C, 8 Fed. Reg. 11463 (1943), 54 Stat. 1191, 50 U.S.C.A. § 583 (Supp. 1940); sanctions against strikers and unions by the National War Labor Board by denial or conditional grant of union security, *Monsanto Chemical Co.*, WLB Case No. 292, Aug. 18, 1942, and *Semet-Solvay Co.*, WLB case No. 347, March 19, 1943; denial of reinstatement by WLB to employees who strike in violation of "no-strike" contract clause, *Borg-Wagner Corp.*, WLB Case No. 111-5665-D, May 16, 1944; denial of reinstatement by National Labor Relations Board to em-

ployees who strike to force employer to violate Economic Stabilization Act, *In re American News Co., Inc.*, 55 NLRB 1302 (1944).

11. Ralph Linton, *The Cultural Background of Personality*; "He who desires or attempts to reform the government of a state, and wishes to have it accepted and capable of maintaining itself to the satisfaction of everybody, must at least retain the resemblance of the old forms; so that it may seem to the people that there has been no change in the institutions, even though in fact they are entirely different from the old ones for the great majority of mankind are satisfied with appearances, as though they were realities and are often even more influenced by the things that seem than by those that are. The Romans understood this well."—Machiavelli in *The Discourses*, Bk. 7, Chap. 25.

12. See Chap. IX.

13. "The means which Nature employs to bring about the development of all the capacities implanted in men, is their mutual antagonism in society, but only so far as this antagonism becomes at length the cause of an Order among them that is regulated by Law."—Immanuell; Kant in *Principles of Political Right*; Catlin, *Principles of Politics*, 137-186.

14. See Chaps. I, II and IV; Marx and Engels, *The Communist Manifesto*; Monsignor Ryan's essay, "Religion as the Basis of the Postulates of Freedom" in the symposium, *Freedom, Its Meaning* (R. N. Anshen, ed.).

15. First Book of Samuel.

16. Compare More, *Utopia*; Bacon, *New Atlantis*; Campanella, *City of the Sun*; Rousseau, *Social Contract*; St. Augustine, *The City of God*.

17. Thomas Hobbes, *The Leviathan*.

18. Compare J. G. Fichte, *Political Theory*; "The State is the Divine Idea as it exists on Earth."—Hegel, *Philosophy of History*, 41; Heinrich von Treitschke, *Politics* and *The History of Germany in the Nineteenth Century*.

Index

Abnormal power drive, 8
Adjustment, to environment, 4-6, 7-8; freedom through government, 233; as power control, 17; of state to environment, 193-195
Administrative integration, 222-231
Administrative Procedure Act of 1946, 226-228
Administrative state. See State, The
Agencies (See also Bureaucracy), administrative integration, 224-231; government cycles, and, 214-215; law and government, 191; planning, 73-74; reorganization, program, 222-224, proposal for, 228-229; state, 200; war, 178
Aggression sublimation, 13
Agrarian economy, 39, 41, 52, 54
Airpower, 221
Alexander, 22, 43
Alliances, political, 196-197
Amalgamated Clothing Workers, 184
Ambition and satisfaction, 6, 8
American Federation of Labor, C.I.O. conflict, 123, 142, 143, 180-181; political role, 175-176, 178; Taft-Hartley Act, and, 176, 178
American Labor party, 176-177, 179
American Revolution, 43, 197, 217
Anarchy, government cycle, 214; property, and, 128
Annual wage, 175
Anthropology and Man, 7
Antidemocratic forces. See Subversive elements
Anti-Semitism, Soviet, 201
Antisovietism, 16
Antistrike legislation, 139-150, 150-158
Antitrust. See Trusts
Arbitration, federal, 156-157; freedom through government, and, 237; labor in the administrative state, and 140, 147-150, 155; labor union democracy, and, 165; "mediation," 148
Aristocracy (See also Kingship), 105, 107; property, and, 129-130, 132; source of leadership, 111-112

Aristotle, 99, 199, government cycle of, 213; leadership, and, 112; on Man, 7; power quest, and, 20
Army, class, and, 124; Russian and U. S. compared, 117
Art, government aid to, 70; liberties under planning, 87-88; transfer to in power socialization, 11
Articles of Confederation, 197
Ascetism, 13
Assembly, antidemocratic forces, and, 96; liberties under planning, 87, 89
Atheists, liberties under planning, 87
Atomic energy, aided by exiles, 118; government integration, and, 221; resources planning, and, 67, 69-70; vested interest, and, 193; warfare, 74, economic planning to avoid, 56
Atrocities, German, 13
Attlee, Clement, 186
Authority (See also Sovereignty), freedom through government, 231-239; leadership, and, 11; organization, and, 26-27
Autocracy, integrating environment, 193; leadership, and, 111-114, 118; power and responsibility problem in, 193

Balkan States revolutions, 108
Balloting. See Voting
Banks, failures, 57; in Rusisa, 133
Beck, Dave, 176
Behavior. See Human Behavior
Bevin, Ernest, 186
Bill of Rights, 82
Biological drive. See Sex
Birth (See also Heredity), family state, and, 32-33; freedom through government, 233; leadership, 104-105, 108, 111-112
Black market, Russian, 133
Bluntschli, 192
Bolsheviks. See Russia
Bonapartism, 212
Boss rule, 199
Boycotts, secondary, 173
British Labor party, 106, 129, 177, 186

260

INDEX

Brophy, John, 182
Budgets, administrative integrating, 225; government spending, 59; planning, 65, 71
Bukharin, 16
Bureaucracy, 113, administrative integration, and, 225; reorganization proposal, 228
Burnham, James, 224
Business (*See also* Capitalism, Corporations, Industry, Management), small, 198

Cabinets, administrative reorganization proposal for, 228-299; British system, 215-216, 218-219; government reorganization program for, 222-224; planning agencies, and, 74
Caesar, 212, 214
Canada spy trials, 98
Cannibalism, 102
Capitalism, absolute, return to, 56; approaches to planning, 55-62; comparisons, 37; control by government, 51-55; contract, and, 207-208; cultural and political liberties under planning, 87-98; development, labor unions, and, 168, modern world, in, 41-43; distribution approaches to full employment, 61-62; early, 123; freedom under planning, 79-86; government ownership, and, 58-59; government spending, and, 58-61; idea identification, as, 15; leadership, and, 110-119; planned economy for, 62-75; power distribution and political system, 99-119; precapitalist economics, 37-41; property and social order, 128-136; psychological weakness, 24-25; Russian scapegoat, as, 11; shortcomings of, 46-51; social structure and leadership, 100-110; sovereignty, and, 32
Carnegie, Andrew, 130
Cartels, 51, 68, 71, 172; labor relations, and, 141; warnings against, 97
Catholic Church. *See* Roman Catholic Church
Celibacy, heredity leadership, and, 107; power control, and, 14
Certification. *See* "Policing" certifications, NLRB
Chamber of Commerce, U. S., 97
Chambers of commerce and politics, 185
Checkoff system, 144
Chinese state and kinship, 35
Choice (*See also* Will), employment freedom, and, 171; freedom through government, 231-232, 233
Christianity and competition, 25
Churches (*See also* Religion), development of capitalism, and, 42; leadership, and, 107; liberties, and, 89; organization, and, 24, 25; power control, and, 14, 24; separation from state, 89; state, competition, and, 25, opposition to, 10
Churchill, Winston S., 130
Cities, 51, 108; boss rule, 199; early political integration of, 197, 200, 210, 213; functional federalism, and, 199-200; precapitalist economies, 39-40; strikes, and, 145
Civil liberties and rights (*See also* Freedom), antidemocratic forces, and, 96-98; family state, and, 36; freedom through government, and, 238-239; idea identification, as, 15; industrial democracy, and, 159-163; leadership, and, 113-116; Nazism, and, 82-83; planning under, 87-98; struggles for, 45
Civil Service Commission, 229
Class (*See also* Mass), democracy in planned economy, 120-128; divisions and leadership, 101-110; family state, and, 34; labor-union leadership, 167-168, 185-186; leadership, recruitment, 112-119; source, 110-112, organization, and, 27-28; power socialization, as, 14, 18, property, and, 37, 103-104, social order, and, 128-136
Closed shop, 144, 164-165
Coal, collective-bargaining, 146-147, 174; 1946 strike, 140, 148-149, 158; wage-price relationship, 152
Codes, legal, 205
Collective bargaining 52-53, 130-131; contract and law, 208; employment freedom, and, 170-171; freedom through government, 235-237; industrial freedom, and, 161-163; intra-union democracy, and, 163-168; labor's role in politics, 178, 184; state, and the, 139-142, 146-150, 155-156; union restrictive practices, and, 172, 174-175
Colonies, American pattern and political integration, 197; state, and the, 40-41, 43
Color (*See also* Race), freedom, and, 233, 234; political integrating, and, 199
Commerce (*See also* Mercantile economy), 39, 201; labor, and, 178; return to absolute capitalism, 57; resources planning, and, 67-69
Commercial economy, 39
Communication, free, 90-91
Communism, business control, and, 54; civil liberties and rights under planning, 79-98; economic freedom, and, 80, 128-136, planning, and, 56; identification as, 15-16; leadership, and, 116, 118, success in, 102; mass religion, and, 10; property, and, 98; public ownership, and, 57-58; revolution and leadership, 105, 109
Communist party, American labor movement, in, 181; antidemocratic elements, 96-98; infiltration in labor, 181-182; labor's role in politics, 176-177, 181;

outlawing in U. S., 96; outside Russia, 123; Taft-Hartley Act, and, 97
Community, administrative integration, 225-226; capitalism emerges, 45-46; differentiation of law and government, and, 203-206; family state, 35-37; freedom through government, 237, 239; government's role in, 191-195; industrial freedom in, 160; labor relations and, 145-147; law's role in, 191-195; political power, and, 21; power control, and, 18; precapitalist economies, 37-44; State, and the, 29-32
Companionship, drive for, 3
Company unions, 161
Compensation, unemployment, 173
Competition, emerging capitalism, 45-46; freedom through government, 233-234; government control, and, 53-55; monopoly, and, 48-51; organization, 24-25
Conciliation. See Arbitration
Confederations, 196, 197
Congress, U. S., administrative integration, 224-231; antidemocratic forces, and, 97; labor relations, and, 158; political integration, 197-199; Presidential system, and, 217-222; reorganizational program for, 222-224; Taft-Hartley Act information, and, 167
Congress of Industrial Organizations, 146, 178; A.F.L. conflict, 123, 142, 143, 180-181; elections role, 182, 184; General Motors strike, 140; industrial councils, and, 174-175; Labor's Non-Partisan League, 176, 182; Political Action Committee, 176-177, 184; U.E.W. *Guide to Political Action*, 183
Conservation, 67, 194
Constancy of human nature, 5-6
Constitution, 217
Consumer, freedom, 84-86; needs, 61-62, 83
Contract, 206-209, 234-235; negotiations, 139-158
Control of leadership. See Leadership
Controlling Man's wants. See Power
Controls. See Government regulation
"Cooling-off" period, 140, 147-148, 157
Corporations, compared with unions, 166; labor relations, 146; monopolies, and, 48-51; organization, and, 28-29; production planning, and, 72; struggle against, 82
Costs, production, 151, 152-153
Council of Economic Advisers, 55-56
Courts (*See also* Judicial function), 206; administrative integration of, 226-228
Craft unionism, 157; democracy, and, 165; restrictive practices, 172, 174-175
Creativeness (*See also* Art, Science), liberties under planning, 87-88
Credit, 133
Criminal law, 204

Culture, environment, and, 4; freedom through government, 231-232; human nature, and, 5; liberties under planning, 87-89
"Curse of bigness," 51, 72
Custom and law, 203-204
Cycles, business, 46, 47, 213; government, 212-216

Darwinism, 82
Death (*See also* Hereafter), and Man's desires, 3
Declaration of Independence, 18; democracy, and, 100; leadership, and, 113
Decontrol, 140
Demand. *See* Supply and demand
Democracies, administration, microcosm of, 229-231; administrative integration, and, 224-231; administrative reorganization, proposal for, 228-229; American Presidential system, 217-222; civil liberties, and, 87-89; control of business, 54; economic freedom, and, 79-80; employment freedom in, 170-171; fatherhood symbolism, 209-211; freedom through government, 231-239; government, reorganization program, 222-224, spending, and, 59-60; graveyard of, 215; industrial freedom, and, 159-175; integrating representative government, 212-224; intra-union democracy, 163-168; labor relations, 139-158; law and government in, 191-202; leadership and political system, 99-119; mass religion, and, 10; nature of the state, and, 32; organized labor in, 168-170; planned-economy in, 120-126; power and responsibility in, 194-195; power control, and, 14; property in social order, 128-136; public ownership, and, 58; transition problems, 126-128; union restrictive practices, 171-175; war economy, and, 63, 74
Democratic party, labor, and, 176-177; Presidential elections and U.M.W., 182
Depressions, 152
Descent. *See* Birth, Heredity
Desires of Man (*See also* Power, Satisfaction), drive for, 3-4, 6-8; environment, and, 5; freedom through government, 231-239; labor and government, and, 192; power control of, 13-20; quest for satisfaction, 6-8; satisfaction increase mechanisms, and, 9-13, 18-19
Destiny (*See also* Desires of Man, Planning Power), human nature, and, 5
Dewey, John, 17
Dictatorships, absence of civil liberties, 89-90; American Presidential system, and, 222, 223; cultural regimentation, 87-88; democracy of, 99; democracy transition, 126-128; economic freedom, and, 79-80, 83; economic planning, and, 56; evolution of, 212-214; fatherhood

symbol, 209-211; freedom through government, 231-239; integrating environment, 193; leadership, and, 105, 109, 111-119; mass faiths, and, 10; nature of the state, 32; power and responsibility in, 194; power control, and, 14; property in social order, 128-136; scapegoats of, 211; tenure, and, 216; war economy, and, 63
Dies committee, 97
Disarmament, 15
Discrimination (See also Race), freedom of organized labor, and, 169; functional federalism, and, 201; labor union democracy, and, 164-165; union restrictive practices, 174
Diseases, 68, 193
Dismissal grievance, 161
Displacement and power control, 16-17
Distribution of power. See Power
District Court, U. S., 227
Divine rights of royalty. See Kingship
Division of labor, 33, 74; emerging capitalism, and, 44-45; leadership need for, 101, 102-103; organization, and, 26-28; political integration, and, 198, 212
Divorce laws, 198
Drives, Man's. See Desires of Man
Dualism, freedom through government, 232; reason, and, 17-18; role of man in society, 3, 7
Dubinsky, David, 177, 178, 184
Due process. See Law

Economic environment. See Planning
Economic freedom. See Planning
Economic integration, 48, 54-55, 60, 75, 195
"Economic man," 45, 134
Economic needs. See Desires of Man
Economic organization, 23, 71; freedom and, 231-239
Economic power (See also Power), 21-23, 50-51, 54
Economic weapons, labor, and, 145, 148-149, 155, 235; political strike, 178-179
Economics (See also Planning, Power), "economic man," and, 45, 134; human destiny, and, 5; power socialization, and, 11-12, 18
Education, British leadership, and, 106; freedom in, 88-89; opportunity, and, 121; political integration, and, 198-199; property, and, 131-132
Efficiency, 71-72; labor unions, and, 172; spoils of, 50
Ego, emerging capitalism, and, 42; leadership propaganda, and, 114; power, control, and, 14-15, 16-18, quest, and, 7-8; socialization mechanism, 11; property, and, 38; superego, 17
Eisenhower, Dwight D., 117
Elders, 204-205, 208

Elections, American Presidential system, and, 219-220; government reorganization, and, 222-223; labor's role in, 165, 169-170, 175-187
Electoral college, 219
Elevator operators' strike, 147
Employers. See Management
Employment (See also Labor, Labor Unions, Unemployment), 47, 50-51; cultural freedoms, and, 87; distribution approach to, 61-62; economic planning, and, 55-56; freedom, through government, 233-235, under planning, 170-171; government, aid, and, 83-84, spending, and, 59-61; labor, and, 139-144, 149, 154-155, 157; planned economy, 124; planning program, 63-67, 70, 73; property, and, 131; public works program for, 69-70; right to a job, and, 170; security, and, 83-84; union restrictive practices, and, 171-175
Employment Act of 1946, 56
England, 37, 199; American Presidential system, and, 217-219, 222-224; Cabinet system of, 215-216; control of business, 54; economic freedom in, 80; family state, 203-204; fatherhood symbol, 210-211; government spending, and, 59; House of Lords decision vs. Labor party, 177; labor, freedom, 170, public ownership, and, 154-155, union conflicts, 181, leadership opportunities, 108; 1926 general strike, 186; precapitalist economies, 43-44; public ownership, and, 57-58, 128-130, 133-134, 154-155; reparations, and, 68; Russian idea identification, 16; shifting manpower, 170; socialism of, 127; society and leadership, 105, 106; strikes in, 144, 145; work drive in power socialization, 11-12
Entertainment and sex drive, 6
Entrepreneurs, 47, 52-53; distribution, and, 61-62; Europe role, 122; free entrepreneurs, 86; labor relations, 146; planning program for, 64
Environment, 74; adjustment, and, 3-5; contract law, and, 208; early law, and, 204-205; effect of science and technology on, 192-193; evolution of the state, and, 192; freedom through government, 231-239; industrial, 54; Man's drive, and, 4-5; political power, and, 21-23; power socialization, 20; quest for control of and power, 6-8
Envy and satisfaction, 6
Equality, democracy, and, 100, 126; freedom through government, 234-235; human nature, and, 5; leadership, and, 109, 113, 117; Man's differences, and, 121; property, and, 129-130, 133
Escape of reality. See Reality
"Escape period," union, 144

INDEX

Espionage and treason, antidemocratic elements, 98; leadership opposition, and, 116
Ethics, freedom through government, 231-232; power socialization, and, 9
Europe (*See also* names of countries), capitalism, 43-44; government regulation in, 53; middle class fascism, 122; public ownership, 128-136
Evolution, human nature, and, 5; leadership, of, 115; Maine contract theory, and, 208; quest for power, and, 7
"Excess of liberty," 213
Executive function, 204, 206, 209; administrative integration, and, 224-231; American Presidential system, and, 217-222; British Cabinet system, and, 215-216; government, cycles, and, 214-215, reorganization, and, 222-224; reorganization proposal for, 228-229

Fact-Finding Board, 140
Failure, fear of, 85
Family, 21; family state, and, 33-34, 102, development of, 202-208, growth of, 197; fatherhood symbolism, 208, 210, leadership in, 111, origin of, 32-37; idea identification, 16-17; Man's satisfaction, and, 6; organization, 23; property, and, 37-38
Farm groups, 53; labor, and, 147, 178; political integration, and, 198; politics, and, 185; wage-price relationship, 153
Fascism, antidemocratic elements, and, 96-98; business organization, 181; control of business, 54; economic, freedom, and, 80, 83, planning, and, 56, labor, and, 150, freedom, and, 169-170, parties, and, 181, propaganda, and, 143; leadership, and, 116, 118; mass religion, and, 10
Fatherhood symbolism, 209-211
Fear, 119, freedom from, 83, 85, through government control, 235-236
"Featherbedding," 172-173
Federal Communications Commission, 91
Federalism, American pattern, 197-199; functional under planning, 199-202; political integration of the state, 195-197
Federations, 196
Feudality, 51, 54; contract, and, 207-208; guilds, 139; industrial conflict of, 51-52; precapitalist economy, as, 37-40, 45
Fifth columns, 96-97, 119; labor infiltration, 182
Fighting (*See also* War), 11, 12
Florence, Republic of, 233
Ford, Henry, 130
Forecasts, economic (*See also* Planning), 70-71
Foreign investments, 65, 68-69
Foreign policy (*See also* Nonintervention), 221

Force and law, 203
France, 44, 199; chaotic politics of, 223; government patterns, 212-213; 1947 strikes, 98; Revolution, 105, 109; rise of capitalism, 105
Franco, Francisco, 126; democracy claim of, 99
Free enterprise (*See also* Laissez-faire), administrative state, in, 85-86; collective bargaining, and, 139
Free markets, determination of, 48, 50-51; economic planning, 56; emerging capitalism, and, 46; free enterprise, and, 85
Freedom, authority and, 238-239; cultural and political liberties under planning, 87-98; defined, 81; economic, under planning, 79-86; employment of, 170-171; industrial democracy, and, 159-175; leadership, and, 115-116; organization, and, 231-234; organized labor, of, 168-170; price of, 83; struggle for, 81-82; through government, 231-239; union restrictive practices, and 171-175
Freedom in education. *See* Education
Freedom of the press. *See* Press
Freedom of religion. *See* Religion
Freedom of speech. *See* Speech
French Revolution, 105, 109
Freud, conception of religion, 10; conformity and superego, on, 17; duality, and, 7
Fuels, strikes hit, 140; wage-price relationship, 152
Full-employment economy. *See* Employment

General Motors Corp. strike, 140, 157
General strikes, 145-147, 186
Geography (*See also* Territoriality), 47; democratic rule, and, 200; human destiny, and, 5; organization, and, 24; precapitalistic economies, and, 39-40
Germany (*See also* Hitler, Nazism), 37, 116, 127, 199; capitalist development, and, 44; fascism and labor in, 182; government patterns, 212; Jews as scapegoat, 11; Kultur and power control, 13; mass religion, and, 10-11; property, and, 135; rebuilding war potential, 68; socialization of power, 10-11
Gerontocracy, 208-209, 213
God, contract, and, 207; freedom, and, 81; Man's creation, and, 3; power socialization, and, 19, 20
Gompers, Samuel, 176
"Good man," 231-232
Government, administrative integration, and, 212-231; administrative reorganization program for, 228-229; American Presidential system, and, 215-222; business, as a, 206, 209; differentiation of, 202-211; family state, and, 35-36; freedom through, 231-239; history of pat-

terns of, 212-213; integration of representative, 212-224; labor's role in politics, 175-187; leadership, and, 99-119; nature of the state, and, 29-32; political integration, and, 195-198; reorganization program for, 222-224; role in the state, 191-195
Government regulation (*See also* State, The), 41, 45; administrative integration, and, 224-231; approaches to economic planning, 55-62; control mechanisms, 193-195; cultural and political liberties under, 87-98; distribution approach to full-employment, and, 61-62; economic freedom under planning, 79-86; economy control, 52-55; employment freedom, and, 170-171; freedom, and, 238-239, organized labor, of, 168-170; functional federalism, and, 201-202; growth trend, 48; labor relations, and, 139-158; meaning of administrative state, and, 74-75; planned economy, and, 124; power and responsibility, and, 193-195; production planning, and, 71-73; role of law and government, 191-192; strikes, and, 144-150; techniques and agencies, 73-74; union restrictive practices, and, 171-175
Government service, administrative integration, 225-231; democracy, and, 120, 124
Government spending, administrative integration, and, 225; planned economy, in, 58-61; production planning, 71; subsidies, and, 52, 53, 121, 133; vested interests, and, 193
Greece, democracy, 99; early city rule, 200, 213; "fatherhood" symbol, 210
Grievance procedure, 161, 163
Guide to Political Action, 183
Guilds, 139
Gumplowitz, 30

Habit, 204
Hamilton, Alexander, 198, 217
Hartley, Fred A., 176
Hate, fatherhood symbol, 211; propaganda, 11-12; satisfaction, 6
Hayek, Friedrich, 53
Hazlitt, Henry, 53
Health insurance, 66
"Heating-up" period, 148, 157
Heaven, 42; socialization of power, and, 9-10, 13
Hegel, 46
Hebraic religion, 210
Hereafter, The, 42; socialization of power, and, 9-10, 13
Heredity (*See also* Birth), environment, and, 5; government form, and, 208; leadership, and, 105-106; 111-112; property, 129-132
Hierarchy, class in democracy, 122, 124; family state, 34; freedom through government, 232-233; leadership, and, 101-102; organization, and, 26-27; property, and, 129
Hillman, Sidney, 177
History, human nature, and, 5; role of law and government, 191-192; socialization of power, 9
Hitler, 22, 99, 117, 126; democracy claim, 99; idea identification, and, 15, 20; justification of desires, 18; leadership of, 116; power control, and, 14
Hobbes, 45; Man's desires, on, 3
Holmes, Justice, 90
Housing, 64, 178; economic planning, and, 85
Human behavior (*See also* Desires of Man, Man), democracy, and, 100; power socialization, 11
Human nature (*See also* Desires of Man, Man, Satisfaction), 16, 36; constancy of, 5; Man's creation and desires, 3-4; quest for satisfaction, 6-8; satisfaction mechanisms and control, 9-20

Idea identification, 15-16, 20
Identification, 11; power control, 13-16, 20
Idle rich, 130
Ideology, 126, 172; controlling man's needs, 15, 18; freedom through government, 235; Marxist, 5; labor, and, 164; modern dictatorship, of, 11; Russian, 133; social revolutions, and, 127-128; unemployment, and, 142
Immortality as Man's dream, 3
Incentives. See Work
Income, democracy, in, 100, 124; freedom through government, 233-234; labor union leadership, of, 167; needs planning, 65; production planning, 71
Individual, democracy, and, 100; freedom, security of, 84, through government, 231-239; government development, and, 207; labor union democracy, and, 168; law and government, and, 192; "plant democracy" and, 161-163; role of law and government in the state, and, 191-192; role of Man in society, 3, 6-7; "rugged individualism," 157
Individual states, 196
Industrial democracy. See Labor unions
Industrial environment. See Environment
Industrial Revolution, 43-44, 45, 133
Industry (*See also* Capitalism, Economics, Labor, Labor unions, Planning), democracy, in, 120-121; freedom, and, 159-175; labor relations, and, 139-158; national scope of, 198
Industry councils, 174-175
Inequality (*See also* Equality), democracy, and, 163
Inflation in Russia, 133
Information, civil liberties under planning, 90-91; freedom program for, 91-

95; labor union under Taft-Hartley Act, 166-167; leadership, and, 115-116
Inheritance, 38; government, of, 208-209; leadership, and, 104, 106-107, 111; property, and, 129-130, 131
Injunctions, labor, 140, 149, 157-158, 160, 236
Insect society, 4, 168, 192
Insecurity (*See also* Security), antisovietism, and, 16; economic freedom, and, 83-85; idea identification, as, 14; power quest, and, 19
"Instinct of workmanship," 12
"Instruments of production," 124
Integrating, administrative, 224-231; American Presidential system, and, 217-222; British Cabinet system, and, 215-216; civil liberties, 91; economic, 48, 54, 60, 71-75, 80, 195; environment in state, 193; government reorganization, and, 224; information, 91-96; labor and industry, 154-159; law and government, 193-195, 206, 208; organization, and, 26-29; political, 195-202, 204, 206-208; representative government, 212-224; state, the, 195-197, 204-208
Intellectualism idea identification, 16
Intelligence, environment, and, 4; freedom, and, 238; fulfillment of needs, and, 81
Intelligensia, Russian, 129-130
Interest rates, 49; government spending, and, 59
International Ladies Garment Workers, 177, 184
International trade. *See* Commerce
Interstate commerce, 201
Intolerance and leadership, 118
Investments, 49-50; foreign, 65; government spending, and, 58-61; resources planning, and, 73
Isolationism. *See* Nonintervention
Italy (*See also* Fascism, Rome, ancient), 126-127; government patterns, 212; labor under, 170; mass religion, and, 101; 1947 strikes, 98

Jackson, Andrew, 112, 220
James-Lange theory, 148
Japan, kinship, and, 35; Mikado, 111; state, 37; U. S. exports to, 68-69
Jefferson, Thomas, 219, 220
Jews, cultural liberty under planning, 87; German scapegoat, as, 11; purge instrument, as, 118; Ukranian anti-Semitism, and, 201
Job classification, 161
Job discrimination. *See* Employment
Job security. *See* Employment
Joint Legislative-Executive Council, 222
Judicial function, 204-206, 209; administrative integration, and, 217, 224-227, 228

Jurisdictional rivalry, 143-144, 182
Justice, 123; Man's idea of, 202-203

Keynes, J. M., 49-50, 59-61
Keynes-Hansen, analysis, 59; distribution, and, 61
"King's Peace," 204
Kingship, divine right of, 210; fatherhood symbolism, 208, 209-210; government cycle, and, 212-213; heredity, 107; kinship, and, 102, 210; leadership, and, 111, 113, 118
Kinship, 39; family state, and, 34-35; kingship, and, 102, 210; leadership, and, 106, 111-119
Knights of Labor, 175
Knowledge and environment, 4
Kultur, 13

Labor, Department of, 228
Labor (*See also* Division of Labor, Employment, Labor Unions), administrative reorganization, and, 228-229; economic, freedom, and, 80, planning, and, 56; employment, 46, 47, 50-51; freedom through government, 234; government regulation, and, 52-55; planned economy, in, 124-125; political, integration, and, 198, role, 165, 169-170, 175-187; property, and, 130-134; relations in administrative state, 139-158; social reforms, and, 230; Taft-Hartley Act effect, 178; tariff support, 123
Labor unions, antidemocratic elements, 97-98; certifications, NLRB, 165, 235; civil liberties and rights, 159-160; Communist infiltration, 181-182; elections, and 175-179, 182, 184; employment freedom, and, 170-171; freedom through government production, 235-236; government role, and, 154-158; growing strength, 141-144; industrial democracy, and, 125, freedom, and, 159-175; intra-union democracy, 163-168; leadership, and, 106, 163-168; management relations, 159-163; national scope, 198; planning, and, 72; politics, role in, 175-187; property, and, 130-131; restrictive practices, 171-175; right to information, 91; role, 139-141; Russian, 131; security, and, 160-163, 168; strikes, 144-150; wage-price relationship, and, 150-154
Labor-Management Committees, 183
Labor-Management Conference, 139-140
Labor-Management Relations Act (*See also* Taft-Hartley Act), 179, 182
Labor's Non-Partisan League, 176, 182
Laissez-faire, approach to economic planning, 55-62; contract, and, 207; democracy, and, 80; enthronement of, 41; free enterprise, and, 86; government regulation, and, 151-155; greatest development, 43; labor relations, 139; police

state, as, 74; political democracy, and, 126; power socialization, 11-12; property, and, 128-129, 133; return to absolute, 56-57; risks, and, 84; shortcomings of, 46-51; struggle against, 82; wages in, 235

Law (*See also* Government, Politics, State, The), absence of and freedom, 238-239; administrative integration, 224-231; differentiation of, 202-211; due process and injunctions, 157, 237; freedom of organized labor and, 164-167, 169; freedom through government, and, 231-239; liberties, and, 98; political integration, 195-202; role in the state, 191-202

Lea Act, 173

Leadership, American Presidential system, and, 217-222; British Cabinet system, and, 215-216; competition for government, 208; father symbol, and, 208, 209-211; government, cycles, and, 212-214, reorganization, and, 222-224; labor union democracy, and, 163-168; planned economy, and, 120-122; power control, and, 14, 20; recruitment, and control, 112-119; social structure, 100-110; sources of, 110-112; transition, and, 127-128; union practices, and, 185-186

Leagues, 196

Legislative function, 204-205, 206, 209; administrative integration, and, 224-231; American Presidential system, and, 217-222; British cabinet system, and, 215-216; government reorganization, and, 222-224; reorganization proposal for, 228-229

Legislative Reorganization Act of 1946, 222, 225-226

Lenin, 109, 118; order of, 134; property, and, 129, 310

Lewis, John L., backs Willkie, 176, 182, 184; coal strike, 140, 148; labor conflict, 142; Labor's Non-Partisan League, 176; miners' political opposition, 177, 182, 184-185; wage-price, on, 148

Liberal party of N. Y., 176-177, 179

Liberty. *See* Civil liberties and rights, Freedom

Lincoln, 16, 99, 220; malignment, 211

Literature, liberties under planning, 87-88; romantic, 6

Lobbies, 220

Localism, 199

Locke, 45

Lockout, 237

Love, father symbol, 211; freedom of art, 88; satisfaction, and, 6

Loyalty as power control, 16, 17

Luther, 43

Machiavelli, 18, 43, 45, 233

Maedanek, 160

Magic and law, 203, 207

Maine, Sir Henry, 206-208

Majorites, labor politics, and, 168, 184-187; tyranny, and, 124

Make-work schemes, 172-173

Man (*See also* Desires of Man, Human behavior, Human nature, Satisfaction), creation of and desires, 3-4; environment, and, 5, 8; freedom through government, 231-239; history of freedom struggle, 81; power quest, 7-9; satisfaction quest, 6-7; state, and the, 29-37

Management, democracy, and, 120, 125-126; employer groups, 145-146, 156; freedom through government, 236-239; industrial civil liberties, and, 159-163; labor, and, 139-158, 171, 178; labor-management committees, 183; politics, and, 185; power and responsibility, 194 "prerogatives," 172; property, and, 130; union relations, and, 160-163

"Managerial revolution," 125, 132

Manpower, employment freedom, and, 170-171; union restrictive practices, 173-175

March Revolution, 109

Maritime trades union, 167

Markets, *See* Free markets

Marriage (*See also* Family, Sex), origin of state, and, 33, 35

Marshall, George C., 117

Marx, Karl, business control, and, 54; class conception, 123; conception of religion, 10; ideology and idea identification, 15; nationalism, and, 35; nature of the state, and, 30; ownership concentration, and, 48; precapitalist economies, and, 44; private property, on, 103, 128, 132-133; production control, on, 128-129

Mass (*See also* Class), behavior and environment, 5; faiths, 10; freedom through government, 234-235

"Mature man," 231-232

Meat strike, 141, 237

"Mediation." *See* Arbitration

Medicine needs planning, 66

Megalomania, 8

Mercantile economy, 39, 41, 43, 45, 54; labor conditions under, 133; U. S. struggle against, 82

Mergers, 48-49

Merit, 161; labor restrictions, and, 171, 174; sanctions, and, 233

Middle Ages (*See also* Feudality), 44; precapitalist economies, 37-41

Middle class (*See also* Class), 104; labor union leadership, 167; position in society, 122; property, and, 131; wage-price relationship, 152

Military, class control, and, 117, 124-125; force, 21; needs planning, 66-67; power and leadership, 103

Miners and John Lewis, 177, 182, 184-185, 237
Minimum-wage laws, 161
Minority, control, 102; functional federalism, and, 201; labor union democracy, and, 164-168; leadership, 115; the lot of, 118
Monarchy. *See* Kingship
Money, precapitalist economies, and, 39; Russia, in, 133
Monopoly, civil liberties and information, 90-91; determination of, 48-49, 50-51; emerging capitalism, and, 46; freedom and security against, 82, 85-86; government control, 52-55; information freedom against propaganda, 93; labor relations, and, 141, 178; leadership, of, 112-116; organization, and, 24-25; production planning, 71-72; program against, 93; sanctions, and, 232-233; union restrictive policies, and, 171-172; wage-price relationship, and, 152-153
"Monopoly capitalists," 11, 69
Montesqieu, 217
Morrison, Herbert, 186
Movies and satisfaction, 6
Murray, Philip, 140, 178, 182
Music and government aid, 70
Mussolini, 126, 212; democracy claims, 99; idea identification, as, 15; leadership of, 116

Napoleon, 22, 212
Napoleon complex, 23
National Association of Manufacturers, 52, 134
"National emergencies," 140, 148, 156-158, 237
National Labor Relations Act, 97, 126, 157; administrative integration, and 226-228; industrial civil liberties, and, 159-163; intra-union democracy, and, 163-168; union restrictive practices, and, 174
National Wage Stabilization Board, 140
National War Labor Board, 74, 140, 144, 150; administrative integration, and, 227-228; labor union democracy, and, 165; labor's role, and, 178; wage-price relationship, 151, 155
Nationalism, family state, and, 34-35; labor union democracy, 169; power socialization, 18; state alliances, and, 196
Natural resources. *See* Resources
Nature, human. *See* Human nature
Nature and power socialization, 11
Navy and class, 124
Nazism, atrocities and power control, 13, 20; business control, and, 54; cartel agreements, 68-69; civil liberties absent, 87, 89-90; cultural regimentation, 87; economic freedom, and, 79-83; government ownership, and, 58; idea identification, 15; Jews as scapegoat, 11; labor under, 170; leadership, and, 116-118; mass religion, and, 10; political democracy, and, 126-127; property, and, 136; revolution and leadership, 105
Needle trades, 146, 155, 174
Needs of Man. *See* Desires of Man
Negroes and union democracy, 164-165
New Deal, 126, 220; opportunity, and, 120; recovery policies, 59
"New despotism," 225
New York (State), 200
New York, N. Y., elevator operators' strike, 147; labors' role in politics, 176-177, 179-180
New Zealand, 170
Newspaper Guild, American, 165-166
Newspapers. *See* Press
Newton complex, 23
Nomads and state evolution, 31, 38
Nonintervention, 116, American Presidential system, and, 220; idea identification, 15
Normal power drive, 8, 9
North America work drive, 12
No-strike policy, 150, 165, 177, 178-179

Oedipus complex, 211
Office of Price Administration, 74, 151
Officer class, 101
Old Testament and contract, 207
Oligarchy, 120; cycle, 214; "iron law of," 27, 167; labor union democracy, and, 167; leadership, 111-112
Oppenheimer, 30
Opportunity, 83-84, 85; democracy, in, 120-122, 126; leadership, and, 108; property, and, 131-132
Opposition. *See* Right of opposition
Organization (*See also* Reorganization), freedom, and, 231-239; nature and principles of, 23-29
Organized labor. *See* Labor unions
Osborne, 177, 180
Ownership. *See* Private ownership, Public ownership

"Parity wage-price," 153, 154
Parties, *See* Political parties
Partisanship, 175-176
Patents, 72
Patriarchism, 203-205, 208-209; fatherhood symbol, 210
Patriotism, 118; labor and, 143
Patton, George S., Jr., 117
Peacetime economy, 47-50; consumer freedom, and, 84-85; effect of war economy, 63-64; freedom, and, 80; labor freedom, and, 170; needs planning, 66, 74; postwar labor, and, 139-158
Personnel practices, 161
Petrillo, James C., 173

Petroleum, coal prices, and, 152; exports to Japan, 68; tidelands conservation, 67
Philosophy, power drive, 8; will, and, 81
Physical environment. *See* Environment
Planned economy. *See* Planning
Planning, administrative integration, and, 224-231; approach to economics, 55-63; cultural and political liberties, under, 87-98; democracy in planned economy, 120-128; differentiation of law and government, and, 202-211; economic, development stages, 132-134, freedom under, 79-86, security, and, 82-84; employment freedom under government, 170-171; federalism, and, 195-202; freedom through government, 231-239; government role in the state, 191-202; labor freedom, and, 168-170; law's role in the state, 191-202; leadership and political systems, 99-119; needs, 65-66; political integration, and, 195-202; production, and, 70-73; program for direct, 63-65; property, political stystems, and, 134-136, social status, and, 128-132; resources, 66-70; techniques and agencies, 73-74; transition problem, 126-128; union restriction practices, and, 171-175
"Plant community," 162, 168
Plato, 105, 107, 117, 163, 199; government cycles, on, 213; "royal lie," 99, 126, 234
Police state, 74
"Policing" certifications, NLRB, 165, 235
Political Action Committee. *See* Congress of Industrial Organizations
Political integration, 195-202, 204, 206-208
Political organization (*See also* Political Parties, freedom, and, 231-239; nature and principles of, 23-29
Political parties, 124; American Presidential system, and, 217-222; labor as third party, 179-182; labor's role, and, 175-187; tenure, and, 216, 218-219
Political power (*See also* State, The), 51; organization, and, 23-29; purpose and function, 21-23
Politics (*See also* Government, State, The), administrative integration, and, 224-231; American Presidential system, and, 219-220; civil liberties and rights under planning, 87-98; freedom through government, 231-239; identification as power control, 14-16; industrial democracy, and, 159-175; integration of representative government, and, 212-224; labor compulsives, and, 139-158; labor's role in, 165, 169-170, 175-187; law and government differentiation, 202-211; law and government in, 191-192; leadership, and, 99-119; property, and, 134-136
Polls. *See* Public opinion
Popular-frontism, 181, 182
Population, 65

Power, conformity and control mechanism, and, 17; control mechanisms, 13-20, capitalism, in, 44-46; dangers of misuse, and labor, 169; defined, 81; democracy in planned economy, 120-128; differentiation of law and government, and, 202-211; displacement control mechanism, 14-15; family state, and, 32-37; freedom through government, 231-239; idea identification control mechanism, 16; identification control mechanism, 14-15; industrial civil liberties, 159-163; integration of representative government, 212-224, 228; labor in the administrative state, 139-158; nature of the state, and, 29-32; organization, and, 23-29; political integration of the state, 195-202; political power, 21-23; property in social order, 128-136; reason, and, 17-18; religion drive, and, 9-11; responsibility, and, 193-195; role of government and law in the state, 191-195; satisfaction increase mechanism, 9-13, 18-19; shortcomings of capitalism, and, 46-51; state, political integration, 195-202, precapitalist economies, and, 38-41, regulation of, 52-55; sports drive, and, 12-13; war, and, 11-12
Prejudice (*See also* Discrimination), state government, 201
Presidents, U. S., administrative integration, and, 224-231; father symbol, as, 211; government reorganization, and, 222-224; labor party, and, 179; labor's role in politics, and, 176-177; planning agencies, 74; political integration, and, 197; postwar labor relations, 139-141, 149, 156-158; reorganization proposal, and, 228-229; representative government system, 217-222
Press, 113; antidemocratic forces, and, 96; freedom program for, 91-92; functional federalism, and, 200; labor, civil liberties, 159, relations, 143, Taft-Hartley Act, and, 186; liberties under planning, 87, 89-91
Pressure groups and labor relations, 143
Prestige system, 108
Prices (*See also* Wage-price), direct planning program for, 64-65; economic planning, 56-57; emerging capitalism, and, 46; government control of, 53; government spending, and, 60; production planning, 71, 73
Priesthood, "father" symbol, as, 208-209; government leadership, and, 208-209; judiciary function, 204-205; power control, 14
Private enterprise. *See* Capitalism
Private ownership. (*See also* Capitalism, Laissez-faire), 128-136
Privation, 12, 235-236

Privileges, leadership, and, 106; property, and, 131-132; Russia, in, 133-134
Production, 60-61; agencies, 73-74; class control, and, 125; costs, 151-153; employment freedom, and, 170-171; labor relations, and, 141-142, 147, 150-153; planning, 63-65, 70-73; planning of needs, 65-67; property, and, 129-131, 134; techniques, 73-74; union restrictive practices, 171-175
Professional organizations, 171, 174; political integration, and, 198; sanctions, and, 233
Profit, direct planning program, and, 64-65; emerging capitalism, and, 46; free enterprise, and, 85; monopolies, and, 48-49, 50; production planning, and, 71, 73; Russia, in, 133; security for risks, 84; wage-price relationship, 151
Promotion, grievance, 161; sanctions, and, 233
Propaganda, antidemocratic elements, and, 98; class leadership, and, 103, 114, 116, 119; cultural and political liberties under planning, 87-88
Property, corporation ownership, 49; family state, and, 33-34, 36, 37; freedom through government, 237; government leadership, and, 208-209; leadership class division, and, 102-103; nature of the state, and, 31; political systems, and, 134-136; precapitalist economies, and, 37-41; private and public ownership, 57-58, 128-132; social status, and 128-132
Protection (See also Security), drive for, 7
Protestantism, 42; liberties under planning, 87
Psychiatry and work, 11
Psychology, 233; Man's needs, and, 7-8; power socialization, 9
Ptolemaic world, 42
Public debt, 59
Public health and safety, 156-157, 237
Public opinion, freedom program for, 93-95; leadership, and, 115; union restrictive practices, and, 172
Public ownership, economic planning, and, 57-58; industrial civil liberties, and, 162; labor relations, and, 154-155; leadership, and, 103; planned economy, in, 128-136
Public relations freedom program, 91
Public works, 56, 59; resources planning for, 69-70
Pump priming, 60
Purchasing power, 60, 63; consumer freedom, 85; labor and, 147, 155-156; strikes, and, 147
Purges, leadership, 114, 118-119; transition, and, 127

Quest for power. See Power

Race, environment, and, 4; family state, and, 32-33; freedom through government, 233-239; functional federalism, and, 201; labor union democracy, and, 164-165, 169; political integration, and, 199; power socialization, 11, 19
Racketeers and contract, 207
Radio, civil liberties, and, 90-91; freedom program for, 91-93; functional federalism, and, 200
Railroads, 141; strike, 147-148, 158
Railway Labor Act, 147, 157; labor union democracy, and, 165
Rankin committee, 97
Rationalization, 3, 18; freedom through government, 233; political, 198, 200
Rationing, 84-85
Raw materials. See Resources
Reactionaries, controls, and, 56; labor unions, and, 169; state government, and, 201
Real state, 196
Reality escape and power socialization, 9
Reason (See also Rationalization), Man's drive for, and, 4-5; power control, and, 17-19; satisfaction, and, 4-5
Reconversion and industrial councils, 175
Recruitment of leadership. See Leadership
Regionalism, 123, 199
Relief, 56; labor, and, 142
Religion, control mechanisms, 13-14; family state, and, 34; freedom under planning, 87, 89; labor union democracy, and, 169, 185; law, and, 203, 207; nature of the state, and, 31, 42; satisfaction mechanisms, 9-11, 18; state opposition to, 10; will, and, 81
Religious education, 199
Renaissance, 43, 88, 197
Reorganization, government, 222-224; proposal for administration, 228-229
Reparations, 67-68
Representative system, administrative integration, and, 224-231; American Presidential system, and, 217-222; British Cabinet system, and, 215-216; evolution of, 203-211; government reorganization, and, 222-224; integration of, 212-224
Reproduction, drive for, 3, 6-7; family organization, and, 23, 33
Republican party, labor and, 176-177, 182, 184-185; 1947 controls, 225
Resources, planned economy, and, 64-67; planning, 66-70; raw materials foreign sources, 67
Responsibility, control mechanism, and, 194-195; differentiation of law and government, and, 202-211; freedom through government, 238-239; integration of representative government, and, 212-224; political integration of the state, and, 195-202
Rest-periods, labor, 173

Revolution, culture, and, 88; democracy transition, 127-128; industrial civil liberties, and, 162; leadership, and, 105, 108-110, 114; liberty, and authority, and, 238; social, 105, 108-110
Right of opposition, leadership, and, 113-116; property, and, 131-132, 133
Right to organize. *See* Labor unions
Robber barons, 133
Roman Catholic Church, 42; celibacy and leadership, 107; competition, and, 25; identification as power control, 14; liberties under planning, 87; organization, and, 24; socialization of power, and, 10
Rome, ancient, 22; fatherhood symbol, 210-211; historical patterns of, 212; jurisdiction rise, 205; precapitalist economies, 39; senate, 197
Roosevelt, Franklin D., 16, 94; American Presidential system, and, 220; father symbol, as, 211; labor strength in 1933, 141; labor's role in elections, and, 175-177, 182; leadership of, 116-117
Rotarianism, 45
"Royal lie," 99, 126, 234
"Rugged individualism," 57
"Rule of law," 226
Russia, capitalist development, 44; civil liberties absent, 87-90; cultural regimentation, 87-88; distribution schemes, 61-62; economic freedom, and, 79-80, 83-84; idea identification and power control, 14-16; leadership, and, 100; propaganda, 115; mass religion and socialization of power, 10-11; nationalism, and, 35; nature of the state, and, 30-31; property and leadership, 103; public ownership, and, 57-58, 128-136; purges of, 118-119; religion under, 89; Revolution and leadership, 105, 109; Trotskyites as scapegoat, 11; U. S. trade with, 68-69
Russian Orthodox Church, revival and absorption in the state, 10; under planning, 89
Russian Revolution, 105, 109, 132-133

Sabotage, 98
Sadism sublimation in power socialization, 13
Safety and health measures *(See also* Public health and safety), 173
Sanctions, economic, 66; freedom through government, and, 234-238; law and government, 203-205; political, 232-239; socialization of power, and, 18-19
Satisfaction *(See also* Desires of Man), consumer freedom, and, 84-85; control mechanisms, 13-20; freedom through government, and, 234; increasing mechanisms, 9-13, 18-19; Man's reason, and, 4; organizations for, 23-29; political power, and, 22; quest for, 6-8
Savings, 49-50; government spending, and, 58-61
Scandinavia, 199
Scholarships, 121; Russian, 132
Schools, 69; political integration, and, 198-199
Science, 136; effect on environment, 192-193; freedom through government, 231-232; power, quest, 6-8, 16, socialization, 19, 20; resources planning, and, 69
Season employment, 175
Sectarianism, 199
Security *(See also* Insecurity), civil liberties, and, 98; economy, 61-62; employment freedom, and, 170-171; freedom, and, 82-84, through government, 231-239; leadership, and, 103; "plant community," and, 160-163; property, and, 129-130; union restrictive practices, and, 172-175
Self-regulated economy, approaches to planning, 55-63; industry-labor relations, 154; mechanisms of, 44-46; planned economy, and, 63-75; precapitalist economies, 51-52; shortcomings of capitalism, 46-51
Seniority practices, 161
Sex, drive for, 3, 6-7, 20, 81, 84; familial grip, and, 33; family organization, and, 23
Shelter *(See also* Housing), drive for, 6, 20
Shifts, employment, 172-173
Slavery, freedom through government, and, 235; Greek, 23; leadership, 102
Slowdowns, 173
Smith, Adam, 45, 53, 82, 134
Smith, Alfred E., 14
Smith, Repr. Howard K., 177
Smith-Connally Act, 177
"Social contract," 234
Social environment. See Environment
Social evolution. *See* Evolution
Social revolutions, 105, 108-110, 127-128
Social sciences, cultural liberties under planning, 88; planning of, 69-70
Social security, 178; economic planning, 56, 66; political integration, and, 198
Social values and freedom through government, 231-239
Socialists, 127; Communist conflict, 181; public ownership, and, 57-58, 128-138; third party, as, 179-180
Socializing power. *See* Power
Society, capitalism emerges, 45-46; civil liberties, and, 87-98; culture and political freedom in, 87-98; democracy in planned economy, 120-128; differentiation of government, and, 202-204; economic freedom, and, 79-86; freedom and security in, 81-86; freedom through government, and, 231-239; government

INDEX

regulation, 51-55; industrial freedom, and, 159-175; leadership, and, 99-119; organization, and, 25-26; organized labor, and, 139-158; planning for capitalism, 163-175; precapitalist economies, 37-44; property, and, 128-136; role of law and government, 191-195; shortcomings of capitalism, 46-51; state, and the, 29-37
Sociology and power socialization, 9
Socrates, 123
Solopsism, 9
Sources of leadership. *See* Leadership
South America, dictator-ridden republics, 199; revolutions, 108
Sovereignty *(See also* Authority), democracy, and, 99-100; nature of the state, and, 31-32; role of law and government, and, 191; union politics, and, 185
Soviet Constitution, 129, 131
Spain, 99, 126-127
Specialization and organization, 26-27
Speech, 113; antidemocratic forces, and, 96; freedom program for, 93; labor civil liberties, 159; liberties under planning, 87, 89-90
Speed-ups, work, 173
Spencer, 82, 192
Spending. *See* Government spending
Spies. *See* Espionage and treason
Spinoza, 45
Sports in power socialization, 12-13
Stabilization Director, 151
Stakhanovism, 12, 133
Stalin, 99; democracy claim, 99; early anonymity, 108; idea identification, 16; leadership of, 116, 118; power control, and, 14
Standard of living, 11; leadership, and, 103; needs planning, and, 65; property, and, 129-134
State, The, 21; administrative integration, 224-231; approaches to economic planning, 55-62; capitalism shortcomings, 46-51; culture and political liberties, and, 87-98; democracy in planned economy, 120-128; developments in modern world, 41-44; differentiation of law and government, and, 202-211; distribution approaches to full employment, 61-62; economic, control, 51-55; freedom and security, and, 79-86; planning, 63-75, regulations, 44-46; environment changes, and, 192-193; family state, 32-37; industrial freedom, and, 159-175; labor's role in politics, 165, 169-170, 175-187; law and government role in, 191-195; leadership, and, 87-98, 99-119; meaning of administrative state, 74-75; microcosm of democratic administration, 229-231; nature of, 29-32; organization, 23-24; organized labor, and, 139-158; origin of, 32-37; political integration of, 195-202; precapitalist economies, in, 38-41; public ownership, and, 57-58; reorganization, program for, 222-224, proposal for, 228-229; representative government, integration of, 212-224; spending, and, 58-61; techniques and agencies, 73-74
State government *(See also* "States' rights"), American pattern, 197-198; functional federalism, and, 199-202; government reorganization, and, 223
State religion, socialization of power, and, 10-11; warning against, 87
"States' rights," 52; labor, and, 142-143; political integration, and, 198-199
Statesmanship, leadership, 116-117; transition, and, 127
"Status of contract," 206-208
Steel, price monopoly, 152-153; strike, 140, 147, 157
Stockownership, 48-50, 72
Storage-problems, strike, 147
Strikes, civil liberties, and, 159-160; general, 145-147, 186; government policy, and, 236-237; intra-union democracy, and, 165, 167; labor in the administrative state, and, 139-158; labor's role in politics, and, 178-179; modern economy, and, 144-150; no-strike policy, and, 165, 177, 178-179; political, 178-179; Smith-Connally Act, and, 177
Sublimation and power drive, 12
Subsidies, government, 52, 53, 87-89, 121; Russian, 133
Subversive elements *(See also* Fifth Columns), 96-98
Suffrage *(See also* Voting), democracy, 100; leadership, 114
Superego, 17
Supply and demand, 54; determination of, 47-48, 50; direct planning program, and, 63, 74; emerging capitalism, and, 45-46
Supreme Court, U. S., father symbol, 210; Presidential system, and, 217; Railway Labor Act, and, 165; union restrictive practices, and, 173, 236; Wagner Act, and, 165, 201
Sweatshops, 155
Symbols, authority, 238; cultural, 203; fatherhood, 209-211; mass religion, 10; political parties, and, 180
Synthetic industry, 67

Taff-Vale, 177
Taft-Hartley Act, 97, 179, 230, 237; administrative integration, and, 226-227; A.F.L. support, 176; effect on labor, 178; labor, opposition to, 142, 144; union democracy, and, 166, 168; political integration, and, 198; role, 156-158; union restrictive practices, and, 173-174

INDEX 273

Tariffs, 52; class support of, 123; England removes, 43-44; need for, 68
Taxation, competition, and, 120; economic planning, and, 56, 59-60; laws, 198; production planning, and, 73; Russian, 133
Teachers' pay, 198-199
Technology, 51, 55, 136; effect on environment, 192-193; Man's power quest, and, 6-7
Telephone strike, 141
Tennessee Valley Authority, 58, 200
Tenure, 216; American Presidential system, and, 218-219
Territoriality, citizenship, and, 210; family state, and, 33-34; nature of the state, and, 31; precapitalist economies, and, 38
Theatre, government aid to, 70
Third Republic, French, 212
Third-party, 179-182
Thirst, drive for, 3, 6-7
Thomas Aquinas, 18
Thomas committee, 97
Tidelands oil conservation, 67
Time and Man's desires, 6
Tort law, 204
Total war, 55, 66
Totalitarianism. *See* Dictatorships
Transition. *See* Planning
Trotsky, 16, 109
Trotskyites, democratic revolution, and, 126; as Russian scapegoat, 11
Truman, Harry S., labor relations, 139-140; Roosevelt death, and, 209; Taft-Hartley Act veto, 186
Trusts, 48-49; law's effects, 71; labor unions, and, 155-156; production planning, and, 71-72

Ukraine anti-Semitism, 201
Unemployment (*See also* Employment), 46, 47, 50-51, 53, 178; economic planning, and, 56-57; government spending, and, 59; organized labor, and, 142-143; right to a job, and, 170-171; temporary, 173
"Unfair labor practices," 163-164, 171-175
"Union responsibility," 163-168
Union shop, 174
Unionization (*See also* Labor Unions), middle class, of, 122
Unions. *See* Labor Unions
Unitary state, 196-197, 204
United Mine Workers, 177, 182, 184-185
United States, 31, 37; administrative integration, 224-231; antidemocratic forces, and, 96-98; British Cabinet system, and, 215-216; control of business, 53; distribution schemes, 61-62; Economic Advisory Council, 55-56; economic freedom, 80, 82; Employment Act of 1946, 55-56; functional federalism, and, 199-202; government reorganization program, 222-224; labor, aristocracy, 151, freedom, 168-170, relations, 139-158, role in politics, 175-187; political integration, and, 197-199; precapitalist economies, 43-44; Presidential system, and, 217-222; property, and, 131, 132, 134-135; public opinion checking, 94-95; public ownership, and, 57-58; reparations, and, 68; return to absolute capitalism, and, 56-57; Russian, idea identification, and, 16, leadership propaganda, and, 115; scapegoat, as, 11; scarcity economy, 61-62; society and leadership, 105, 120; spending, and, 58-59; work drive in power socialization, 11-12; World War II leadership, and, 117
Upper chamber, 224
Upper class (*See also* Class), 103-104
Utilities Holding Company Act, 72
Utopia, 117, 121, 133, 167, 180

Vacations, union, 173
Values. *See* Social values
Vanity, 119
Veblen, 12
Veterans, war, government aid, 121; labor relations, and, 142-143
Veto power, 218-219
Victory, spoils of, 102; efficiency, and, 50
Vigilantism, 160
Voting (*See also* Suffrage), 234; American Presidential system, and, 219-220

Wage-price, 57, 60, 124, 236; control need, and, 53; economic planning, and, 71, 73; government regulation of, 141; Lewis attitude toward, 148; relationship, 150-153, 154, 158
Wages (*See also* Wage-price), annual, 175; economic planning, and, 56-57; emerging capitalism, and, 46; freedom through government, 235; government spending, and, 60; production planning, and, 71, 73; structure, and employment freedom, 170; work incentive, as, 66
Wagner Act, 201; democratic administration, and, 229-230; freedom, and, 238; industrial civil liberties, and, 159-163; labor union democracy, and, 163-168; union restrictive practices, and, 172
Wagner-Murray-Dingell bill, 66
War (*See also* Total war, War economy), encirclement myth, and, 11; sublimation in power socialization, 12-13
War economy, 47, 55; consumer freedom, and, 84; economic freedom, 80; functional federalism, and, 200; labor, and, 139-144, 147, 152, freedom, 170, policy, 165; military planning, 66; planning agencies, 73; resources planning, and, 67; unions, and, 172, 178-179
War Labor Disputes Act, 148

War of Independence. See American Revolution
Washington, George, 117, 219; father symbol, as, 210
Waste, resources planning, and, 67; union contracts, and, 172
Wealth (*See also* Property), concentration of, 49-50
Weimar Republic, 212
Wildcat strikes, 149
Will, choice, and, 81; freedom through government, 234; government control, and, 53; leadership, and, 101-102; organization, and, 21, 25-26; property development, and, 133
Willkie, Wendell, 176, 182, 184-185
Wilson, Woodrow, malignment, 211; New Freedom, 220
Women in industry, 142
Work (*See also* Employment, Labor, Workers), incentives for, 66, 73; power socialization, and, 11-12
Workers (*See also* Labor, Labor unions), free enterprise, and, 86; incentives for, 66, 73; loss of privileges, 131-132; resources planning, and, 68
Workers' committees, 130
World War I, 55; American Presidential system, and, 218; labor and, 144; reparations, 68
World War II, 48; labor, and, 141, 144, 147; property development, and, 134; reparations, 67-68; resources waste, 67
WPA, benefits of, 70; cultural liberty under planning, 88
Writers' projects, 70, 88

Augsburg College
George Sverdrup Library
Minneapolis, Minnesota 55404